Europe's Strategic Future:
From Crisis to Coherence?

Sarah Raine

Europe's Strategic Future:
From Crisis to Coherence?

Sarah Raine

IISS The International Institute for Strategic Studies

The International Institute for Strategic Studies

Arundel House | 6 Temple Place | London | WC2R 2PG | UK

First published June 2019 by **Routledge**
4 Park Square, Milton Park, Abingdon, Oxon, OX14 4RN

for **The International Institute for Strategic Studies**
Arundel House, 6 Temple Place, London, WC2R 2PG, UK
www.iiss.org

Simultaneously published in the USA and Canada by **Routledge**
52 Vanderbilt Avenue, New York, NY 10017

Routledge is an imprint of Taylor & Francis, an Informa Business

© 2019 The International Institute for Strategic Studies

DIRECTOR-GENERAL AND CHIEF EXECUTIVE Dr John Chipman
EDITOR Dr Nicholas Redman
ASSISTANT EDITOR Clea Gibson
EDITORIAL Vivien Antwi, Jill Lally, Gaynor Roberts, Sam Stocker
COVER/PRODUCTION John Buck, Kelly Verity
COVER IMAGES: Getty

The International Institute for Strategic Studies is an independent centre for research, information and debate on the problems of conflict, however caused, that have, or potentially have, an important military content. The Council and Staff of the Institute are international and its membership is drawn from almost 100 countries. The Institute is independent and it alone decides what activities to conduct. It owes no allegiance to any government, any group of governments or any political or other organisation. The IISS stresses rigorous research with a forward-looking policy orientation and places particular emphasis on bringing new perspectives to the strategic debate.

The Institute's publications are designed to meet the needs of a wider audience than its own membership and are available on subscription, by mail order and in good book-shops. Further details at www.iiss.org.

British Library Cataloguing in Publication Data
A catalogue record for this book is available from the British Library

Library of Congress Cataloging in Publication Data

ADELPHI series
ISSN 1944-5571

ADELPHI 468–469
ISBN 978-0-367-35775-7

Contents

ACKNOWLEDGEMENTS

This book is written in response to all those friends, colleagues and intellectual sparring partners who have rolled their eyes at me whenever the role of Europe, and in particular the EU, has crept into our conversations on issues of international security and defence. Its central thesis, that Europe's deteriorating security environment is belatedly now informing the development of strategic thought and action on the continent and within its Union in ways that look set to have genuine significance, is not offered naively. The disappointments of what has gone before will continue to inform the developments of what will come tomorrow, but they will not define them. Even as the EU faces critical challenges in other areas, its collective contribution to the continent's foreign, security and defence policy interests is evolving, with implications that stretch beyond its borders. This development reflects the changing forms in which challenges of international security and defence present. It also reflects the reality that the continent's leading powers are becoming more pragmatic about the forms of cooperation that they pursue to defend interests and cultivate influence, both within EU structures and beyond.

But the story is an evolving one. At the time of publication for example, the ultimate destination of the process that has become known as 'Brexit' remained unclear. Likewise, the nature, programme and priorities of the next European Commission (2019–24) were unknown. Developments will overtake some of the judgements in the book, but the underlying themes will endure. The issues brought by Brexit will not be quickly or easily resolved, whatever the eventual end state. Any new Commission, whatever its composition, will put greater emphasis on the development of the EU's impact and influence on issues of continental, and by extension international, security.

My sincere thanks to all those who have helped me with this book, whether directly and deliberately or in more indirect ways, through thought-provoking conversations and supportive collegiality. I remain forever appreciative of the consistently nurturing and welcoming professional environment that is the IISS. My particular thanks in this instance to Jeff Mazo for his thoughtful editing of the manuscript, to Nick Redman for his ever-insightful input and commitment, and to my former boss, Adam Ward, for first giving me the chance to write this.

GLOSSARY

AfD	Alternative für Deutschland
AI	artificial intelligence
ASEAN	Association of Southeast Asian Nations
AU	African Union
AWACS	airborne warning and control system
CARD	Coordinated Annual Review on Defence
CBRN	chemical, biological, radiological and nuclear
CFSP	Common Foreign and Security Policy
CSDP	Common Security and Defence Policy
DEVCO	Directorate General for International Cooperation and Development
ECB	European Central Bank
ECJ	European Court of Justice
ECSC	European Coal and Steel Community
EDA	European Defence Agency
EDC	European Defence Community
EDF	European Defence Fund
EEA	European Economic Area
EEAS	European External Action Service
EEC	European Economic Community
EII	European Intervention Initiative
ENISA	European Union Network and Information Security Agency
ENP	European Neighbourhood Policy
EPC	European Political Cooperation
ESDP	European Security and Defence Policy
ESS	European Security Strategy
ETAC	European Tactical Airlift Centre
EU	European Union
EUBAM	EU Border Assistance Mission
EUCAP	EU Capacity Building Mission
EUFOR	EU Force
EUGS	EU Global Strategy
EULEX	EU Rule of Law Mission in Kosovo
EUTM	EU Training Mission

EW	early warning
FDI	foreign direct investment
FTA	free-trade agreement
G7	Group of Seven
HR/VP	High Representative for Foreign Affairs and Security Policy/Vice President of the European Commission
IMF	International Monetary Fund
JCPOA	Joint Comprehensive Plan of Action
MEP	member of the European Parliament
MFF	Multiannual Financial Framework
MoD	Ministry of Defence
MPCC	Military Planning and Conduct Capability
NATO	North Atlantic Treaty Organization
NDPP	NATO Defence Policy Planning
NSA	(Bahrain) Naval Support Activity
OCCAR	Organisation for Joint Armament Cooperation
OCHA	United Nations Office for the Coordination of Humanitarian Affairs
ODA	official development assistance
OECD	Organisation for Economic Co-operation and Development
OMT	outright monetary transactions
OSCE	Organization for Security and Co-operation in Europe
PESCO	Permanent Structured Cooperation
PiS	(Polish) Law and Justice Party
QMV	qualified majority voting
R&D	research and development
SDIP	Security and Defence Implementation Plan
SPV	Special Purpose Vehicle
TEU	Treaty on European Union
TFEU	Treaty on the Functioning of the European Union
TTIP	Transatlantic Trade and Investment Partnership
UAV	unmanned aerial vehicle
UNSC	United Nations Security Council
V4	Visegrad 4
VJTF	Very High Readiness Joint Task Force
WEU	Western European Union
WMD	weapon of mass destruction
WTO	World Trade Organization

INTRODUCTION

This past decade has been difficult for Europe. Multiple, simultaneous and overlapping crises have threatened the security of the continent and the stability of its Union. These crises, moreover, came while Europe was still struggling to adapt to more structural shifts in global affairs, and to what these shifts heralded for the global rebalancing of geo-economic and geopolitical power. This *Adelphi* book considers the strategic consequences that these crises have wrought for the foreign, security and defence policies of Europe, the European Union and its member states. It looks at how respective strategic outlooks and practices on the continent are changing in light of the challenges that continue to unfold within and beyond the EU's borders, and it analyses what these developments might mean for the continent's strategic influence in the future.

Europe is no stranger to crises. Indeed, European integration has often advanced because of them. Recent developments, however, do not so much present an opportunity to forge a more collective response, as demand it. Coming as they do against a backdrop of declining influence and growing illiberalism, a failure to respond adequately will sentence the continent to the strategic sidelines of world affairs.

Europe's decade of crises was preceded by what might be the EU's greatest foreign-policy achievement: the 2004 expansion that cemented a peaceful transition across most of the former Warsaw Pact, fundamentally altering the future prospects and outlook of these countries. Yet the EU's international engagements have subsequently become unimaginatively dependent on the story of past accessions and the accompanying narrative of the transformational lure of the EU. Geopolitical developments from a reassertive Russia to questions over the future of the transatlantic alliance and the rise of a more self-confident and authoritarian China have all highlighted the limits of a policy whose potential is largely exhausted. As a result, European states and the EU now have to reinvent themselves as actors on the international stage.

The pressures of crises within, around and beyond the EU's borders have led the European political establishment increasingly to focus on the EU's future capacity and appetite for *Weltpolitikfähigkeit* (roughly translated as the ability to play a role in shaping global affairs). This focus includes a push towards closer cooperation in security and defence policy, often framed in the context of developing a more sovereign Europe. As French President Emmanuel Macron told the German Bundestag in November 2018, Europe cannot let itself 'become a plaything of great powers, [it] must assume greater responsibility for its security and defence'.[1] Should Europe fail to build and exercise its credentials as a global power, its future will be defined by the rules and demands of external actors.

In 2016, a new EU Global Strategy (EUGS) suggested that 'a more fragile world calls for a more confident and responsible European Union, it calls for an outward and forward-looking European foreign and security policy'.[2] Plans for a renewed push on European security and defence were duly drawn up, aimed at addressing the continent's declining security environment and its struggle for strategic relevance. Yet previous pushes in this direction have fallen far short of their accompanying rhetoric. Indeed, many of the latest ideas for improving Europe's substance as a strategic actor have been proffered before, to little effect.

What are the prospects that this time will be any different? Will Europe and its Union live up to its ambition, as laid out in the EUGS, of being a 'global security provider', 'handling global threats and local dynamics'? Can the continent develop its foreign, security and defence capabilities more effectively to project both power and stability, and can it summon the political will and unity of purpose to agree on *how* and *where* this power should be exercised, not just in theory but also in action?

Changing global and regional environments

The global strategic environment has become more congested and contested. Not only are there more active actors (both state and non-state), there is also greater competition between them. As the bipolar and unipolar moments of the late twentieth century have been overtaken by a more complex dynamic that has been labelled everything from 'G-Zero' to 'G-Plus', and 'multipolar' to 'multiplex', the ability of Europe, the EU and its member states to defend interests and project influence was always going to come under stress. Indeed, the very development of the EU has been fuelled, at least in part, by the anticipation of increasing competition for strategic influence. With many of the world's most populous nation-states, fastest-growing economies and largest militaries now located in the Indo-Pacific, some sort of collective rebalance in strategic influence has long been inevitable.

The scale of the structural challenge Europe now faces should not be underestimated. A 2012 McKinsey report showed how the global economic centre of gravity shifted dramatically within the space of the decade from 2000–10 back towards Asia, reversing the trends initiated by the industrialisation and urbanisation of Europe and the United States.[3] Should the current trajectory continue, by 2050 no European country would qualify to be in the Group of Seven (G7) most advanced industrialised nations.[4] China's economy could be as much as 50% bigger than that of the US; the EU's leading economies will follow far behind.[5] Europe also faces major demographic challenges: by 2020 the continent will host a significant number of the world's 'super-aged' societies (where more than 20% of the population is 65 or older), including Croatia, France, Germany, Italy, the Netherlands, Portugal and Sweden.[6]

China's presence is likely to continue to grow not just in Europe's markets but also in its politics. Beijing will seek to influence European behaviour in international affairs, and to capitalise on Washington's weakening interest in the continent. China will also continue to draw US attention away from the Atlantic and towards the Indo-Pacific. The challenges Asia itself faces, to be sure, should not be discounted. Asia is not immune from its own demographic pressures; China will have six working adults per elderly person in 2020, but just 1.5 by 2050.[7] Nevertheless, the future of global security and prosperity will likely be written more in the Pacific than in the West,[8] and what (if any) role European powers will play is uncertain.

Europe's quest for strategic relevance is further complicated by a relative weakening in its transatlantic partner and protector's ability to influence and shape international affairs. This reflects, in part, the rise of alternative narratives, for example that the West writ large is not so much the source of solutions to the world's problems as part of those problems.[9] Asia's rise in general, and China's in particular, challenge many of the assumptions on which the Washington Consensus had been based. The West stands accused of incompetence in its handling of global affairs. It is, moreover, charged with undermining existing multilateral institutions by failing to support their modernisation in alignment with the changing distribution of global economic power.

Meanwhile, although the transatlantic alliance continues to lie at the heart of Europe's territorial defence, the foundations on which this alliance rests have slowly been weakening. Well before the 2017 arrival of President Donald Trump in the Oval Office, US attentions had been pivoting to Asia. With China now firmly established as Washington's principal foreign-policy concern, US interest in and relations with its European allies look set to be subordinated to this overarching agenda. Under Trump, transatlantic strategic dissonance has sharpened still further, in particular as the president has become increasingly unconstrained in showing his personal hostility to the EU and its perceived desire to 'take advantage of the US'.[10] Indeed, as Trump sets about his 'America First' agenda, attacking multilateral institutions and approaches that have helped secure Europe's peace and prosperity, European counterparts are, for the first time, being forced to consider what steps they might need to take to protect these institutions not only from their adversaries but also from their ally. As European Commission President Jean-Claude Juncker opined in his 2018 State of the Union speech, Europe can no longer be sure that the alliances of yesterday will look the same in the future. With the US focused on Asia, Europe has to prepare for the possibility that it will not just have to contribute more to its own defence, but that it will have to take the lead.

Other powers of course have contributed to Europe's shifting strategic circumstances. With the annexation of Crimea and the invasion of eastern Ukraine, a revanchist Russia confirmed its return to the strategic front lines. Moscow has shown an increasing appetite for hybrid engagements, while simultaneously investing in new advanced weapons systems as part of an ongoing programme of military modernisation. This includes the development of missiles that resulted, in early 2019, in the collapse of the more than 30-year-old Intermediate-range Nuclear Forces treaty that removed ground-based missiles with ranges of 500–5500 kilometres from Europe. Russia has also used its intervention in Syria to try to reposition itself as a major power in international affairs, able to shape military outcomes and tip geopolitical balances.

In addition to this global structural repositioning, Europe has faced a complex range of multi-rooted and interlinked regional crises. The 2009 eurozone debt and banking crises heralded a decade of turmoil. A crisis of competition and growth in turn brought further crises of cohesion, confidence and even policy creativity. Heads of state and government lurched from one 'make or break' summit to the next. Events in Europe's eastern and southern neighbourhoods saw refugees and migrants make their way to the continent in unprecedented numbers, creating an immigration crisis that peaked in 2015–16. It was against this backdrop that the membership crisis that was Brexit would unfold. For the first time in the Union's history, changes to the EU's membership looked as likely to involve departures as arrivals. The shock of the UK's June 2016 vote to leave the Union was compounded in November by the looming threat of a transatlantic crisis. Trump's electoral victory was, in his own words, 'Brexit plus plus plus'.[11]

There have, of course, been periods of respite. In elections in 2017, pro-European politicians in France and the Netherlands – both founding members of the European Community – defied fears and defeated populism (albeit by worryingly close margins). Macron's victory in the French presidential elections that March provided a particular boost to continental confidence. Standing on perhaps the most pro-European platform of any leading politician on the continent, he defied sceptics not just once, but twice as his newly established political party secured victory in the country's legislative elections a few months later. But the pendulum soon swung back. In Italy in 2018 a new populist coalition entered government, and the Italian president was forced to use his veto on cabinet posts for only the third time in the past 25 years to ensure that the new finance minister was someone who was not on record as favouring unilateral withdrawal from the euro. In the run-up to the EU parliamentary elections in 2019, clashes between European leaders such as Macron and Italian Deputy Prime Minister Matteo Salvini intensified, fuelled by competing visions over the future of Europe.

Europe as a strategic player

From the perspective of many of Europe's global partners, these crises meant that, just when the continent had promised it would start looking outwards, it instead became even more preoccupied with its own affairs. The 2009 Lisbon Treaty – which amended previous treaties to create today's Treaty on European Union (TEU) and Treaty on the Functioning of the European Union (TFEU) – aggrandised the position of High Representative for Foreign Affairs and Security Policy and established a European External Action Service (EEAS).[12] The measures were designed, at least in part, to make the Union's position on the world stage both more secure and more influential. A newly empowered EU would outgrow its stereotype as a 'geopolitical pygmy' and push back against the broader global structural shifts that seemed set to diminish the continent's strategic relevance. Instead, facing shrinking financial resources, the EU found its status as an economic giant reduced and its soft power undermined by its chaotic and rancorous handling of its crises and the surge of populism these helped fuel.[13]

Even in the midst of crises, there nevertheless remain areas, such as aid and trade, where Europe and its Union maintain a serious strategic presence and influence. Though this *Adelphi* does not focus on such areas, they should be recognised as a critical part of the continent's strategic presence.

For example, EU development policy has long been designed and promoted as a major contribution to international security. Europe is by far the world's largest aid donor, collectively accounting for almost 59% of global assistance in 2017.[14] In the midst of the EU's austerity crisis, as the Arab Spring spread from Tunisia to Egypt, the EU and its member states still donated more money to both countries than the US did. The EU is also trying to work more closely with the private sector in development cooperation, including with regard to strategic infrastructure investment.[15]

Meanwhile, as global trade policy has turned more protectionist, the EU has remained open for business. The new free-trade agreement (FTA) between the EU and Japan that came into effect in February 2019 covers around one-third of the global economy and some 40% of global trade. This deal, notably, had been stalled for years before it was finally agreed in December 2018. Its conclusion is testimony to the ability of both sides to recognise the broader strategic imperative to act now to uphold the values and order that have served them so well. Meanwhile, the streamlining of the EU's ratification process and the deal's quick implementation should bolster a more robust narrative on EU trade-policy capabilities than that which emerged in 2016 in the wake of efforts by the Walloon parliament in Belgium single-handedly to hold up the ratification of the EU–Canada FTA.

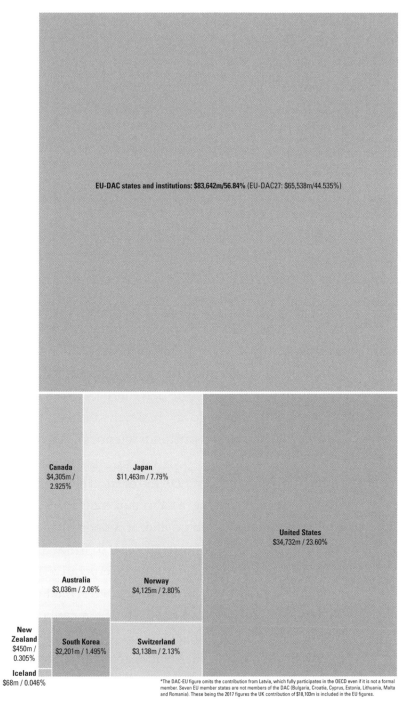

EU-DAC states and institutions: **$83,642m/56.84%** (EU-DAC27: $65,538m/44.535%)

Canada
$4,305m /
2.925%

Japan
$11,463m / 7.79%

United States
$34,732m / 23.60%

Australia
$3,036m / 2.06%

Norway
$4,125m / 2.80%

New
Zealand
$450m /
0.305%

South Korea
$2,201m / 1.495%

Switzerland
$3,138m / 2.13%

Iceland
$68m / 0.046%

*The DAC-EU figure omits the contribution from Latvia, which fully participates in the OECD even if it is not a formal member. Seven EU member states are not members of the DAC (Bulgaria, Croatia, Cyprus, Estonia, Lithuania, Malta and Romania). These being the 2017 figures the UK contribution of $18,103m is included in the EU figures.

Source: Organisation for Economic Co-operation and Development (OECD)

Figure 1. **Development Assistance Committee (DAC) net ODA, 2017**

In light of the Trump administration's protectionist instincts, there are obvious opportunities for the EU to expand its global leadership in this area. This includes not just the maintenance of commitments to a free and open economy, but also an insistence on meaningful standards, for example with regard to environmental protection or labour law. With the Lisbon Treaty committing the EU to encourage 'the progressive abolition of restrictions on international trade', the manner in which these dynamics play out will have broader implications for the credibility of one of the ideological foundations on which not just the EU, but the liberal international order, has been constructed.

As the EU places itself at the centre of the world's largest free-trade network, the Union's profile on the international stage will be amplified (especially as a sanctioning power). But this will also increase Europe's stake in the preservation of the open rules-based order on which such networks depend. Whether Europe is ready or not, the strategic periphery in which it has too often conveniently taken cover is slowly shrinking. The consequences for European security and defence engagements are unavoidable.

The continent's common currency, the euro, is also systemically important globally, acting as the currency for 36% of international transactions by value and accounting for some 20% of international reserves of foreign central banks. Efforts to develop further the international role of the euro are likely to find increasing favour in a world where the perceived advantages of dependence on US global financial hegemony appear to be shrinking, even for Europe.

More generally, as Japan's first National Security Strategy noted in 2013, 'Europe has the influence to formulate public opinion' and 'the capacity to develop norms in major international frameworks'.[16] Meanwhile, as freedom and democracy continue to retreat around the world, more attention is inevitably drawn to the EU and its role as one of the standard-bearers for multilateralism and democracy.

The question this *Adelphi* considers is whether Europe and its Union can evolve into what Juncker once referred to as being not just a 'global payer' but a 'global player'.[17] Although the focus is on Europe and the EU's evolving engagements in foreign, security and defence policies, it should be acknowledged at the outset that the full programme of EU external actions is far broader, ranging from support for multilateralism, to the consolidation of democracy and human rights, to the sustainable development of global natural resources.[18] The EU aims 'to preserve peace, prevent conflicts and strengthen international security'[19] using tools that go beyond the realm of foreign, security and defence policies. In these other realms of strategic relevance, then, Europe and its Union already have a substantive strategic presence. Similarly, even as European developments under a specifically NATO platform have been deliberately excluded from consideration from this book given its already extensive scope, it is important to acknowledge the reality that NATO is the primary organisation for guaranteeing European territorial defence.

A *sui generis* union

Hard power cannot be the only metric of strategic influence. The EU's evident preference for civilian-based security interactions might yet find a niche in a world where the Western appetite for military interventionism is declining and the array of threats to global security stretch beyond state militaries to include private companies, organisations and individuals. Although the role of military power remains critical, the demand for police and other civil law-enforcement and capacity-building capabilities is likely to grow as Europe seeks to shore up its crisis-management capabilities in its neighbour-hood. The EU is underselling itself (and its transatlantic ally is missing a trick) if it cannot persuade others that the prospects for survival of the rules-based international order will be deter-mined not simply by the willingness to use hard power in its defence, but also by the inclusive appeal of the broader model that this hard power has been developed to defend.

In focusing on European prospects for a more collective and effective presence in foreign, security and defence policy, however, it is important to recognise the peculiarities of the system in which such efforts are evolving. It is, for example, not too surprising that an institution created to preclude hard-power conflict does not naturally excel at its projection.[20] Moreover, a European Commission with limited competencies in foreign, security and defence policy will never be effortlessly inclined to think strategically about the Union's geopolitical and strategic heft. Anyone designing from scratch a 'European Union' intended to give weight to Europe's strategic ambitions would not construct the EU of today. The audacity of the EU's initial ambition has been matched only by the eccentricity of its evolving design as a half-formed experiment in the extremes of multinational joinery.

But imperfect efforts can still be consequential. The EU will never evolve into a muscular superpower, able unilaterally to impose its will on others. But it does have at its command an array of tools which could be highly effective influencers in its neighbourhood, and at times beyond. If Europe is to develop greater strategic substance, however, it will need the military capabilities and political will to back up its economic presence and enable it to take action in its immediate neighbourhood when crises come.

The uniqueness of the EU's 'comprehensive approach' to issues of international security is often over-stressed. But

Europe does have near-unrivalled expertise in bridging the civil–military divide in crisis-management operations. In Asia, for example, which arguably suffers from a surfeit of hard power, Europe could make obvious contributions to international security not by any vain attempt to masquerade as a regional military power but through the development of a more substantive set of security partnerships. The EU's skills in risk management, mediation, crisis prevention and preparation are all crucial aspects of security policy; demand for such skills is growing, both close to home and further away.

Crises matter

Against a backdrop of rising illiberalism and a growing rejection of multilateralism globally, the EU's strategic future has taken on a symbolism that transcends geography. How Europe and the EU respond to what UK journalist Gideon Rachman has referred to as a 'bonfire of agreements, norms and rules' will help determine the prospects for what he labels as a 'world based round rules and rights, rather than power and force'.[21] Certainly the prospect that other mid-sized powers might similarly step up in defence of this world of rules and rights will be greatly improved if Europe and its Union are willing and able to play their full part.

The imperative for the EU to serve as an avatar for post-nationalist politics and effective multilateralism, and to act as an antidote to resurgent nationalism not just within its continent but beyond, has never been clearer. European nations have asserted a determination to stick to their multilateralist course. They have reiterated their commitments to foreign-policy agreements from which the US has unilaterally retreated, such as the Paris Agreement on climate change and the Joint Comprehensive Plan of Action (JCPOA) that they helped conceive as a mechanism for managing Iran's nuclear ambitions.

Statements of European intent are everywhere to be found. Following her experiences at the 2017 NATO and G7 summits, German Chancellor Angela Merkel obliquely suggested that 'the times in which we can fully count on others are somewhat over ... we Europeans must really take our destiny into our own hands'.[22] The day after Trump addressed the UN General Assembly, in an isolationist speech that referred no fewer than 21 times to the importance of 'sovereignty', EU High Representative for Foreign Affairs and Security Policy/ Vice President of the European Commission (HR/VP) Federica Mogherini declared, perhaps optimistically, that 'the rest of the world is now looking at Europe for leadership'.[23]

In reality, much of the rest of the world might reasonably have given up on European and EU leadership in international security. They have seen too many past promises go unfulfilled. But Europe and its Union have proven capable of exporting stability and security in the past. In today's more competitive and unstable strategic environment, the requirement to do more at times appears unsustainable. Together, European states will have to forge a greater unity of purpose in foreign policy. They will have to develop better their collective military capabilities to help lend meaning to their policies. And they will have to summon the political will to act, if necessary without their transatlantic partner, where circumstances dictate.

CHAPTER ONE

The context and anatomy of crises

The desire to preserve Europe's strategic relevance in a changing global environment has informed the evolution of the European Union from the outset. Already in 1951, when six states signed the Treaty of Paris to establish the European Coal and Steel Community (ECSC), cooperation was about more than just coal and steel. French economist and diplomat Jean Monnet was one of the community's chief architects and a founding father of what has become the EU. Writing in 1954, when Europe still represented 37% of global GDP and 13% of the world's population, he warned that 'our countries have become too small for today's world, faced with the ... America and Russia of today and the China and India of tomorrow'.[1] Decades later, he remained steadfast in his outlook: 'The problems that our countries need to sort out are not the same as in 1950. But the method remains the same: a transfer of power to common institutions, majority rule and a common approach to finding a solution to problems are the only answer in our current state of crisis.'[2]

The progress of process

The early concept that a European Community could become a key security provider for the continent was given impetus by the demands put upon the US during the Korean War and the impending tensions of bipolarity. In late May 1952, two months before the Treaty of Paris came into force, the ECSC's six foreign ministers signed a treaty creating a European Defence Community (EDC), with the intention that it would last for 50 years. In the event, the treaty did not reach its second birthday. After a toxic debate over the loss of national sovereignty and the revival of German militancy that the initiative appeared to promote, in 1954 the French National Assembly refused to ratify the EDC. With America's direct engagement in the future of European security increasingly embedded in the developing institutions of NATO, defence discussions under a strictly European umbrella were taken off the table.

The 1957 Treaty of Rome, which launched a more general common market in Europe, was explicit in the qualification it gave to its new venture: the European *Economic* Community (EEC). Although the EEC had no official mandate covering foreign and security policy, the European Commission was given responsibility for negotiating EEC trade policy with third parties, initiating a presence for the community on the international stage and beginning the development of today's dense web of FTAs that serve not just Europe's prosperity but also its profile and influence. The Treaty of Rome also established a multilateral European Development Fund to contribute to the economic and social development of the African colonies (and former colonies) of EEC member states. By 1963, the first seeds of EU development policy were in place. Here, too, the EU's profile would grow over time as EU member states and institutions collectively became the world's leading donor of official development assistance (ODA), with the possibilities for global partnerships and influence this entails.

Following the departure from the international stage of French President Charles de Gaulle, with his suspicion of supranational institutions, in 1970 community members finally agreed a format to enable foreign-policy coordination. Labelled 'European Political Cooperation' (EPC), it created a process for consultation in which ministers of foreign affairs would meet twice a year to discuss world affairs, supported by structures below them meeting with greater regularity as well as the appointment of a representative to handle EEC affairs in the foreign ministry of each member state. All business was to be conducted on a strictly intergovernmental basis. Regard for concerns of sovereignty was strict. It was not permitted to discuss foreign policy towards former colonies of member states, nor was it permitted to discuss defence policy. No mandate or role was given to the EEC's institutions. Issues with the EPC's capacity and efficacy quickly arose, in particular as more member states joined the community.

The EPC enjoyed a smattering of successes, most obviously with its sponsorship of the 1973 Conference for Security and Cooperation in Europe. Conceived as a forum for promoting dialogue between East and West, this was the predecessor of today's Organization for Security and Co-operation in Europe (OSCE). Yet the limitations of the EPC were also clear. Europe was, in the words of François Duchêne, one of Monnet's key advisers, 'long on economic power and relatively short on armed force'.[3] Indeed, by 1982, international-relations theorist Hedley Bull would issue a clear indictment of the EU's 'civilian power', arguing that '"Europe" is not an actor in international affairs, and does not seem likely to become one'.[4]

From Maastricht to Lisbon

The 1991 Gulf War highlighted Europe's geopolitical irrelevance and disunity. Though the European Commission quickly rejected Iraq's annexation of Kuwait as 'contrary to international law', as it became apparent that diplomatic statements alone would not dislodge Iraqi forces from Kuwait, national foreign-policy interests diverged. The UK and France, as permanent members of the United Nations Security Council (UNSC), both dispatched forces to the region. Anglo-French differences were on display, however, over the possibility of continuing the fight on Iraqi soil. Germany, by contrast, decided against deploying troops, confining its contribution to pledges of money and limited logistical support. Belgium reportedly refused to provide British troops with ammunition.[5]

As US leadership united a coalition to remove Iraqi forces from Kuwait under the aegis of UNSC Resolution 678, Europe's lack of a united approach to the use of military force precipitated a wider fracturing of its political responses to the crisis. One month prior to the war, the European Parliament voted to approve a resolution calling for no military action while there was a prospect for peaceful settlement. Fifty Members of the European Parliament (MEPs) wrote to their counterparts in the US Congress to note that European opposition to war was 'broader and deeper' than that being represented by European governments.[6] French efforts to pull off a diplomatic coup through last-minute bilateral negotiations immediately prior to the UN deadline for Iraqi withdrawal were conducted without consultation or sanction from France's allies. Not only was Europe a 'political dwarf', then Belgian foreign minister Mark Eyskens concluded, it was also 'a military worm'.[7]

When the EU Common Foreign and Security Policy (CFSP) was established two years later as the second of three pillars (alongside European Communities and Justice and Home Affairs) under the 1993 Maastricht Treaty, it was evident that the institutions and processes being created would not quickly be matched by meaningful policies. And although foreign and security policy were now formally brought under the umbrella of the European project, the CFSP was excluded from the 'community method', limiting the influence of the supranational powers of the community – the commission, the parliament and the European Court of Justice (ECJ). This made sound political sense but had practical disadvantages. The CFSP had no instruments of its own and no EU institutional actors to represent its interests. It also lacked direct links to any of the instruments where a common policy could most readily make itself felt. Trade and development cooperation, for example, fell under the first pillar of the commission. For at least some of its participants, moreover, the CFSP was as much about furthering integration, forging identity and even salvaging credibility as it was about having real external impact.

In 1999 the Treaty of Amsterdam put a single 'face' on the CFSP for the first time, in the form of a High Representative for Common Foreign and Security Policy. The treaty also strengthened links to the Western European Union (WEU) (a parallel military structure grounded in NATO), adopting its 1992 'Petersberg Tasks' including 'humanitarian and rescue tasks; peacekeeping tasks; [and] tasks of combat forces in crisis management including peace making', as the military mission for the CFSP.[8] That same year, EU heads of state and government adopted a 'Declaration on Strengthening the Common European Policy on Security and Defence', expressing their determination that the Union should 'play its full role on the international stage'.[9] The birth of a European Security and Defence Policy (ESDP) marked the long-delayed inclusion of a military element to European integration. The CFSP was starting to get the mandate and processes to enable it to evolve into something more than a display of good intentions.

In December 1999 the Helsinki Headline Goal set a clear target for these emerging ambitions for defence cooperation. By 2003 the EU should have 'an autonomous capacity to take decisions and, where NATO as a whole is not engaged, to launch and conduct EU-led military operations in response to international crises'. The Union should be able to deploy military forces for operations up to army-corps level (50,000–60,000 troops) capable of conducting the range of Petersberg tasks. These forces should be deployable within 60 days and sustainable for one year. Concerns that 'militarisation' of the EU would weaken its unique selling point as a civilian actor helped fuel parallel EU efforts to boost civilian crisis-management capabilities, including in the areas of policing, rule of law, civil administration and civil protection.[10] In March 2003, in what is known as the 'Berlin Plus' arrangements, the EU was permitted to make use of NATO assets and capabilities. This development helped facilitate the EU's first-ever military operation when, in December 2003, it took over from NATO's *Operation Allied Harmony* in Macedonia.

The gap between ambition and delivery nevertheless remained a persistent feature of EU foreign and security policy-making. Some critics have blamed this not so much on missed opportunities as on unrealistic expectations, arguing that what the EU can achieve in this sphere amounts to nothing more than 'eternal fantasy'.[11] Certainly events did not take long to re-expose the underlying differences that the EU's progress on process had helped partially to conceal. The 2003 Iraq War was another low point in European unity in international affairs, as European countries differed between themselves and with their US ally over the threat to international security posed by Saddam Hussein's Iraq and the legitimacy of military intervention.

In December 2003 the EU adopted its first European Security Strategy (ESS). 'A Secure Europe in a Better World' called for the EU to be 'more active' in pursuing its strategic objectives. One key challenge, as NATO's 1999 Strategic Concept had already noted, was the transformation of Cold War defence systems and practices to meet new collective security threats. The threats prioritised by the ESS – terrorism, the proliferation of weapons of mass destruction (WMDs), and the threats of failed states and organised crime – could not be managed by individual member states on their own. In a changing world, cooperation in foreign and security policy was becoming not so much a question of ideology but of practicality.

The ESS was a good document, well-timed. In addition to its new operation in Macedonia, the EU had also begun two missions in the western Balkans and launched a modest military stabilisation mission in the Democratic Republic of the Congo. In October 2003, moreover, France, Germany and the UK had sent their foreign ministers to Tehran with the support of EU High Representative Javier Solana, giving European nations a front seat in the efforts to negotiate a curtailment of Iran's nuclear ambitions. The ESS prompted a new 2010 Headline Goal expanding the range of EU military tasks to include counter-terrorism training for third countries, support for security-sector reform and the development of EU rapid-response capabilities. It also laid the groundwork for new initiatives such as a European Defence Agency (EDA) to work on correcting European capability shortfalls, an EU Civilian–Military Cell and the establishment of EU Battlegroups.

In 2008, the European Council raised the bar further. The EU had now to strive to be capable of simultaneously planning and conducting two major stabilisation and reconstruction operations (up to 10,000 troops, up to two years), two rapid-response operations using EU Battlegroups, an evacuation operation for European nationals, a maritime or air surveillance/interdiction mission, a civilian–military humanitarian operation (up to 90 days) and a dozen ESDP missions including one major mission (up to 3,000 experts, lasting several years). The level of ambition for EU civilian crisis management was also updated.

This included the capability to run several civilian missions (including a larger substitution mission in a non-benign environment and an enhanced rapid-response capability) as well as steps to ensure the close interlinking of civilian and military crisis-management operations.[12]

These upgrades in strategic ambitions continued, however, to be undermined by uncomfortable questions over the degree to which member states were willing to make good even on the promise of collating the capabilities these upgrades demanded, let alone deploying them in operations. Yet the EU had long developed through process- and institution-building, in the expectation that the substance to populate these initiatives would follow. In this respect, defence was being treated no differently to any other area of concern.

The 2009 Treaty of Lisbon was meant to be another turning point in increasing the coherence, effectiveness and visibility of the EU on the international stage, including through its engagements under the CFSP and ESDP. While making it clear that member states' competencies in foreign policy would not be infringed, it brought all EU foreign policy under one treaty title, ending the pillar system of Maastricht.[13] It also gave the EU its own legal personality, meaning that the EU could now sign international treaties in its areas of competence and join international organisations. The EU's global standing and ambition would be represented and prosecuted by its High Representative for Foreign Affairs and Security Policy who now became one of the vice presidents of the commission (HR/VP) and who now chaired a newly created Foreign Affairs Council. The work of the HR/VP would be supported by a European External Action Service, a quasi-diplomatic service with delegations around the world.

The idea was to give EU foreign policy greater prominence and consistency. The ESDP was rebranded as the Common

Security and Defence Policy (CSDP), with the range of Petersberg tasks expanded specifically to include activities such as disarmament operations, military advice and assistance, and post-conflict stabilisation. A mutual-defence clause obliged member states to 'provide aid and assistance by all the means in their power' if a member state were 'the victim of armed aggression on its territory'. A new solidarity clause was intended to facilitate the mobilisation of the Union and its member states in the provision of mutual assistance following natural or man-made disasters, including terrorist attacks, on the territory of a member state.[14] The treaty also provided for the possibility of 'Permanent Structured Cooperation' (PESCO) between member states on defence, activated in consultation with the HR/VP and with the support of a qualified majority.

Other provisions with foreign-policy implications included a policy objective on the security of energy supplies and a move to develop a European space policy. While calling for consistency between the different areas of EU external action and between these and other policies, the treaty cemented 'the comprehensive approach' as the 'guiding principle for EU external action across all areas, in particular in relation to conflict prevention and crisis resolution'.[15]

With the Lisbon Treaty, structural divisions between the EU's institutions and its member states were meant to be diminished, a common understanding of what European external action should look like evolved, and institutional barriers to effective follow-through on this understanding decreased if not quite removed.

Beyond CFSP/ESDP

At least as significant as any of the progress on the road from Maastricht to Lisbon were developments taking place outside the CFSP and ESDP. In May 2004, EU membership leapt from 15 to 25 states following the accession of eight Central and Eastern European countries, along with Malta and Cyprus. The enlargements that followed brought EU membership numbers by 2013 to 28 (operating in 24 different official languages); it was a major foreign-policy success for the Union, even as it brought new challenges for cohesion.[16] Most notably, EU institutions and processes were beginning to creak under the weight of numbers, while the challenge of agreeing common approaches inevitably increased.

These accessions brought other tests. As the EU's borders moved further outwards, the foreign-policy challenges of countries such as Belarus, Moldova and Ukraine were brought into sharper focus. New neighbours demanded new policies, and a European Neighbourhood Policy (ENP) was devised to cover 16 countries to the EU's east and south. The 2003 ESS had called for the EU to promote a 'ring of well-governed countries' on the Union's periphery, and the ENP was intended as the vehicle to deliver this. But the collapse in 2005 of ambitious plans for a European constitution and the interplay this had with growing concerns about the EU's absorptive capacity for new members marked the onset of enlargement fatigue. While Commission President Romano Prodi referred to the ENP offer as 'everything but the institutions',[17] few of the intended beneficiaries were impressed by the qualification. The plan to promote economic integration and EU values without the carrot of EU membership was always going to face some challenges. These strategies to promote security, stability and prosperity in the EU's neighbourhood would later be adjusted and subdivided into eastern and southern offshoots, in recognition of the differing geopolitical environments. Further revisions and updates to ENP followed in 2011 and 2015.

The process in practice

Europe's advances in process and ambition from 1954 to 2009 did little to improve fundamentals. Despite a series of incremental steps aimed at recalibrating the historic imbalance, a notable asymmetry remained between the size of the EU's internal market and its profile in international trade on the one hand and its profile in international affairs on the other. Similarly, gaps between grand ambitions and domestic realities did not prove easy to bridge. European allegiance to a Westphalian view of nationhood did not magically disappear in the wake of the continent's experiment with supranationalism. For a believing few, integration may have been a matter of ideology, but for most this project was about interests. Where the EU and its predecessors could add value in terms of peace, power and prosperity, member states proved open to cooperation. But the commitment to ever-closer union was greeted with ambivalence in some quarters; institutional mission-creep was more of a challenge to be guarded against than it was the hidden agenda of modern-day Monnets.

If European states remained protective of their diplomatic sovereignty of action, sensitivities over defence were even more acute. As the narrative of the twenty-first century as the 'Asia-Pacific century' took root, the hope of the Arab Spring disappeared and talk of a new cold war revived as a result of developments to Europe's east, it became evident that not all member states would support a repeat prescription of further integration as the antidote to the continent's troubles. Meanwhile, those open to such a course of action disagreed on the necessary mechanisms and priorities for progress. In short, conferring a competence in foreign and security policy on the EU did not come at the expense of the ongoing competencies of EU member states. Nor did the TEU define the nature of this competence, merely that one existed that would allow the

EU to 'define and implement a common foreign and security policy, including the progressive framing of a common defence policy'.

This has had practical consequences for the growth and capability of the EU's Brussels-based institutions. In contrast to member-state engagement on issues of trade and development policy, EU institutional engagement on foreign policy has been notably less consistent or consequential, while turf wars quickly break out. Competition over who gets to set what agenda in which institutional format – always a problem in the confusing bureaucracy of Brussels – is rife. For example, even in a member-state capital such as Berlin, where officials have long seen German and EU interests as broadly aligned, it is not hard to find officials who fret over the European Commission's slow encroachment into defence affairs and the consequences for member states' interests this is seen to threaten.

While different institutions compete among themselves for political profile, in times of crisis the same institutions can find themselves overloaded by the sheer range of issues that urgently need addressing. In theory, for example, the European Council, the EU's ultimate decision-making body made up of heads of state and government, meets four times a year to define policy principles and general guidelines. In reality, and particularly in times of trouble, it meets considerably more often. Yet even increasing the frequency of interactions has failed to ensure that non-existential issues receive sufficient attention. There was, for example, much fanfare around the December 2013 Council meeting at which heads of government were scheduled to debate the EU's defence agenda for the first time since 2008. In the run-up to the meeting, excited policy observers and advisers produced paper after paper with constructive proposals for an ambitious agenda.[18] In the event, the discussions proved distinctly modest, marginalised by the challenge of forging agreement on a rescue scheme for overly indebted banks within the EU. The meeting came to the underwhelming conclusion that the CSDP and CFSP were not being utilised to their full capacity under Lisbon. A June 2015 follow-up discussion mandated that the HR/VP review the EU's strategy, resulting in the June 2016 EUGS.

Even as the Lisbon Treaty was coming into force, the EU was again looking divided, its reputation and soft power diminished by the onset of the euro crisis. Indeed, Ireland's initial failure to ratify the treaty in 2008 was at least partly connected to the country's recognition of its own deteriorating economic outlook. For all the promise of Lisbon, a series of crises was set to distract and detract from EU operational capabilities and ambitions in foreign and security policy, cruelly exposing Europe's ongoing strategic dissonance.

A euro crisis and a crisis of credibility

As an ambition, European economic and monetary union dates back at least to the late 1960s. Deeper economic integration was supposed to promote political bonds and protect the common market, allowing member states to benefit through the removal of business costs that the existence of multiple currencies and unstable exchange rates inevitably incurs.

In time, more than a few economists would talk wisely about the fundamental flaws in the euro's design. But many of their forebears highlighted the fundamental long-term incompatibility of the 'impossible triangle' of free movement of capital, exchange-rate stability and independent monetary policies. Indeed, it is often overlooked that the conception of the euro was, in some ways, itself a response to a financial crisis – or at least to the turmoil on the international currency markets that had forced a revaluation of the German mark and a devaluation of the French franc, and had threatened the common price system within the EEC's common agricultural policy.

The 1991 Maastricht Treaty finally confirmed the target and agreed the mechanism by which economic and monetary union would be secured. Maastricht may have fallen short in its specific impact on foreign and security policy, but its impact on the European project would be lasting.

The problematic potential of the EU's disconnect between its political, fiscal and monetary cooperation was clear even before the birth of a single European currency in 1999, and the subsequent introduction of euro notes and coins in 2002 to more than 300 million European citizens across 12 countries. The euro was, at its inception, an incomplete currency, gifted a central bank (the ECB) but lacking a common treasury. There were obvious risks in countries with diverging productivity and budgetary policies using the same currency. Yet global growth and low inflation in the years that followed the introduction of the euro helped shield its adopters from the repercussions of the currency's design flaws. Although some modest steps were taken in recognition of the consequences that would likely follow were the developing bubble to burst, the measures were not substantive in their design, serious in their enforcement or sufficient in their numbers. The Stability and Growth Pact of the late 1990s (designed to try to commit eurozone members to limiting budget deficits) was, for example, never properly enforced. Yet, as the eurozone flourished on the back of global growth, and the Union took in new members, the first whispers of a day when the euro might replace the dollar as the world's leading reserve currency began to be heard.

Then came the turbulent years of the US subprime mortgage-induced global financial crisis that began in 2008. The crisis crashed into a European architecture that had none of the usual shock absorbers for combatting the negative effects of demand shocks, yet was lumbered with a central bank unable and unwilling to act as a lender of last resort. Further weaknesses, previously largely unidentified, were also uncovered. It became clear, for example, that member states, unable to print their own money and thus effectively borrowing in a foreign currency, were now exposed to more than simply a theoretical risk of default. (Much of Italy's post-war economic success, for example, was built on frequent devaluations, a mechanism no longer available once it joined the euro.) Government bonds were simply not as risk-free as they had been perceived, while the resulting convergence in interest rates encouraged divergences in economic performance in ways that Maastricht had not foreseen. A voluntary association of sovereign and equal member states was morphing into a complicated mesh of creditor and debtor countries that no longer felt, for more than a few on the continent, either so equal or so voluntary.[19]

Economic distress and political discord followed as some member states lost access to capital markets and found it increasingly difficult to roll over their sovereign debt under reasonable conditions. When, in July 2011, Belgium took over the rotating EU presidency, it seemed somehow fitting that a country whose political landscape was so fragmented that its politicians were unable to form a government was now representing the EU. Tensions spilled out from the eurozone to distract and infect the EU as a whole, before seeping in turn into some of the EU's key international relationships.

In May 2010, Greece became the first eurozone country to request an official bailout from the 'troika' of the IMF, the European Commission and the ECB. It was followed by Ireland in November 2010, Portugal in May 2011, Spain in June 2012 and Cyprus in March 2013. Minds were particularly focused by the prospect that contagion from the Greek crisis might spread to Italy, which by November 2011, with a debt of €1,900 billion (the fourth-largest in the world), appeared to be days away from being cut off from global financial markets. The EU and IMF knew that they would struggle to raise anywhere near the €600bn it was estimated that a three-year bailout programme would cost.[20]

Europe became engulfed in a flurry of crisis-management initiatives. In the window from November 2011 to the end of 2012, which *Financial Times* journalist Peter Spiegel has suggested will be remembered as 'the months which forever changed the European project', budget rules were made inviolable, banking oversight was removed from sovereign control and the ECB was established as the lender of last resort for failing eurozone states.[21]

Befitting a currency whose origins were deeply political, the turning point in the crisis – or at least its transition from acute to chronic – was not so much an institutional as a political response. In July 2012, ECB President Mario Draghi offered his 'big bazooka' pledge to do 'whatever it takes to preserve the Euro'.[22] A process known as Outright Monetary Transactions (OMT) was authorised to allow the ECB to buy bonds issued by eurozone member states in secondary, sovereign bond markets, albeit under conditions. Soon after Draghi's announcement, bond yields for the embattled eurozone periphery countries fell and stock markets began, cautiously, to rally. Crucial time had been bought. Yet even as the crisis peaked, low growth and high unemployment continued to blight Europe's periphery. Unemployment in Greece peaked at 27.9% in 2013, with youth unemployment at 58%. Gross domestic product in periphery countries remained well below pre-crisis highs.

The depth and persistence of the euro crisis affected international perceptions of the continent and its Union. At best, Europe appeared incapacitated, too distracted by the fate of its common currency and Union to be a reliable partner on the world stage. More often, especially when set against the narrative of the shift of global power to the East, Europe appeared to be facing a 'lost decade' of economic stagnation that would inevitably diminish its role in world affairs.[23]

It did not bode well that the EU could not even agree on a common diagnosis for the crisis, let alone a solution.[24] It was problematic, too, to talk (as the Lisbon Treaty did) about doing more on the international stage when the budgets necessary to support such activity were shrinking. For anyone following the merry-go-round of summits, prioritisation of domestic order and fiscal politics was obvious. Issues of banking union were simply more of a priority than operationalising the newly established EEAS. As the euro crisis claimed the career of politician after politician – in 2011–12 heads of state and government in France, Greece, Ireland, Italy and Portugal either resigned, fell or lost re-election bids – friends of the EU could be forgiven for wondering how a common strategic perspective could possibly be agreed among such an unstable line-up of leaders.

The euro crisis not only highlighted intra-Union tensions on the international stage, it fuelled them. When Greek Prime Minister Alexis Tsipras travelled to Moscow in April 2015 to meet President Vladimir Putin in his ongoing bid to ease EU conditions for extending financial assistance to Greece, it highlighted the challenge of maintaining a common European front towards a Russia isolated following its March 2014 annexation of Crimea and its subsequent invasion of eastern Ukraine. That Tsipras returned from his visit largely empty-handed did little to quiet fears about the opportunities the euro crisis afforded hostile third parties to undermine Union solidarity.[25] The EU was, meanwhile, forced to recognise that it could no longer expect the lure of association agreements to be sufficient to pull neighbouring countries smoothly along the path of liberal reform. This was made clear not just by developments in

Ukraine, but also by Putin's ability to persuade Armenia in the space of one afternoon to torpedo three years of negotiations on an association agreement with the EU in favour of joining the Russian-dominated Eurasian Customs Union.

The euro crisis also increased tensions with the US, where senior figures watched the EU's handling of the crisis with mounting frustration and concern. Germany's prescribed medicine, many believed, was not only late in coming but misguided in its formulation. Moreover, the country's persistent current-account surpluses were seen as at least partly to blame for the weakness of the eurozone's subsequent recovery. Under president Barack Obama, the US Treasury placed Germany on its watch list of currency manipulators. By March 2018, as the Trump White House was announcing tariffs on steel and aluminium imports from foreign competitors, Germany appeared a particular target for the president's ire. Trump's language and approach may have been unusually direct, but at least a part of the argument was familiar.

Transatlantic tensions were also raised in interactions between the IMF and its European members, who together constituted one-third of the fund's executive board. There was particular frustration with the early bailout of Greece, where the IMF sidestepped its own rules against lending to countries whose debt was not sustainable. This move also damaged the credibility of the fund among the usual subjects of its attention in the developing world, supposedly proving that the IMF treated its Western founders more favourably.

Economic pain, exacerbated by rounds of unpopular austerity measures often enforced on member states by external governments and institutions, contributed to the rise of populist and nationalist parties in many member states. Anti-EU parties made unprecedented gains across the continent. In Greece, four decades of political domination by left-leaning

Pasok and right-leaning New Democracy were forgotten following the rise of the far-right Golden Dawn movement and Pasok's replacement as the second-largest party in Greece's 2012 elections by the far-left Syriza party. Even founding members of the European project were not immune from this trend, with the continued rise of the National Front in France and the Freedom Party in the Netherlands in the early years of the euro crisis. (It is important to note that these trends predate the euro crisis, even as they were exacerbated by it.) In Italy, a new generation reached voting age familiar only with the euro and a revolving door of political and economic crises that its politicians appeared incapable of resolving. In these circumstances it was perhaps unsurprising that the country's 2018 election saw far-right and populist forces enter government, having together garnered more than 50% of the popular vote.

The development of populist nationalist autocracies within the EU poses an increasingly uncomfortable challenge to the Union's integrity on the international stage, not least because, as British historian Timothy Garton Ash has noted, it questions the degree to which the EU aspires to be a 'community of democracies'.[26] It has also adversely affected the Union's ability to manage its foreign policy with other autocratic states, as shown, for example, by the close ties that have developed between Putin and Hungarian Prime Minister Viktor Orbán.[27] Many of Orbán's methods have been copied by the right-wing Law and Justice party (PiS) in Poland, even as the country takes a very different policy stance with regard to Russia. Indeed, given its size and past symbolism as the poster child for European integration, Poland's political evolution presents the EU with an even greater challenge.

This surge of populist parties also limited the political space in some of the affected countries for weak governments to push through unpopular structural reforms in the face of entrenched special-interest groups. It constrained, too, the political space for considered compromise and debate, in the process weakening the political norms that lie at the heart of EU foreign policymaking.

A neighbourhood crisis

By early 2013, just as Commission President José Manuel Barroso was declaring the 'existential' phase of the euro crisis over, the crisis in Europe's neighbourhoods was entering full swing. The EU neighbourhood policy lay in tatters both to the south and to the east. The hope engendered by the revolutions of the Arab Spring was fading in the face of the bloody realities of state failure and conflict, particularly in the hell of Syria's civil war. Meanwhile, a resurgent Russia had mounted an illegal invasion and annexation in Ukraine, presenting the continent with the challenge of responding not just to this violation but also to the more general reassertion of Russian power and the return of geopolitics to centre stage that it heralded.

The demands made by these twin crises and their respective consequences opened up, in theory, space for a grand bargain on EU foreign-policy priorities between member states in the east and south of the Union. Calling for greater strategic convergence in threat perceptions, Macron noted that 'Russia is not a German problem or a French problem … interventions in Africa are not the sole responsibility of France'.[28]

In reality, especially against a backdrop of limited financial, bureaucratic and military resources, the crises in Europe's neighbourhoods contributed to a further fracturing of EU efforts to develop common strategic agendas, as member states sought to prioritise their own immediate foreign- and security-policy concerns. Mutual recriminations over deficits in solidarity were commonplace. The frustration of Polish MEP Jacek Saryusz-Wolski was representative of the challenge; he warned that 'the southern flank of the Union will not enjoy the understanding of its eastern flank on immigration, it if continues not to understand, or to refuse to understand, the eastern existential threat'.[29]

A fracturing southern neighbourhood

As ordinary people in the EU's southern neighbours took to the streets and populist uprisings spread outwards from Tunisia and Egypt in the early days of the Arab Spring, EU leaders regularly reiterated their commitment to the region. Some of these uprisings occurred in places long-since forgotten, for the most part, in the chaos of the story that would follow. In Morocco, for example, protesters called for social justice and reform. And even as revolutions followed in Tunisia and Egypt, Bahrain's security forces were violently quelling the demands of their population for greater political freedom and equality for the Shia majority. When Saudi Arabia, joined by Gulf states, mobilised to crush the uprising across the King Fahd Causeway, strategic calculations on wider regional dynamics with regard to Iran, as well as the utility of Naval Support Activity Bahrain (NSA Bahrain), ensured a notably muted response not just from the US but also from Europe.

As unrest spread, in June 2011 the EU appointed a Special Representative for the Southern Mediterranean. EU Task Forces were set up with Egypt, Jordan and Tunisia. The EU instinctively understood the deep connection between economics and political progress, yet its efforts to support transitional forces to move in a positive direction were to prove largely insufficient. Talk of timely engagement by EU representatives was soon replaced by talk of the need for strategic patience and the long road to democracy.

In January 2012, Syrian President Bashar al-Assad launched his attack on Homs, blaming foreign interference for the uprisings he was facing. By July the Syrian uprising had morphed into a civil war, with a death toll that had reached 70,000 by February 2013.[30] In Egypt, democratic elections in May brought a strongman back to the scene in the form of Muslim Brotherhood candidate Muhammed Morsi. In Libya in September, Islamic militants murdered US Ambassador Christopher Stevens during the storming of the US embassy in Benghazi.

One of Morsi's first foreign trips was to Brussels, to agree the resumption of bilateral contacts through the structures of the EU–Egypt Association Agreement and the restart of negotiations on a new ENP Action Plan. But the limits of European influence were highlighted when, only two months later, Morsi

Libya: the missed turning point

When civil war broke out in Libya in February 2011, EU leaders largely agreed on their political objective – an orderly transition of power – but they could not agree on the mechanisms by which to achieve it. Efforts at a coordinated response soon unravelled. Germany, three months into a rotating seat on the Security Council, abstained on Resolution 1973 authorising 'all necessary measures' to prevent attacks on civilians, while France, the UK and the US used the resolution to launch airstrikes against government forces and installations. This soon became a NATO operation, yet as NATO took over the naval enforcement of the UN arms embargo as well, Germany withdrew its warships and Airborne Warning and Control System (AWACS) staff from NATO operations in the Mediterranean.

Germany's behaviour raised practical questions about the utility of the CSDP, since military action under its rubric is dependent on agreement among EU member states. Further tensions within the EU came to the fore in the wake of France's decision to airdrop weapons to the Libyan rebels as well as in their reactions to Libyan strongman Muammar Gadhafi's promise to 'unleash an unprecedented wave of illegal migration'.

Aspirations for a robust EU military mission came to nothing. In April 2011, European Union Force (EUFOR) Libya was 'stood up' to provide military support for humanitarian-protection operations. An operational headquarters was decided, a commander appointed and a budget granted himself unlimited powers to protect the nation, including the power to legislate without judicial oversight or review. A new constitution was adopted in a vote plagued by allegations of widespread irregularities that in turn sparked further protests. By July 2013, Morsi had been deposed in a *coup d'état*, marking Egypt's second revolution in two years. While the EU reiterated that it remained 'unequivocally committed to supporting the Egyptian people in their aspirations to democracy and inclusive governance', it stopped short of objecting to the junta's intervention, calling instead for the rapid organisation of new elections.[31]

In Iraq, a country still rebuilding in the wake of the US-led invasion of 2003 and its bloody aftermath, violence again

agreed. But deployment was made conditional on a request from the UN Office for the Coordination of Humanitarian Affairs (OCHA). When this was (perhaps unsurprisingly) not forthcoming, the operation was stood down – an outcome that suited the interests of more than a few member states. OCHA's reluctance to blur the line between military and civilian responses was well known.

The divisions on display did not, however, stop the European Council from calling for Gadhafi to relinquish power immediately, or from recognising the National Transitional Council as 'a political interlocutor' less than a week after its official formation. In May 2011, HR/VP Catherine Ashton visited the rebels in Benghazi, pledging long-term support as she opened an EU Representative office in the rebel stronghold. As the rebellion unfolded, the EU went beyond the sanctions demanded by the UN. For example, it implemented what amounted to an oil and gas embargo when it froze the assets of 26 Libyan energy companies with close ties to the regime, and sanctioned the country's port authorities.

In April 2019, as the situation in Libya again deteriorated, the governments of France, Italy, the United Arab Emirates, the US and the UK issued a joint statement promising to hold accountable 'any Libyan faction that precipitates further civil conflict'.[32] It is likely that, in Libya, European political willingness and capabilities to protect and promote even a fragile stability will continue to be put to the test.

spiralled upwards. Through 2011 and 2012, the sectarian Shia-led government of Nuri al-Maliki faced waves of popular protests. Demonstrators initially focused on demands to end political corruption, unemployment and foreign occupation. With confrontations between the predominantly Sunni-organised protesters and the Shia-led security forces increasing, it seemed as if Syria's sectarian civil war was expanding into Iraq. The defeat of the Iraqi Army at Mosul in June 2014 by forces of the Islamic State, also known as ISIS or ISIL, effectively ended the Maliki government. Neither European nor Western engagement more broadly could contain the spiralling violence.

With the declaration by ISIS of a caliphate stretching from Aleppo in Syria to the eastern Iraqi province of Diyala, Europe's perception of the region's more subtle shifts and dynamics was complicated, perhaps even subsumed, by its focus on the terrorist threat it now faced. Concerns were further heightened by the flow of European citizens to supplement ISIS's ranks of foreign fighters. In the wake of the deadly terrorist attacks by ISIS in Paris in November 2015, France significantly increased its contribution to a US-led coalition conducting airstrikes that had been under way since September. In a largely political act aimed at securing support in kind for French interventions in Syria and Iraq, it also invoked Lisbon's previously unused solidarity clause, requiring the EU and its member states to furnish it with 'aid and assistance' in the wake of these attacks. The perceived lack of responsiveness by many fellow member states to this rallying cry further fuelled French frustrations with the prospects of developing a credible common European defence policy.[33] Nevertheless, France introduced a UNSC resolution (quickly co-sponsored by the UK) to encourage member states to take 'all necessary measures' to defeat ISIS (and its affiliated Al-Nusra Front). Its adoption by the UN was then used to secure UK parliamentary approval in December to join the medley of bombing.

As terrorist attacks continued in Europe, some modest measures were taken to improve the coordination of European responses, including the introduction of improved firearms controls and the establishment in January 2016 of an EU Counter Terrorism Centre as part of a wider push to promote expertise and improve information sharing. A new commissioner was also established, charged with developing the EU's 'Security Union'.

Collectively, the developments that followed the Arab Spring raised serious questions about the EU's strategic coherence and the limits and potential of its security and defence policies. Libya might have been a military coming-of-age for European defence cooperation, not least given the direct stakes EU member states held in Libya's security, as the refugee crisis would go on to prove. Instead, EU governments agreed in April 2011 to offer military support to the UN's humanitarian agency in Libya. Yet EUFOR Libya (as the mooted mission was labelled) never came to pass as no request for such support was made, leaving EU states to take action unilaterally and under the aegis of NATO. That the military action that did unfold showcased continuing European dependence on US military support says much about the scale of the challenges that still lie ahead for the continent in its search for strategic substance.

As the prospect of EUFOR Libya came and went, and as even the modest civilian CSDP mission that was the European Union Border Assistance Mission (EUBAM) in Libya was downsized and had its mandate adjusted in the wake of the country's worsening security situation, the EU struggled for strategy. Yet, in the midst of the financial crisis, EU money still continued to flow. Although few member states reach the ODA objective of 0.7% of GDP, the EU has nevertheless cemented its position as the world's leading donor to the Middle East and North Africa, with EU institutions and member states accounting for one-third of all aid received by the region.[34] European ODA to the region rose from €4.4bn in 2010 to €6.7bn in 2015 (using 2017 rates). Under its European Neighbourhood Instrument, EU institutional spending alone in its southern neighbourhood is set to come in at around €7.5bn–9.2bn between 2014 and 2020.[35]

Though ISIS might have been militarily defeated, so were the majority of those who had peacefully protested for dignity and democracy across the Arab world. In the meantime, the growing youth population of the Middle East continues to experience stunted opportunities under autocratic, often sclerotic governments. Egypt, the world's most populous Arab nation, is once again under military dictatorship. Syria lies in ruins and still under the control of a war criminal, supported by Iran and Russia. Large areas of Libya have been reduced to rubble. Civil war in Yemen brings with it staggering human costs, including the threat of starvation for millions. Proxy conflicts are proliferating across the region. A low-level Shia insurgency in Bahrain is sponsored by Iran and countered by Saudi Arabia. And even as the hope that is the Tunisian Spring stumbles on, thankfully, Tunisia served as the largest source of foreign fighters who left their homes to join the ranks of ISIS.[36]

A stable 'ring of friends' to the EU's south this is not. A 2016 UN Arab Development report warned of more conflicts to come, noting that in 2014 the Arab world accounted for 5% of the world's population, but 45% of the world's terrorism, 68% of its battle-related deaths and 58% of its refugees. By 2020, it concluded, three of every four Arabs in the world would be living in countries designated as 'prone to conflict'.[37] The strategic implications for Europe and the demands that this will make of its Union are brutally clear.

The eastern neighbourhood and the revenge of geopolitics

In November 2013, Ukrainian President Victor Yanukovych opted to delay a planned signing of an association agreement with the EU. He was encouraged in his decision by a package of sovereign loans and cheap gas from Russia designed to help his campaign for re-election. His action brought protesters onto the streets, many waving EU flags, only to find themselves opposed by rubber bullets and then live fire. This set in motion a series of events that culminated in Yanukovych's flight from Kiev and the occupation of the Crimean Peninsula by Russian special forces in February 2014, followed by annexation in March. A pro-Russia insurgency then spread into Ukraine's eastern Donbas region. Referendums on 11 May 2014 approved the secession of the 'people's republics' of Donetsk and Luhansk.

With the election of a new, pro-Western president in Kiev, the landmark trade deal with the EU spurned by Yanukovych was revived and signed into law. In the wake of the downing of a Malaysian airliner by a Russian *Buk* surface-to-air missile, the EU extended the sanctions it had imposed on Russia after the annexation of Crimea. It also cancelled the EU–Russia summit, with EU member states agreeing not to hold regular bilateral summits. Instead, at the 70th anniversary commemorations of the Normandy landings, an informal grouping of the leaders of France, Germany, Russia and Ukraine met for tentative discussions in what would become known as the 'Normandy format'. Although the absence of EU institutions was noticeable, Europe, or at least Germany, would nevertheless lead the way in handling crisis negotiations in its eastern neighbourhood.

With a G8 meeting in Sochi scheduled for June 2014 cancelled in favour of a G7 meeting in Brussels, EU countries also led the way in supporting Russia's suspension from the Organisation for Economic Co-operation and Development (OECD) and the International Energy Agency. An array of sanctions was developed, from asset freezes and travel bans, to specific sectoral sanctions, to restrictions on economic cooperation.[38] Attention shifted to the more pragmatic challenge of restoring stability in Ukraine beyond Crimea. In March 2015, under German stewardship, EU leaders agreed to align their sanctions with the implementation of the updated 'Minsk II' agreement they had helped negotiate the previous month. This agreement laid out a 13-point road map to resolving the conflict, beginning with a ceasefire and the withdrawal of heavy weaponry from the front lines. As progress on the implementation of Minsk II has remained unsatisfactory, the EU has surprised its critics by the unity it has shown in consistently rolling over these sanctions as required. Western goodwill towards Ukraine, however, was sorely tested by growing concerns about the incompetence and corruption of the administration in Kiev. It was, as the Russian government delighted in pointing out, not just Russia that was failing to deliver upon its commitments under Minsk. The result was a political stalemate unsatisfactory for all involved.

By mid-2017, the UN estimated that 10,000 people had been killed in the crisis in Ukraine, with more than 23,500 injured.[39] This was no frozen conflict in Europe's backyard. Indeed, 2017 proved to be more deadly than 2016. Some 27,000 armed separatist personnel, supported by more than 3,000 Russian soldiers, continued to face off against some 30,000 Ukrainian troops, while 3.5m Ukrainians found themselves living in occupied territories. Approximately 1.4m Ukrainians fled as refugees abroad, while some 1.7m were internally displaced. Even with all the turmoil to Europe's south, in 2015 the fourth-largest source of internally displaced people globally lay within the wider European continent itself.[40]

Yet Russia's actions in Ukraine are just one part of the test that the EU now finds itself facing to its east. The broader concern is the challenge that the revival of an assertive, even aggressive, Russia poses to European security and internal EU cohesion. Europe can no longer deny that its efforts at a 'modernisation partnership' with Putin have failed. Instead, Russia is engaging in international affairs according to Putin's own terms and conditions, with little regard for the rule of law and other values that the EU seeks to protect and promote.

Russia's geopolitical ambitions can be seen not just in Putin's actions in Ukraine, but also in his intervention in Syria in 2015. This intervention, nominally targeted against ISIS, was critical in helping restore the authority of a beleaguered Assad over his fractured country. Russian ambitions can also be seen in Putin's cultivation of closer relations with other actors in the region including Egypt, Iran, Saudi Arabia and Turkey, as well as the bolstering of Moscow's ties to North Korea, where Russia's record on proliferation appears questionable.[41] Meanwhile, the military reforms that Russia embarked upon in 2008, supported by a large increase in defence spending, have begun to pay dividends. Russian warplanes restarted their Cold War-era patrols in 2007, but Russian incursions and aerial encounters became more frequent following Russian aggression in Ukraine. In 2013, NATO jets intercepted Russian jets just 43 times over the Baltic; by 2015 this figure had risen to 160.[42] In 2016, Estonia reported six violations of its airspace by Russia. Other EU member states, including the UK, also reported an increase in activity near and sometimes inside their airspace and territorial waters. Russia also bolstered its capabilities elsewhere, including in the Arctic, where it has been both reactivating military bases abandoned after the collapse of the USSR and building new ones.[43] The scale and nature of the military exercise *Zapad* 2017 in September, conducted by Russia and Belarus along the latter's western border and in the exclave of Kaliningrad, served as a further lightning rod for growing European concerns.[44]

While the primary focus for the military response lay with NATO, Europe was left to grapple with the implications these developments had for the EU and for the defence requirements and capabilities of its individual member states. These concerns became more acute following the election of a US president with an apparently transactional commitment, at best, to the cornerstone of European security.

A migration crisis

Pressure on EU frontier states, most notably Greece and Italy, from growing numbers of migrants fleeing instability in the EU's neighbourhoods raised uncomfortable questions about European solidarity. Combined with the ongoing threat of deadly terrorist attacks, these pressures also cast doubt on the future of the Schengen area (the 26 member states with no passport or other border controls along their mutual borders). It became clear that, if free travel between Schengen states was to be sustainable, stronger, better functioning external controls would be required.

The EU had faced refugee crises before, for example during the break-up of Yugoslavia and in 2006 when tens of thousands of migrants from West Africa made their way to Spain's Canary Islands. And the 11 September 2001 terrorist attacks had already sparked a conversation within the EU that linked the security of its external borders to the future of the Schengen zone. Yet the institutional arrangements the EU put in place to deal with these challenges were unfit for purpose in the face of the 2015–16 refugee crisis, which peaked in October 2015 when more than 10,000 migrants arrived in Greece in a single day. At one point, Slovenia faced refugee numbers equivalent to 0.6% of its population on a daily basis. Between January and November 2015, an estimated 1.5m people entered the EU illegally.[45] First-time applications for asylum in EU member states doubled in 2016 over the previous year, reaching around 1.2m.

The EU's external-border management force, Frontex, had long included a surge in refugee numbers in its risk analysis. After all, by July 2013, the UN Refugee Agency was reporting that 6,000 people were leaving Syria daily. These flows were supplemented by other events such as ISIS's takeover of Mosul, Iraq in June 2014. Yet Frontex continued to go underequipped and underfunded. A simple coordinating agency, its budget for hiring its equipment and forces from national agencies was a mere €143m in 2015 (increased to €254m in 2016).

When Italy failed to persuade fellow member states to provide further funding to its expensive *Operation Mare Nostrum* in its southern waters, Frontex stepped in to replace this bilateral operation with a smaller, more tightly mandated multinational mission. The primary focus of *Operation Triton* was on border patrol and surveillance closer to the Italian coast than the national operation it replaced, although *Triton's* area of responsibility expanded over time to a line 139 nano-metres south of Sicily.[46] (In early 2018, the mission, renamed *Themis*, was given an expanded mandate; a key change was that rescued migrants would no longer necessarily be processed on Italian soil.) A counterpart, *Operation Poseidon Rapid Intervention*, covering the Greek sea borders with Turkey and the Greek islands and providing technical assistance to the Greek authorities, replaced the *Poseidon Sea* that had been ongoing since 2006.

In April 2015, two mass drownings of migrants in the Mediterranean in quick succession led to the tripling of funding for *Triton* and *Poseidon*. Reinforcements for the CSDP civilian mission EUCAP Sahel Niger (aimed at combatting irregular migration, or migration outside regulatory norms, at source) soon followed. A military CSDP mission, EUNAVFOR Med (nicknamed *Sophia*), was also agreed, targeted at disrupting people-smugglers in the south-central Mediterranean.

By July 2015, however, Hungary was erecting razor wire along its external border with Serbia, closing its borders with Romania and Croatia, and allowing its army to use tear gas against increasingly desperate irregular migrants. Others, including Slovenia and Austria, would soon follow Budapest in spirit, if not in method. On 20 August, faced with more than 3,000 refugees arriving daily, Macedonia declared a state of emergency and closed its border with Greece, forcing a stand-off that saw migrants tear gassed, with batons and stun grenades also deployed. Media images of drowned children combined with the ineffective EU response to the surge in migration had created a crisis well before Merkel's unilateral decision four days later to suspend, for Syrian refugees, Germany's implementation of an EU regulation that obliged refugees to claim asylum from the first EU country they reached. As member states struggled to deal with the influx of refugees, a growing number of them temporarily reintroduced border controls, as was their sovereign right as a last resort in the face of an established serious threat to public policy or internal security.[47]

In September, member states showed some rhetorical solidarity when they agreed to redistribute among themselves (with EU budgetary support) 120,000 refugees then based in Greece and Italy (on top of the 40,000 previously agreed) over the following two years. Some former Communist countries from which refugees had once fled to Western Europe now opposed these mandatory quotas, which were only adopted thanks to qualified majority voting (QMV). In a sign of the degree to which norms were breaking down even within the Union, Orbán described his opposition to the measure as fighting 'the Islamisation of Europe'. Slovakia and the Czech Republic also made their preference for Christian refugees clear.

The attempt to impose mandatory quotas certainly divided the EU, but a policy of inaction had already proved similarly divisive, with front-line member states left to bear the brunt of the crisis. Weak member-state follow-through on the quota allocations reflected the EU's constant struggle between rhetoric and reality. By the end of April 2018, a mere 34,694 refugees had been relocated across 24 European countries, with Germany alone taking 10,825.[48] In December 2017, the European Commission referred the Czech Republic, Hungary and Poland to the ECJ for non-compliance with their legal obligations under the emergency relocation scheme, which the ECJ had already affirmed.[49]

The 2015 Paris attacks highlighted the security threats posed by weak external borders. One of the perpetrators was discovered to have entered Europe disguised as a refugee. France quickly followed the example set by others and reimposed border controls. In December 2016 internal border issues were again highlighted when a terrorist, who had arrived in Italy as a migrant from Tunisia five years earlier, drove a stolen truck through a crowded Christmas market in Berlin. The attacker, who already had a criminal record in Italy and was facing deportation from Germany, then fled unchallenged through four countries before being shot dead by Italian police.

If the Schengen zone was to survive, action to shore up the EU's external border was needed. This would not come quickly, or easily. Some modest measures were taken, such as the triggering of integrated political crisis-response arrangements on information sharing which resulted in the development of a common web platform to monitor, amongst other things, developing migratory flows. A strategy began to emerge based around first reception facilities (known in EU parlance as 'hotspots') located at the EU's external borders, where coordinated efforts by EU and national agencies were meant to ensure the identification and registration of asylum seekers, followed up by a policy of relocations and returns. Yet the strategy was insufficiently resourced in terms of finance, personnel and political will.[50] As migratory flows continued, so too did the suspensions of Schengen and the rise of populist forces. In January 2016, for example, Sweden and Denmark joined the ranks of those member states suspending Schengen. Meanwhile, in Germany, reports of organised sexual harassment and assaults by migrants in Cologne on New Year's Eve 2015 galvanised the rise of an anti-immigrant populist party, the Alternative für Deutschland (AfD). By September 2017 the AfD had won sufficient seats in federal elections to become the third-largest party in the Bundestag.

Only in March 2016, with a controversial EU–Turkey deal (effectively secured by Merkel in a display of bilateral diplomacy), did the flow began to lessen. The deal offered Ankara a package of political incentives and financial aid in return for Turkish cooperation policing its border with Greece and its acceptance of returned migrants. While the initial effect was dramatic, the flow did not stop entirely, and the agreement involved several unpleasant moral compromises for the EU. The need to secure Turkish assistance with regard to the EU's migration difficulties clashed with EU efforts to promote democracy and human rights in a state that was turning towards authoritarianism. With thousands stranded on Greek islands such as Lesbos in overcrowded and often desperate conditions, Médecins Sans Frontières condemned the EU's 'policy of cruelty', 'trapping people in these dire conditions to deter other refugees from coming'.[51]

In September 2016, Frontex became the European Border and Coast Guard Agency, with new competencies, including the ability to buy its own equipment and to draw upon a permanent pool of member-state experts. With the Balkan route and the Greek border with Turkey now stabilised, the attention of authorities and migrants alike turned to the Mediterranean Sea and to Italy's 7,600km coastline in particular. Some refugees who would have entered Europe through the Balkans diverted to Libya, a country with even less infrastructure, money and interest in satisfactorily housing the rising number of migrants than Turkey.

In February 2017, EU leaders endorsed a further deal between Italy and the new UN-backed Libyan government aimed at curbing the Mediterranean route. Amongst other measures, the EU would help train and equip the Libyan coastguard, support the establishment of 'safe' refugee camps within Libya and assist with the voluntary repatriation of asylum seekers. In 2017, an EU Emergency Trust Fund for Africa helped 20,000 migrants return home from Libya. As with the EU–Turkey deal, the numbers crossing the Mediterranean soon dropped. But conditions in Libyan camps continued to deteriorate. In November 2017, UN High Commissioner for Human Rights Zeid bin Ra'ad Zeid al-Hussein called the camps 'an outrage to the conscience of humanity', complaining that the EU had done 'nothing so far to reduce the level of abuses suffered by migrants'.[52]

The numbers of migrants reaching European shores fell by more than half in 2017, to 186,768.[53] Italy now bore much of the brunt, while by early 2018 Spain surpassed Greece in the numbers of migrant arrivals registered. However, even arrivals in Italy fell from a June 2017 peak of 23,524 to 3,895 in May 2018. Yet the political effect of the refugee crisis continues to reverberate. Political scientist Ivan Krastev reflected in October 2017 that the migration crisis had become a point of no return for the EU.[54]

The apparent lack of EU solidarity for Italy's front-line role likely contributed to the formation of a populist government there in June 2018, with an interior minister who had campaigned on a pledge to deport 500,000 migrants living illegally in Italy and whose hardline stance threatened another full-blown crisis of European disunity. Later that month, with arguments over migration management once again appearing to pose an existential challenge to the EU (or at least to the political future of Merkel, the EU's most influential leader), EU leaders committed to a series of measures to improve the security of the EU's external borders, which Amnesty International promptly condemned as 'dangerous and self-serving policies which could expose men, women and children to serious abuse'.[55]

It is almost inevitable that any policy will fail both to be fully effective and to be fully in line with EU values. Proliferation of Turkey-style deals will be expensive for countries, most notably Germany, concerned about secondary migration by refugees arriving in the EU. The challenge of resettlement remains central for EU strategy and solidarity. Meanwhile, it is perhaps more reasonable to cut off irregular migration flows if the EU is perceived in the world beyond its borders to be making legal channels for migration both more available and more efficient. Simply paying others to keep the hordes from the gates is unlikely to work as a stand-alone strategy in anything but the short term. Meanwhile, European states will need to remember that the right to seek asylum is protected in the Universal Declaration of Human Rights and the UN Refugee Convention. This includes a prohibition on penalties for refugees for irregular entry.

A membership crisis

The migration crisis was an important part of the backdrop against which the UK voted, in 2016, to become the first member state to leave the Union since its foundation as the

European Economic Community in 1957. The timing – from the euro crisis to the migrant crisis to concerns over the security ramifications of insecure borders – was particularly favourable for the 'Leave' campaign. Conservative Party maverick Boris Johnson, in his new-found role as Brexit's cheerleader-in-chief, was able to talk of the EU as the 'graveyard of low growth' and berate it for a 'self-inflicted economic disaster' while presenting a picture of a UK restrained by the 'sclerotic one-size-fits-all Brussels approach to regulation'.[56] He would be rewarded for his efforts by his subsequent appointment as UK foreign secretary.

Although there were also both more domestic and more global drivers behind the UK's decision to leave the Union, the euro crisis exacerbated the perception of EU and eurozone weakness, and of the potential liabilities to which the UK was exposed as a result of its membership. Brexit campaigners used images of refugees queuing to cross the Croatia–Slovenia border as a warning of the price of EU solidarity. More generally, the argument that the UK's power and status benefitted from EU membership was undermined by the EU's obvious lack of satisfactory influence on dynamics across its periphery. Years of austerity politics and of government underfunding of key public services enhanced the allure of a supposed Brexit 'dividend' from the UK's EU contributions that could be redirected to help redress this underinvestment. Meanwhile, broader cries to 'take back control' played neatly into the idea that the Union had evolved into something radically different from that to which the UK had signed up, encouraging a sense of perceived unfairness.

The 1975 referendum that asked UK voters 'do you think the UK should stay in the European Community (the common market)?' passed with 67.2% approval, on a turnout of 64%. UK prime minister Harold Wilson had called the referendum to address splits in the Labour Party, and campaigned to remain on the basis of a reformed deal. By contrast, the Conservatives were united in their desire to stay, as was the tabloid press. (The UK tabloid newspaper, the *Sun*, that would in June 2016 run with the headline 'BeLEAVE in Britain', had argued in 1975 that 'We are all Europeans now'.) In 2016, divisions within the Conservative Party triggered a similar referendum. The tabloid press largely opposed continued EU membership, while Labour's party machinery was, at best, unenthusiastic in its support, and was overseen by a leader who had voted to leave in 1975. Asked if the UK should remain a member or leave the EU, 51.9% voted to leave, on a turnout of 72.2%.[57]

The divisions in Europe before the vote not only played directly into the referendum's outcome, they had an indirect impact on UK prime minster David Cameron's room for negotiation once he had decided to copy Wilson's ploy. Cameron's attempt to deliver some sort of 'reformed EU' over-estimated the political appetite of his fellow EU leaders for further substantive discussions on reform that risked opening a Pandora's box of differences. Indeed, the investment made by some of Cameron's people in considering mechanisms for treaty change that might avoid the need for referendums in some member states to ratify the reforms Cameron sought was, with hindsight, the stuff of fantasy.[58]

The palpable tensions between the UK and the rest of the EU (the EU27) in the wake of the Brexit vote were already evident in the run-up to it. Before the referendum, the UK was warned against an 'à la carte Europe'; after the decision to leave, EU27 warnings shifted towards a slimmed-down diet of cherries not for picking. Both before and after the referendum, the UK pushed for flexibility and adaptability; the EU27 emphasised the sanctity of rules and procedures. Both parties had their own logic and own self-interests to support their arguments. But these arguments are also a microcosm of the broader challenges the EU faces as it decides how to steer its Union in the wake of the UK's prospective departure. Might the gap between European elites and citizens be closed by efforts further to embed EU institutions with the capacities they need to function effectively, even with the loss of sovereignty such measures likely involve, or might it instead be further exacerbated by such efforts? Would more flexibility in the crafting of a far-reaching deal, as required, on the closest possible future relationship risk opening the door for others to exit? Or is it instead an abdication of strategic credibility and vision for the EU27 to fail to pursue such an arrangement?

Yet, as the EU27 rallied to protect the Union and an exercise in damage limitation began, a renewed momentum and sense of purpose also began to emerge. Early acts of solidarity helped create, at least while negotiations focused on the terms and conditions of the UK's exit, something of a virtuous circle for EU27 unity and influence. While the UK is rightly criticised for having triggered Article 50 (the TEU provision requiring two years' notice for withdrawal) without any apparent strategic plan, EU27 unity in insisting on 'no negotiation without notification' was at least a consideration in the UK's premature move. Activation of the clause inevitably gave the EU27 an advantage in negotiations but it also contributed, in a relatively minor way, to the confusion and uncertainty that followed.

In the immediate aftermath of the Brexit vote, Mogherini presented the new EUGS to EU leaders as an opportunity for progress now that the traditional stumbling block for closer defence-policy cooperation was leaving the Union. The EUGS attempted to set clear strategic priorities: the EU would protect its Union and its citizens; it would respond to external crises and conflicts using an integrated approach; it would build the resilience and capacities of its partners; and it would promote cooperative regional orders and support a global governance fit for the twenty-first century. The statement 'our Union is under threat' – intended to refer to crises both internal and external – took on even greater significance.[59] The EUGS's call for a more realistic framework for external engagement through the exercise of 'principled pragmatism' appeared more apposite in light of the impending departure of one of the two largest spenders on defence on the continent. But if the overall strategy was perhaps more realistic, the section dedicated specifically to defence cooperation was notably more ambitious.

The challenge of Brexit for Europe's partners around the world is clear. The UK is likely to be preoccupied by managing the fallout from the vote for some time to come. A UK departure also risks the EU27 becoming less outward-looking with regard to key strategic issues of defence and security beyond its immediate neighbourhood. Meanwhile, the knock-on effect of the management of the Brexit process on Europe–US relations remains unclear. Certainly, Trump's apparent support for a harder Brexit than many Europeans (and perhaps even UK Prime Minister Theresa May) consider desirable would appear to be another indication of transatlantic problems ahead.

A transatlantic crisis

On 8 November 2016, the superpower that has historically enabled European integration elected a president ideologically hostile to the Union's integrationist conceit and multilateralist ways. Beyond his attitudes to the EU, Trump was the first US president since the end of the Second World War who appeared not to consider himself the leader of the Western world, with its accompanying values and institutions. Indeed, American scholar John Ikenberry argued, 'the world's most powerful state has begun to sabotage the order it created'.[60] The president was generous in his praise for autocrats from Putin to North Korean leader Kim Jong-un, whereas relations with allied European leaders, most notably Merkel, came under increasing strain. As the US, informed by an America First approach, began questioning the validity of or withdrawing from institutions of global governance, the narrative within Europe began to shift in response. European states had no alternative but to take seriously the prospect that they might need one day to be able to fend for, and to defend, themselves. If they wanted multilateralist institutions to endure, too, they would need to act to defend them.

The substance of Trump's challenge to Europe on its security contribution is, to be sure, far from new, even if the nature and directness of its expression is. Seen in narrow terms, Trump is not the unpredictable anomaly he is so often presented as, but rather the incarnation of what US defense secretary Robert Gates warned of publicly in 2011, after years of futile American cajoling behind closed doors: 'if current trends in the decline of European defence capabilities are not halted or reversed, future US leaders … may not consider the return on America's investment in NATO worth the cost'. In these circumstances, Gates warned, the future for the transatlantic alliance would be 'dim if not dismal'.[61]

European leaders understandably reject the view that Trump's threats can be credited with any of their decisions to invest more in their own security and defence. The revival of the Russian threat and the prospective departure of a serious contributor to the EU force catalogue as a result of Brexit are more likely to be cited as drivers. If there is any credit due to Trump, the bluntness of his rhetoric has ensured that it is a questionable sort of credit. Insofar as the unfolding developments explored in the rest of this *Adelphi* are aided by concerns coming from across the Atlantic, the context is not a positive one. They are motivated as much by a desire to hedge against the risk of a failure of the transatlantic alliance, as to save it.

These developments do, however, appear to be having some positive effects on the compromises member states are willing to consider within Europe in order to develop cooperation further. The progress made at the June 2018 Franco-German summit in Meseberg, for example, where Macron and Merkel agreed a modest agenda for EU reforms long contested in their substance, came in the wake of the shared experience (and public display) of transatlantic discord at the G7 summit in Quebec two weeks earlier, which included Trump's subsequent retraction of the closing joint statement.

As evidenced by the 1956 Suez crisis, transatlantic relations have gone through crises before, and survived. Moreover, considerable overlaps in interests are deeply embedded into the US and European systems. Nevertheless, the scale of the challenge for Europe should be clear as it seeks to shore up what it can of its transatlantic alliance, even as it begins to consider alternatives. In August 2018, centre-left German Foreign Minister Heiko Maas intervened in the debate that continues to unfold across European capitals over the degree to which shifts in Washington's international outlook are a short-term crisis to be managed or a longer-term structural shift that requires a more fundamental continental rethink. His pitch was clear: 'the US and Europe have been drifting apart for years. The overlapping of values and interests that shaped our relationship for two generations is decreasing. The binding force of the East–West conflict is history.'[62]

Crisis contained is not crisis solved

It is unsurprising that Europe's partners abroad tend to see a continent beset by its own concerns to the detriment of its strategic aspirations, but such generalisations do a disservice to the

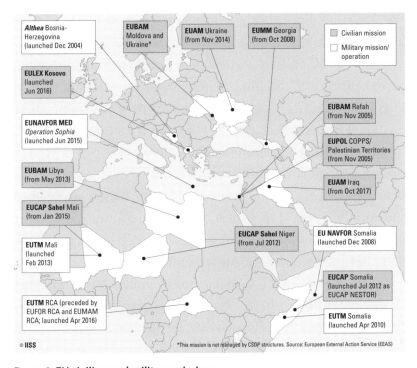

Figure 2. **EU civilian and military missions**

complexity of what is happening within Europe, not to mention the boundaries of what is possible for Europe and its partners in a more nationalist geopolitical order. In the midst of all these crises, the stereotype of a European foreign and security policy entirely distracted and frozen in inaction is unfair. While CSDP mission mandates and reach remain generally underwhelming, three new CSDP missions were launched in 2012 even as the euro crisis raged. The EU may have been able to do little to prevent the withering of the Arab Spring, but the EU's first High Representative, Catherine Ashton, did make a meaningful contribution to stability in the Balkans as the EU facilitated the 2013 agreement between Serbia and Kosovo. The same year, Croatia became the 28th EU member state. In 2015, the EU and individual member states played key roles in the agreement of the JCPOA to tackle the Iranian nuclear crisis, even if, to secure the deal, they deliberately left unaddressed other undesirable aspects of Iran's behaviour on the international stage.

In the midst of, and in reaction to, these cumulative crises, signs of recovery and progress have begun to emerge, even if largely born out of necessity and in the face of adversity. There are some important stories to tell from the crisis years, both institutionally and geographically. Construction of a European banking union is far from complete, but that it is under way is significant, whilst its Single Resolution Board, established during the crisis years, has proved itself capable at key moments. Similarly, the ECB has grown in its role, becoming increasingly effective and assertive in enforcing discipline on eurozone members. (The departure of Italian prime minister Silvio Berlusconi from office in 2011 was in no small part due to the ECB's decision to stop buying Italian bonds.) Meanwhile, Portugal has become one of Europe's relative economic success stories; in 2017, its economy recorded its strongest rate of expansion since 2000, consolidating an economic recovery that began in the wake of Lisbon's exit from its three-year economic-adjustment programme.[63] None of the crises described in this chapter have gone away, even if the nature of some of them – most obviously the membership crisis – may have changed shape.

High public debt, inflexible labour-market structures and persistent high rates of non-performing loans are only a few of the obstacles that blight much of the eurozone, particularly across Southern Europe. Greece will be repaying its bailout loans until 2060.[64] In April 2018, its economic recovery was so modest that it was still 23.5% poorer than it was in 2007.[65] Modest eurozone stabilisation has been achieved through intervention and the European Stability Mechanism, rather than through more radical and sustainable progress on fiscal integration. The analogy made by Draghi in 2012 remains largely valid: the euro is a bumblebee, an insect that is popularly believed to fly in defiance of the laws of physics. Structural reforms, he noted, were required within the eurozone in order for the bumblebee to turn into a honeybee.[66]

External challenges likewise persist. In November 2018, three Ukrainian naval vessels were intercepted by Russian border-patrol vessels in the southern approach to the Kerch Strait between Russia and the Crimean Peninsula, and later fired upon in international waters; Russia detained the 24 Ukrainian crew members. A bid by Moscow to establish unilateral control over passage through the Kerch Strait and the Sea of Azov likely looms ahead. Tensions in Ukraine continue; in January 2019 the head of Russia's Security Council, Nikolai Patrushev, warned Kiev against 'implementing the West's scenario to break Ukraine away from Russia'.[67] As of early 2019, progress on the Minsk agreement had ground to a halt.

Even as the number of people crossing illegally into Europe fell in 2018 to the lowest level for five years, tensions around migration and the likelihood of further spikes to come continue to take their toll on European politics, fuelling populist parties across the continent.[68] Meanwhile, in 2018, more than 2,200 migrants are thought to have died in the Mediterranean.[69]

The EU27 may have held together better than many expected through the negotiation of the Article 50 process with the UK, but the membership crisis, too, is far from over. Most populist parties appear to have adjusted their approaches in the wake of Brexit (no longer arguing for immediate withdrawal from the EU but rather for radical reform from within), but this has altered rather than ended the crisis. Membership of the Union threatens to be of questionable value if its institutions are paralysed by anti-establishment parties. Meanwhile, the nature of the UK's future relationship with the EU will do much to determine the continent's strategic prospects.

Most acutely, the transatlantic crisis has not been contained. As key members of the Trump administration who were likely to have had restraining influences on the president have departed, Trump looks set to take on a greater role in the formulation of US foreign policy. This does not bode well for transatlantic relations and for the EU in particular. Even those few countries in Europe with whom Trump has sought to cultivate closer relations, such as Hungary, are likely to experience greater difficulties in their bilateral relationships with the US as they push back against Washington's efforts to enlist their support against Chinese influence.[70]

Powers that aspire to any form of leadership on the international stage will, of course, have to get used to dealing with multiple, multi-faceted crises simultaneously. The capacity for engagement in complex scenarios in difficult contexts is part of what defines major-power diplomacy. In a more unstable world, Europe, the EU and its member states are all called upon to do more in the fields of foreign, security and defence policy. The continent's indulgent respite from strategic thinking is coming to an end.

CHAPTER TWO

The internal consequences of crises

Europe's decade-long 'poly-crisis' has aggravated long-standing differences within and between EU member states with regard to the purpose, design and structure of the Union, whilst also introducing new tensions.[1] The resulting points of departure, debate and compromise inevitably have ramifications for the nature and design of future European engagement in external affairs.

Organising principles
What purpose a union?
Even the founders of the European project differed in their ultimate reasons for pursuing European integration. For Konrad Adenauer, whose clear foreign-policy priority as the first chancellor of the Federal Republic of Germany was reconciliation with France, a 'United States of Europe' held out the promise of bringing lasting peace to his war-ravaged continent.[2] Adenauer's French counterpart, General Charles de Gaulle, spoke more of a Europe of nation-states, albeit one stretching 'from the Atlantic to the Urals'.[3] Indeed, as already noted, it was French discomfort with the prospect of supranational

institutions that helped ensure the stillbirth of the EDC in 1954. The Gaullist conception of France's role informed not just Paris's vetoes of the UK's applications to join the EEC in 1963 and 1967, but also its 1965 staging of the 'empty chair crisis', when France withdrew from the Council of Ministers for six months over objections to federalist proposals such as giving the commission its 'own resources' for financing the Common Agricultural Policy, overseen by the European Parliament, with decisions made by qualified majority voting.

Such tensions over the ultimate ideological goal for the grand European project have reverberated for decades. The story of Europe's management of the euro crisis, for example, is also a tale of inescapable differences about the underlying purpose, philosophy and principles of a union.[4] Germany, in particular, was accused of showing insufficient solidarity with its fellow member states, as what one commentator referred to as an 'ideological divorce' arose between the so-called 'PIIGS' (Portugal, Ireland, Italy, Greece and Spain) on the one hand, and much of the rest of Europe on the other.[5] While Berlin was anxious to see financial aid closely tied to delivery against binding commitments on strict structural reforms, others, for example in Rome, favoured softer fiscal rules that gave greater weight to the 'growth part' of the eurozone's 1997 Stability and Growth Pact. In his first appearance before the European Parliament as Italian prime minister in 2014, Matteo Renzi argued against a single-minded obsession with financial spreadsheets that he saw as threatening to eviscerate the cooperative soul of the Union, while warning ominously of the consequences of the EU acting like 'a boring old aunt'.[6] Similar broad disagreements on principle and purpose were reflected in British prime minister David Cameron's pitch for EU reform in 2016. As he sought to secure greater protection for 'euro outs' within the Union, he inadvertently highlighted the debate over the degree to which the single market still lay at the heart of the European project, and the degree to which it had been supplanted by a broader political project.

Other long-standing philosophical and ideological differences are more directly relevant to the EU's foreign-policy identity and ambitions. There are cultural differences in thinking about the principle and utility of military force as well as the role that EU institutions should play in the further development of the Union's profile in defence and security affairs. There are different relative judgements over the degree to which the CSDP is the most appropriate vehicle to deliver increased European defence capabilities and operational effectiveness, in particular with regard to its relative value alongside existing NATO mechanisms. There is a divergence over the positioning of the EU with regard to its transatlantic ally; well before Trump took office, a debate was under way over the degree to which the Union should stand deliberately and distinctly apart from the US, focused on building its own platform within a more multipolar world.

Those preferring close alignment, and the leadership that a strong transatlantic alliance can offer, generally welcomed, for example, the Joint EU–US initiative on the Asia-Pacific announced by US secretary of state Hillary Clinton and high representative Catherine Ashton in 2012.[7] Others, whether more anxious to seek strategic advantage through distinction or simply to insulate Europe from the complicated dynamics of US–China relations, were more inclined to see the innovation as a detrimental co-option of the EU by the US.[8] This debate is likely to increase in the years ahead as relations between the US and China deteriorate. The US is likely to look for European support in this struggle as it invites its European allies to shore up a transatlantic relationship that is under considerable pressure.

More generally, the announcement by president Obama of the US 'pivot to Asia' in 2010 prompted a renewed bout of reflection in Europe with regard to its own policies towards a region of increasing strategic importance. EU member states disagreed over the extent to which a resource-strapped EU could and should aspire to be a credible security and defence actor in a part of the world where geopolitical threats eclipsed the non-traditional threats on which EU institutions have long preferred to focus. Did it not make sense to recognise the more practical logic of concentrating precious resources on security challenges closer to home, leaving the US freer to focus on its Asia pivot? Certainly many member states, with the notable exceptions of France, Germany and the UK, appeared ready to accept a more geographical approach to partnership and the division of labour.

Prior to the 2016 EUGS, the EU was still formally operating under a security strategy that predated the financial crisis, let alone the US pivot to Asia or the Russian annexation of Crimea. A new strategy had been long resisted because it would require a comprehensive review of strategic priorities that risked bringing underlying differences in foreign- and security-policy priorities and purpose between member states to the fore. A French-led experiment in 2008 to 'update' the 2003 ESS proved unsatisfactory precisely because it threatened to divide more than to unite. Some, but not all, of these differences appeared to have been settled with the adoption of the EUGS. However, the practical interpretation of EU aspirations for 'strategic autonomy', and the implications this should have for defence cooperation with the US, for example, continue to be hotly debated.

More generally, Trump's election has changed the nature of some of the questions long debated in European strategic circles. How openly critical should the EU be of the leadership of its chief ally and protector? What value should the EU and its member states attach to transatlantic relations under Trump, to what lengths should European states go to protect these relations and what compromises should they be prepared to make? How structural are the shifts in US outlook and foreign-policy priorities and to what degree should Europe be preparing for a post-American world order?

What cost a union?

As the capacities of EU institutions have grown along with their reach into the daily affairs of member states, the relative financial and political costs and benefits of EU membership have come under increasing scrutiny. The story of European integration in general, and the stunted tale of European defence cooperation in particular, owes much to differing calculations over the relative pay-off between the benefits of integration and the costs to sovereignty such integration is understood to demand. Europe's decade of crises repeatedly highlighted these tensions from a number of different perspectives.

The migrant crisis, for example, emboldened critical discussions of the costs of club membership for those within the Schengen zone as well as the broader Union. For some states in Central and Eastern Europe in particular, Juncker's call for 'more Europe in our asylum policy' and 'more Union in our refugee policy' proved too demanding.[9] When new commission proposals mandating quotas for refugee relocations were forced through under QMV, the financial, cultural and sovereign consequences of EU membership for dissenters appeared stark. (In the event, after years of internal struggles, an escape clause was effectively agreed in December 2018 for countries that had adamantly refused to implement mandatory refugee quotas, with the commission left to pick up the pieces.)

One of the many challenges the euro crisis brought for the EU's political leaders was how to explain to their citizens that the steps being taken either (for debtor countries) to protect their membership of the single currency or (for creditor countries) to save the currency itself were a price worth paying. The politics of debt relief were formidable. In 2010, the mass-circulation German daily tabloid *Bild* asked: 'will we finally have to pay for all of Europe?'[10] Merkel had to explain repeatedly to a sceptical Bundestag and her bailout-weary citizens why their country should provide bailouts to an apparently profligate government which had cheated on the club's rules, whilst also underwriting the new institutions, such as the European Financial Stability Facility and the European Stability Mechanism, that came into existence over the course of the crisis. Proposals for the creation of eurobonds, long advocated by federalists as well as by more than a few currency professionals, have proved politically unpalatable in countries such as Germany, not simply for the moral hazard they present, but because they suggest the eurozone is evolving into a fully fledged 'transfer union', in which German taxpayers' money would be transferred to weaker countries in the eurozone. Instead, Merkel had already concluded by 2011, what was needed was not a 'debt union' but a 'sustainable stability union'.[11]

The poisonous politics of debt relief seeped into a complex patchwork of internal differences that defies simple characterisation, whether geographic (north–south or east–west) or thematic (creditor–debtor or forms of governance from independent bureaucracies to clientelism).[12] The distinction between core and periphery, for example, seemed moot when Baltic states, which collectively tightened their budgets by 9% of GDP in 2009, found themselves asked to contribute to the bailout of Greece, a country with a higher per capita GDP.[13]

More generally, in the decades of peace that have accompanied the evolution of the EU, attitudes to membership have become increasingly transactional. It is easy for a country to be enthusiastic about EU membership whilst its net budget gains and resulting investments are readily identifiable, reflected in a modernised economy and upgraded infrastructure. Yet what happens when the gains are not so immediate or clear? Or, as in the case of Ireland, when a country switches from being a net recipient to a net contributor? Certainly, debate over the size and merits of the UK's membership contributions figured prominently in the Brexit referendum campaign.

Brexit has sharpened considerably the tone and urgency of debates over the nature and allocation of costs within the EU. Negotiations over the EU's next Multiannual Financial Framework (MFF), due to come into effect from January 2021, will see these tensions on full display. Once again, the EU is being asked to do 'more with less'. The next MFF will have to provide for new policy areas (such as a budget for migration-policy goals) even as the prospective departure of the UK could mean a €12bn–13bn per year drop in contributions. Germany has already accepted that it will have to pay more to help overcome this deficit, but other net contributors appear notably less resigned to the prospect. Meanwhile, net recipients of EU funding are likely not only to receive less, but to find that the money comes with stricter conditions attached.

What structure a union?

Whilst EU member states might willingly recognise the Union's structural deficits with regard to efficiency, transparency, democracy and legitimacy, there is scant agreement over how these deficits might substantively be rectified. The EU's structure is itself an often-underappreciated testament to the collective determination of member states to find a way through even in the most complex and incoherent of circumstances.

The ideal balance between the commission, the council and the parliament remains contested, most obviously between the institutions themselves. The European Parliament, for example, has been keen to act more like a conventional parliament, with powers of economic and budgetary oversight.[14] Meanwhile, the 2014 '*Spitzenkandidat*' innovation, whereby European parliamentary groups each nominated a favoured candidate for commission president with the position going to whichever party won the most MEPs, has been the subject of considerable discontent and pushback on the part of many EU leaders.[15] The initiative certainly failed to generate a noticeable wave of democratic engagement during the 2014 European elections; turnout in Slovakia was just 13%.[16]

In shining a spotlight on the structural underpinnings of the single currency, the euro crisis fuelled an internal debate on the nature of the changes needed to secure the euro's resilience in the face of future global financial crises. Member states differed in their assessments of the extent to which the challenge was structural rather than grounded in the failure of member states to implement necessary reforms. To the extent they acknowledged contributory structural factors, too, they differed on the appropriate prescription for addressing them. To what extent, for example, does the eurozone require, or indeed is it advisable for the eurozone to develop, its own parallel institutions of governance within the EU? The divergent responses such challenges elicited exacerbated tensions across the continent.[17]

Another consequence of the euro crisis was to increase the regularity of contact and range of discussions between eurozone member states. Such euro-caucusing is likely to prove increasingly problematic for non-eurozone members. The creeping institutionalisation of the Eurogroup – which began life in 1997 as an informal forum for policy coordination among eurozone finance ministers, the president of the ECB and the commissioner for economic and financial affairs – heralds an increasing centrality for eurozone affairs within the EU.[18] As answers to these key questions on the future management of the euro incrementally emerge, they will have a knock-on effect on the coherence and nature of the EU as an international actor.

Any decisive shift towards a clearer (yet still outward-looking) core EU, for example, around which non-eurozone member states could orbit to more flexible formulas of integration, would inevitably affect the conduct of European foreign and security policy. One would expect to see central EU institutions, including the commission and the EEAS, slowly win the resources and member-state support necessary to grow into more consequential actors. While there would be no lessening of member-state internal investment in these areas, closer cooperation in other areas, combined with stronger institutions at the Union centre, would confer greater coherence and effect on the structures and action of EU foreign and security policy. On the other hand, if some member states were to push for greater integration in this way and their attempt fell short, it is hard to see how negative geopolitical consequences for the EU's reputation and coherence as a strategic actor could be avoided.

As the EU considers how its structures should evolve, one critical challenge it faces is the management of its future relationship with the UK (as this book will explore in Chapter Five). It is clear that the EU and the UK both have much to gain from the closest possible future partnership on security and defence, yet the current rules with regard to third-party interactions mean that the emergence of such a partnership, with the strategic imagination it is likely to require, is far from guaranteed.

Internal implications

These fundamental differences with regard to organising principles, purpose, costs and structures will continue to affect the EU's efforts to improve its resilience and influence on the international stage, whether through defence integration or economic and monetary union. Where these will lead is unclear, but Europe's decade of crises has exacerbated or given rise to some important trends which offer clues to the EU's strategic future. Five such trends are particularly important for foreign, security and defence policy: the interplay of limited resources and moderated ambitions; the increasing internal power differentials; the impact of unfolding centrifugal forces; the evolution of a multi-speed and multi-track structure; and the requirement to imagine mechanisms for influence in the EU's neighbourhood beyond the promise of enlargement.

Limited resources, moderated ambitions

After the Cold War ended, European defence budgets fell steadily as governments took advantage of the 'peace dividend' to redirect spending. The onset of the financial crisis made matters worse. Even economically resilient countries such as Germany failed to protect already low levels of defence spending from the austerity policies that gripped much of the continent. Deficits in political will were every bit as serious as the real deficits in many government accounts.

Between 2006 and 2010, defence expenditure by the 27 EU member states who participate in the CSDP fell by 7.2%.[19] Appetite for CSDP missions abroad fell, with only six missions launched between 2009 and August 2013 (compared to the 22 missions launched in 2003–08). Four of these six missions were, moreover, small-scale civilian capacity-building missions with a cumulative troop strength of no more than a couple of hundred personnel. Critics understandably questioned whether such missions could have real strategic impact, suggesting that they risked being little more than exercises in flag-waving. Indeed, missions were repeatedly and cynically left chronically under-resourced in money, personnel or equipment. For example, despite its subsequent evolution into one of the largest and most expensive CSDP missions in history, the EU's civilian Rule of Law Mission in Kosovo (EULEX) took more than two years to become fully operational following its launch in 2008, hampered, amongst other things, by poor levels of staffing. The rhetoric of the CSDP may have been grandiloquent, but the reality of its execution was considerably more modest.

Early hopes that financial pressures would help member states overcome long-standing concerns about safeguarding sovereignty and permit a streamlining of European defence capabilities proved misplaced. European governments largely failed to respond to the crisis by doing 'more with less', instead using it as an excuse to do 'less with less'.

Existing bureaucratic inefficiencies combined with austerity to produce a particularly toxic mix of under-reach and low self-esteem. The EEAS, for example, did not develop the teeth envisaged by Lisbon; its record of formulating initiatives was notably better than its record of delivering on them.[20] Regional priorities developed even sharper contrasts: countries in the north and east of the EU engaged more actively with CSDP missions in the Balkans and Eastern Europe, while France led the way among those who looked more instinctively towards security threats proliferating to the south.[21]

The deteriorating external security environment gave more impetus to greater European cooperation in the development of defence capabilities than did the internal demands of the euro crisis. The cuts that had become characteristic of European defence spending finally began to be reversed. While the commitments of the EU's NATO members to spend 2% of GDP on defence (set at the 2014 NATO summit in Wales) remain largely unfulfilled, non-US defence spending as a share of total NATO spending has risen every year since 2014 as Russian revanchism began, slowly and inadequately, to turn philosophical reflections into more tangible reactions.[22] European concerns were then amplified by the urgent need to manage migrant flows which, combined with fears over the threat of terrorism exacerbated by returning foreign fighters, pushed defence and security concerns back up European agendas. In 2017, real-term defence spending grew faster in Europe than in any other region.[23] This upturn in spending, moreover, was largely allocated in 2016 budgets adopted before Trump took office in the US. More money, of course, does not necessarily mean greater capabilities; the 2018 Munich Security Report argues that, without a shift towards more collaborative and cost-effective processes, meeting the 2% target for all NATO members would still not be a game changer for European military capabilities.[24] (These issues are discussed in greater detail in Chapter Four.)

The need for Europe to strengthen both its defence capabilities and its operational capacities has finally become an accepted part of the political narrative within Europe as well as beyond. Although renewed concern in Europe predates Trump's particularly voluble complaints about European NATO defence spending, stresses in the transatlantic relationship have played an important role in bolstering European spending as well as in shifting European strategic thinking. As fears have risen that US military retrenchment from Europe might some day follow America's evident political and diplomatic retrenchment, European conversations on defence spending have been informed as much by doubts over the dependability of the transatlantic alliance as by the growing list of traditional geopolitical threats and complications. If Putin was the driving force behind the 2014 NATO defence-spending commitments, by the time of the 2018 NATO summit in Brussels, Trump's America was playing a key role in focusing European attention. While the push for European partners to increase defence spending was reasonable, the way this push was expressed risked dividing the alliance more than strengthening it.

The EUGS reflected some rebalance in thinking over the two years that preceded its publication. While the ambitions it suggested for European defence were high, ambitions for what the EU could deliver in an 'increasingly connected, contested and complex world' were more modest. This was encapsulated in the 'principled pragmatism' and promotion of 'resilience' the strategy espoused. While the EU committed itself to upholding a 'rules-based global order', some of the ideological excitement of the 2003 ESS had faded. For example, as European defence analyst Sven Biscop has noted, the EU's moderated ambitions for democracy promotion reflected the new global context in which the EU now found itself.[25]

The operationalisation of this strategy and the nature of European engagements to promote a more collaborative and effective approach to defence spending are explored in more detail below. But even as Europe's partners on the international stage might reasonably remain critical of the pace and degree of its implementation, they should welcome what appears to be the beginning of a rebound in resources for foreign and security policy, in particular with regard to defence spending. At least in some European states, concerns about the lack of political will to take military action and the lack of investment in security and defence has moved beyond defence ministries into the mainstream: upwards, into the chancelleries of European governments and, more slowly, outwards to the people these governments have pledged to protect.[26]

A less equal union

The impact of the years of crises on the EU's shifting centres of power is more complex than commonly understood. On the one hand, the crises have exacerbated an existing trend back towards a more intergovernmental approach, which favours larger member states. On the other hand, the European Commission has gained greater authority and influence, especially in areas such as defence research and development. As a result, however, its role as the traditional ally of the smaller member states is in danger of being diluted as the grip on the commission by the larger members has tightened. Contact with the EU at the institutional level has thus become more important for the EU's international partners, even as individual member states appear increasingly willing to stand alone in opposition to EU initiatives, sometimes supported or even encouraged by third parties.

The euro crisis is often portrayed as having precipitated a clear shift during Barroso's second term as commission president (2009–14) towards intergovernmentalism at the expense of the traditional 'community method'. As member states led the way in defining the EU response to the euro crisis, the commission lost power and influence, becoming less the author of new initiatives than the implementer of an agenda established and decided upon by the European Council. British journalist Gideon Rachman wrote in 2014 that the crisis had 'reduced' outgoing president Barroso 'to a messenger boy and scapegoat'.[27]

Intergovernmentalism has a long history within the EU. The Lisbon Treaty's recognition of the European Council as a formal executive body of the EU, chaired for the first time by a permanent president, had already bolstered the central role of the member states and the council meetings of their heads of state and government. At the peak of the euro crisis, these meetings became the big set-piece events at which crunch points were reached and new goals were set. The European Commission was notable largely by its absence. Even in cases of close inter-institutional cooperation, the balance of influence was evident. Although the proposal for reform of the monetary union put forward in December 2012 is known as the Four Presidents' Report, it was ultimately coordinated and led by Council president Herman Van Rompuy. (The others were Barroso, Juncker and Draghi.)

That member states played front-line roles in the management of apparently existential crises – from the euro crisis to the migration crisis – should not be surprising.[28] It was taxpayers' money from member states, after all, that was being risked to save the euro. Heads of the executive branches of the EU member states, and in particular those whose deep pockets were required to counter the crises, therefore quickly came together to ward off any temptation for the EU executive branch to take the opportunity to seek more power. One result, however, was to undercut the European Commission's authority with member states, both big and small, as it interfered where it was not wanted and failed to lead where it was. When, in May 2013, the commission explicitly called for eurozone reform in order to avert a 'social emergency', French president François Hollande was clear in his response: 'the European Commission cannot dictate to us what we have to do'.[29]

The commission also struggled to establish itself as an actor during the peak of the refugee crisis. Its efforts to encourage member states to consider reform of the Common European Asylum System, or at least to push member states to consider modifications to the Dublin system, fell on infertile ground.[30] The suggestion of a 'corrective allocation mechanism' to be activated when countries faced a 'disproportionate number of asylum applications', and that would require other member states to either accept the reallocation of asylum applicants from a member state under pressure or pay a 'solidarity contribution' of €250,000 per applicant, again came up against sensitivities about the Union's organising principles, this time over the financial and sovereign costs that should be associated with membership.[31] The commission learned to self-moderate even as it continued to present legislative proposals for reforming the Common European Asylum System. In December 2017, it tried again, presenting a road map for managing what it described as the 'challenge of a generation'.[32] Yet member states remained largely reluctant to engage. Discussions on migration at the June 2018 council meeting to which this road map pointed were informed more by domestic German and Italian concerns over managing different migratory pressures than they were by policy proposals put forward by the commission. The deal EU leaders agreed was good enough for Merkel to keep her job, but insufficient to deal with the scale of the challenge to come. This dynamic of troubled interactions between member states and the commission spread well beyond managing the crisis of the day. It fed a more general malaise as populist movements flourished across the continent. Member states tried to reassert control across a range of issues.

The central role played by the commission's Article 50 task force in the management of Brexit might appear an exception, but it was not. It was conceived as the answer to a matter of critical national interest for the 27 EU member states: to pre-empt any UK attempts to sow division between them. But this did not stop larger member states from intervening or overruling. When, in October 2017, it appeared that Michel Barnier, the appointed chief negotiator for the EU, was ready to agree that the UK had made 'sufficient progress' on the terms of the UK's exit to allow discussion on the terms of transition to begin, Paris and Berlin orchestrated a pushback to ensure otherwise. Again, as the EU27 drew up their directives for the negotiation of transitional arrangements, member states felt it necessary to clarify that the council, not the commission, was ultimately in charge. In February 2018, the commission unexpectedly contacted British officials to delay confirmation of a negotiating round tentatively scheduled for later in the month following complaints by some member states that they had not been kept sufficiently in the loop.[33]

A more intergovernmental approach inevitably highlights asymmetries of influence between member states. The most obvious lesson of the decade of crises is that Europe's big countries will ultimately always matter more than its small ones. The prospect of a Greek exit from the euro mattered more than the prospect of a Cypriot one. (Indeed, in 2012, Cyprus was effectively allowed to default while remaining in the eurozone.) Even a Greek exit was ultimately rejected not so much over the losses that would be sustained in Greece, but over possible contagion to the more significant economies of Italy and Spain. Meanwhile, it was another big country, Germany, whose influence largely determined the fact and nature of Greece's rescue. Similarly, the migration crisis was not just exacerbated by Merkel's 'open door' policy, it was also largely brought back under temporary control by her initiative with Turkey that was, at least in its initial informal form, negotiated bilaterally. The role that the commission can play in commanding solidarity for smaller member states was nevertheless highlighted by the EU's support for Irish concerns over the post-Brexit future of its border with Northern Ireland, which became all but invisible following the Good Friday Agreement.[34]

The centrality of member states in matters of foreign and security policy is protected through the explicitly intergovernmental nature of the CFSP and CSDP. But here, too, the existential nature of the crises has prompted a shift in power, this time within the member states themselves. The political impact and demands of the 'poly-crisis' on member states have shifted the management of the substance of European foreign policy further towards the cabinets and close advisers of EU heads of state and government and away from foreign ministries. This trend is, of course, far from new; the Lisbon Treaty removed foreign ministers from the European Council even as it confirmed the council's authority 'to adopt the necessary decisions' in the area of EU foreign policy. And the trend mirrors shifts in internal centres of power occurring more globally, spurred on by a blurring of lines between foreign and domestic policy, and the 'all of government' approaches that key policy concerns now demand.

The extent of the shift in Europe has nevertheless been remarkable. In the post-crises world, few issues of foreign and security policy are really important to a government unless they have been escalated to its highest levels. This has caused something of a bottleneck: beset by so many demands, national leaders have limited time to deal with important issues of foreign policy, and are forced to confront only the most urgent.[35] Meanwhile, foreign ministers and ministries with whom the expertise and mandate officially lie often struggle to get sufficient traction within their bureaucracies to make their interests felt.

However, the story of these shifting internal dynamics through recent crises is more complicated than the simple reassertion of member-state control and a changing balance of power between European states. A shift towards intergovernmentalism is not necessarily zero-sum in terms of its effect on the authority enjoyed by central institutions. Sovereignty might not be shared through legal acts, but is rather voluntarily pooled by member states through political agreements. And even though the power to oversee this pooling of sovereignty has not flowed smoothly to the European Commission, the commission has nevertheless found its authority enhanced in some areas at least.

It has, for example, gained greater fiscal and macroeconomic surveillance powers as a result of efforts to contain the euro crisis. The commission now reviews member-state economies more thoroughly and has the authority to penalise rule-break- ers. Indeed, in December 2013, two *Financial Times* journalists argued that the introduction of a commission-controlled Single Supervisory and Resolution Mechanism, established to 'break the link' between the financial credentials of an individual eurozone government and its respective banking sector, marked 'the biggest surrender of sovereignty since the creation of the single currency'.[36] The 'European Semester', a structure designed in 2010 to improve EU economic governance and policy coordination, may not have involved any legal transfer of sovereignty to the EU, but it has begun to give EU institu- tions a higher profile in guiding national policy.

The same is true of commission authority in some aspects of security and defence policy, areas from which it was previ- ously largely excluded. Financing of research and acquisition programmes under the European Defence Fund (EDF), for example, is likely to give the commission influence over member-state defence agendas for the first time. French Defence Minister Florence Parly acknowledged this shift at the 2018 Munich Security Conference, referring to the EDF as a 'cultural revolution in Brussels'. The commission's role in the regulation and control of dual-use exports has similarly expanded, with the prospect that the EU might, for the first time, agree a control list not drawn from one of the multilat- eral export-control regimes.[37] More generally, the commission has tried to deepen the opportunities for defence cooperation through such measures as introducing greater standardisation of certification and licensing systems, whilst also trying to reduce market distortions, including through offsets.[38]

If European defence is to develop the requisite substance, the central institutions in Brussels will have an important role to play in facilitating joint defence-capability planning. In time, especially if the EDF can fulfil its potential, the commission will also develop more of a role in supporting those who wish to build and buy together. The commission's role in the development of the EU's external profile more generally, too, is not to be underestimated. The commission oversees not just the budget for the CFSP, but a range of geographical and thematic instruments in relation to EU external actions, such as the Instrument for Pre-Accession Assistance, the Instrument for Nuclear Safety Cooperation and the Instrument for Contributing to Stability and Peace.

Shifts in internal power dynamics will continue as the EU and its member states try to bolster their collective resilience and effectiveness in foreign and security policy. The trend towards intergovernmentalism can facilitate pragmatic action: member states are more likely to do what it is possible to do if they can act directly in smaller groups, rather than having to persuade collective, consensus-based institutions to come around to their approach. Increased intergovernmentalism should also help the EU reach out beyond its membership to cultivate broader European initiatives, including with a post-Brexit UK.

Yet while this approach might have short-term pragmatic advantages, the seriousness with which member states treat their interactions with the European Commission will be critical. An EU whose member states act with disregard for its institutions risks ultimately falling apart, as smaller states lose one of the key equalising advantages of association. If institutions representing wider European interests are weakened, not only will member states be emboldened to act in smaller groupings, they will be emboldened to act alone. The net effect is likely to be, if not dissolution, a less coordinated and therefore weaker European presence on the international stage. At the other extreme, a Union that acts only through its institutions is unlikely to provide satisfactory answers to challenges to the international order, in particular while decisions have to be taken unanimously. While the commission will never be a true government, it can become more of a force within the institutional ecosystem of the EU. This will require more readiness actively to represent the Union's interests, rather than allow itself to be sidelined, co-opted or scapegoated by the members it is supposed to represent.

One key indicator of, and contributor to, increased commission influence would be the nomination of a political heavyweight as HR/VP. As long as EU members deliberately pass over experienced foreign-policy operators with credible and established reputations on the international stage, it is little wonder that Europe's partners in international affairs are inclined likewise to overlook the EU, treating its central institutions with limited interest. While the prospect of Brexit might remove one obstacle to such a development, the EU27 states are not yet prepared to complicate the Union's sensitive political geography by nominating a high-profile statesperson as their foreign-affairs representative. This means that the EU's international partners will continue to have to divide their attentions, taking account of the influences and interests of individual member states even as they likely begin to pay more attention to EU institutions.

From multi-speed to multi-track union?
Differentiated cooperation between EU member states, or 'variable geometry', has long been a feature of the Union. In 2018,

nine of the EU28 were not yet members of the eurozone, while there were ongoing opt-outs from EU rules and commitments, ranging from the euro (UK, Denmark) to defence (Denmark) to the EU Charter of Fundamental Rights (UK and Poland) to certain areas of justice and home affairs (Denmark, Ireland, UK). Further initiatives are under way. For example, in June 2017, 20 countries reached political agreement under enhanced cooperation to establish a European Public Prosecutor's Office that should take up its function by the end of 2020. Other opt-outs (such as the UK opt-out from the Social Chapter of the Maastricht Treaty) have come and gone.

Intergovernmental agreements integrated within, but extending beyond, the EU legal framework include the Schengen zone (22 EU members and four non-members) whilst others, such as the Treaty on Stability, Coordination and Governance in the Economic and Monetary Union, await integration. Security and defence cooperation is particularly replete with examples of differentiated integration outside EU frameworks, with different constellations of member states participating in different projects from the EU Satellite Centre to the European Air Transport Command.

Before the euro crisis, the migration crisis and Brexit, the EU could at least pretend that member states had inextricably bound themselves together and were heading to a common destination, albeit at different speeds. Opt-outs were largely supposed only to be temporary, whilst intergovernmental agreements were supposed to be brought under the umbrella of EU treaty law at a later date. But the euro crisis persuaded countries such as Poland that they were right to steer well clear of the still half-baked currency.[39] The migration crisis fuelled deep divisions between member states not just over the speed of travel, but over where they were headed. Resistance to a single vision had already led the European Council, under pressure from the UK, to recognise in June 2014 that 'the concept of ever closer union allows for different paths of integration for different countries'. Negotiations in the run-up to the 2016 Brexit vote resulted in an offer of an even more explicit exemption for the UK over the principle of 'ever closer union'. While this offer expired with the vote for Brexit, that it was acceptable for one country raises questions about the broader direction of travel for the EU with or without the UK.

The expression of public support for a multi-speed Europe by the leaders of France, Germany, Italy and Spain at Versailles in March 2017 marked a turning point in the debate over the relative priority of solidarity over effectiveness. A week earlier, Juncker had published a White Paper on the future of the EU, laying out five potential scenarios for its development.[40] The leaders in Versailles seemed to be signalling their support for the third of these: those who wanted to do more would do more. The EU's future would be secured better through pragmatic improvisations rather than obsessive debates on treaty change.

Releasing those who want to do more together actually to do more together under the umbrella of the EU is likely to prove a challenge. That internal bureaucratic bickering can interfere with key strategic issues was on full display in January 2019, with Spain's petty blocking of the European Council conclusions on Iran in protest at the inclusion of Italy alongside the E3 of UK, France and Germany in a new E4 grouping looking at how the EU might address concerns about Iran's behaviour in international affairs without destabilising the nuclear deal. Spain's procedural protest focused on the fact that the E4 had not been discussed and endorsed by the EU28, and thus the grouping and its efforts should not be recognised by the council.[41]

Developing a clearer core group within the EU risks unleashing polarising forces that could destabilise the Union as a whole more than it would strengthen its centre. There will be considerable opposition to any such moves from countries not ready to move forward, but not prepared to be left behind. German officials, for example, aware of stark differences in how the EU's future is imagined in different parts of the Union, are notably nervous about the degree to which it is possible for such flexibility to become a strength in practice. The concern is that any shift towards an EU of 'concentric circles' will inexorably lead to the outer circles feeling treated as second-class citizens.[42] Anxious to avoid anything that might risk destabilising a Union already under attack from without, and mindful of the reactions from fellow member states to its growing geopolitical weight within the continent, Berlin worries about further highlighting existing divisions within the EU.

Precisely because of Berlin's concerns, the initial formulation of Permanent Structured Cooperation on defence was always going to have to be relatively open. This was also a way to minimise opposition, reassuring EU member states that no one who wanted to be involved need fear being left behind. The countervailing risk is that such cooperation could become so inclusive that it would fail to change the dynamic that created years of underwhelming delivery on European 'pooling and sharing'. Yet if the political will for closer cooperation can be sustained, whether through PESCO or in bilateral and minilateral cooperations outside of it, the door is beginning to open for delivery of more serious European strategic ambitions for defence capabilities.

That this cooperation can take place under the umbrella of the EU should be welcomed. In contrast to international treaties, mechanisms for enhanced cooperation under the EU can be left open for other member states to join easily at a later stage. They also provide an in-built mechanism for keeping non-participant states in the loop on developments in a more inclusive way than an intergovernmental agreement.

For the EU's partners, any shift, through the greater use of enhanced cooperation, towards a smaller but more united core EU of the kind envisaged by French President Macron would have several potential advantages. The pursuit of EU unity might no longer be used as an excuse for EU inaction. Working in more flexible coalitions of the willing to mutual benefit, the inner core should find it easier to develop more coherence and credibility in support of EU foreign, security and defence policy. Meanwhile, such a shift could also make for a more credible and attractive outer circle, offering something more graduated and adaptable. This in turn might also make the future of the EU's enlargement policy more credible. At present, the full litany of rights and responsibilities of membership can prove controversial in aspirant countries, even as the alternatives on offer appear all too unsatisfactory a pay-off for the EU's closing of the gates.

Centrifugal forces and the rise of cooperations of convenience

Europe's decade of crises has had a somewhat centrifugal effect on many of the EU's more established internal groupings, from the Franco-German axis to the Weimar Triangle. This has helped spark a search for new strategies and groupings able to facilitate leadership and forge consensus. Some groupings are more institutionalised than others, but all are evolving and few are cohesive on every issue. As concerns over external threats mount, new centripetal forces have also emerged. The difference is that these latter forces – the result of efforts to unify in the face of adversity – are more fragile, transactional and temporary. Efforts at closer coordination between EU member states are, more than ever, usefully understood as cooperations of convenience. This implies no moral judgement; indeed, such issues-based mechanisms could prove more sustainable than artificial geographical constructs.

The groupings briefly examined here are a subset of the complex and evolving web of interrelationships between European states. The sheer number of groupings that could have been considered in more detail is, in fact, an important reminder of the scale of the challenge Europe faces in coordinating effective and speedy action between its states, and a testament to the argument that the EU cannot and should not be judged by the standard for effective action applied to single states.

The Franco-German axis. Close working relationships between officials in Paris and Berlin manifest in near-daily consultations between the two capitals aimed at forging common outlooks and agendas. Such practices are sufficiently ingrained in the bureaucracies of both countries that the technocratic side of the relationship can be sustained regardless of the top-level political dynamics between the two governments at a given time. Nevertheless, when this axis struggles, the EU's energy and appetite for action falters. While Franco-German agreement is, by itself, no longer sufficient to generate EU action, the absence of such agreement is still likely to be an effective blocking mechanism.[43]

However, the shift in relative financial power between these two countries that the euro crisis both highlighted and exacerbated inflicted considerable damage on a bilateral relationship that had already been complicated by the EU's eastern expansion. As Berlin became more likely to see Paris as part of the problem rather than part of the solution, former French president François Mitterrand's vision of an equalising balance between France and Germany looked increasingly like a Walter Mitty dream. De Gaulle once described the EU as 'a coach with horses, with Germany the horse and France the coachman'; now the coachman had become too weak to get the horses to do much more than pay lip service to their desires.

These structural shifts have combined with other, more long-standing structural differences over, for example, nuclear deterrence, or the constitutionally different powers held by a French president and a German chancellor. They have also been matched by a shift in personal dynamics. As former IISS chairman François Heisbourg lamented, the two partners have experienced a 'loss of intimacy'; the days of partnerships such as existed between Válery Giscard D'Estaing and Helmut Schmidt, or François Mitterrand and Helmut Kohl, appear over, lost in a more complex EU and the divergence in outlooks which the Union's enlargement has further widened.[44]

When in 2013 the two countries came together to celebrate 50 years of the Elysée Treaty of friendship, the differences in outlook, including on key issues of foreign and security policy, were stark. The shadows of Germany's UN abstention over the French-led Libya campaign, its minimal support for French troops fighting Islamists in Mali and its veto of a BAE–EADS merger for reasons of short-term national interest loomed large. *Le Monde* labelled the celebrations a 'festival of hypocrisy'.[45] Indeed, in the early days of the Hollande government, as the centrifugal forces of the euro crisis struck, France appeared to be shopping around for new partners as part of a strategy that could have been labelled 'anyone but Berlin'.[46] First came Hollande's outreach to the Mediterranean countries, then a shift in focus to the Latin countries and then, in the face of European Commission scrutiny of the national budgets of both France and Italy, a pivot back to Rome and a more focused cultivation of Renzi, the new prime minister. By the time Macron was planning his extraordinary journey to the Elysée, there were few viable alternatives to Germany left for France to try to romance.

Meanwhile, in Berlin, there was frustration at France's apparent lack of political will to tackle its toxic mixture of high unemployment, high taxes, high debt, high deficits and low growth, all of which appeared to make France a weaker, less attractive partner. Macron's victory in the 2017 French presidential election was supposed to change the nature of this troubled dynamic. But Franco-German rapprochement is fragile, driven, at least in part, by a lack of alternatives rather than being a relationship of first choice between equal partners. While Berlin frets over Macron's ability to sustain domestic political reform and his tendencies towards grand visions, French frustration grows with Germany's slowness to grasp what it sees as the unavoidable consequences of Europe's deteriorating security environment. German support for French-led military deployments has increased in recent years, but many in Paris are well aware that German responses have been informed as much by Berlin's appreciation of the need to show support for Paris as by broader enthusiasm for the substance of the missions.[47]

Helpfully (from Paris's perspective), Germany has supported modest reform of the financing mechanisms for EU military operations, but these efforts have fallen far short of the permanent fund to finance EU military operations requested by a series of French presidents. Whether such modest measures can mollify French frustration over the clumsiness of defence cooperation under the EU umbrella remains to be seen. If not, French military ambitions and operations are likely to be defined and exercised even more unilaterally, or within the context of smaller groupings outside of the EU framework (such as, for example, the 2010 agreement on bilateral defence cooperation between the UK and France).[48] Brexit has increased French determination to improve bilateral defence contacts with Germany, even with a post-Brexit UK expected to argue that, for Paris and Berlin, there are smarter reactions to Brexit than simply doubling down on their bilateral cooperation in recompense.

With the UK set to leave the EU, and as Germany's defence budget grows, France and Germany will together account for approximately half of all military spending by the EU27. Smooth functioning of the Franco-German axis will become increasingly important for European comfort with German influence. This will be particularly the case if uncertainty over the US security guarantee forces Europe to think more about its own power balance and power projection. A functioning Franco-German axis, under a broader EU umbrella, will be critical for avoiding the risks of descent into nationalism and competition that the emergence over time of a more powerful Germany could otherwise herald.

The limits of progress in Franco-German dynamics since the frosty anniversary celebrations of the Elysée Treaty in 2013 are apparent in the modest substance of the 2019 Franco-German Treaty of Aachen. In its tired reiteration of anachronistic promises such as French support for a permanent German seat on a reformed UN Security Council, the treaty inadvertently demonstrated that Franco-German leadership is likely to prove insufficient, on its own, to ensure Europe's successful adaptation to ongoing shifts in global power.

Poland, the Weimar Triangle and the Visegrad Four. Under the leadership of prime minister Donald Tusk from 2007 to 2014, Poland positioned itself firmly in support of greater German leadership through the peak years of the euro crisis and asserted itself as an increasingly significant partner on the European stage.

Even before Russia annexed Crimea, Tusk's centre-right government had prioritised the modernisation of Poland's armed forces, pushing the country ever closer to the NATO target of 2% of GDP for defence. Having weathered the euro crisis better than many (the Polish economy grew by one-fifth between 2009 and 2013), Poland's relatively modest 2013 US$9.5bn defence budget represented an increase of more than 7% on the previous year. More significantly, Poland committed to increasing the percentage of its defence budget to be spent on equipment from 15% to 33% by 2023.[49]

As a result, Germany invested heavily in the bilateral relationship, symbolised by newly elected German president Joachim Gauck's 2012 decision to make Warsaw his first foreign visit – most of his predecessors had opted for Paris. This was not entirely magnanimous; Poland offered a useful counter-balance to the anti-austerity agenda championed by France, Italy and the wider 'Club Med'. Indeed, as one of the fastest-growing economies within the EU, Poland could testify to the benefits of painful economic reforms. Interest in cooperation increased further in the wake of the annexation of Crimea and the return of Russia to the top of Europe's strategic priorities, even as it simultaneously focused Polish minds on closer relations with the US.

This momentum was badly damaged by the 2015 parliamentary election victory of Poland's ultra-conservative and mildly eurosceptic Law and Justice Party, and the stand-offs that followed, most obviously over the migration crisis and on fundamental issues on the rule of law. Indeed, structured trilateral cooperation between France, Germany and Poland (known as the Weimar Triangle) has had limited impact in part because one side of the triangle appears doomed always to be weaker than the other two. French neglect of Poland during Nicolas Sarkozy's presidency (2007–12) was supplanted by Franco-German tensions during the Hollande years (even as Franco-Polish relations improved, as shown by Hollande's support for Tusk's election as president of the European Council in 2014). Now, during the Macron years, the PiS platform has seen the return of Franco-German tensions with Poland. It is thus unsurprising that the closer coordination offered under the more structured format of Weimar has been of fleeting value.

The Czech Republic, Hungary, Poland and Slovakia worked together towards EU accession as the 'Visegrad 4' (V4). The grouping continued even after they joined the Union in 2004, with one objective being to promote further defence integration between the four, including within NATO, in the service of European defence and security. Differences in domestic political orientation, however, ensured that there was little of consequence to the group beyond the bilateral relationships that operated within it. Indeed, the V4 countries themselves have sometimes favoured partners beyond their grouping when promoting initiatives they commonly conceived, as with Poland's dropping of the Czech Republic after their joint early designs for what became the EU's Eastern Partnership initiative.[50]

The financial crisis did stimulate a joint statement by the V4 prime ministers in October 2013 committing the countries to closer defence cooperation. Three further strategic agreements followed in 2014, focused on practical areas for cooperation including training, the establishment of multinational units, and common capability and procurement projects. Yet while the group was able to regain some unity of outlook and common purpose during the migration crisis by adopting policies that set them on a collision course with the EU mainstream, their disparate reactions to Russian aggression have split them firmly down the middle, with Poland and Hungary at opposite ends of the spectrum. These differences encourage the four partners to invest more in the bilateral relations most relevant for a given issue than in their collective partnership.[51]

The trajectory of the Orbán regime in Hungary has, moreover, restricted the V4's utility as a vehicle for influence within the broader EU. A prime minister who, in 2014, openly declared his intent to build an 'illiberal state' had little to offer his neigh-bours in the way of a constructive partnership, at least until the advent of the PiS government in Poland.[52] Shared concerns over the EU's handling of migration have, to be sure, reinstilled some common purpose to the group, but the divides between its members remain clear. As Poland and Hungary have moved closer together, the Czech Republic and Slovakia have moved quietly to strengthen ties with other partners, most obviously Berlin. As the only V4 member in the eurozone, Slovakia has little alternative.

Cooperations of the willing – the new disorder. Divisions within the EU revealed by one crisis are quickly overlaid by divisions laid bare by the next. The search for different ways to exert leader-ship or build consensus within the Union will continue. Some mechanisms have already proved themselves more successful and sustainable than others. Through the Nordic Council, Nordic states (both EU and non-EU) can reasonably claim to be participating in 'one of the most comprehensive regional part-nerships anywhere in the world', even if the influx of migrants and difficulties in dealing with their problematic neighbour to the east have begun to test cooperative relations at the insti-tutional level in recent years.[53] Other patterns of cooperation, most notably between national populist parties in the 2019–24 European Parliament, will be less comfortable for the EU"s future strategic prospects.

The UK's prospective departure from the EU will have considerable impact on the internal balance and functioning of the Union. It will increase Berlin's strategic weight and attrac-tion, but it will also spark a reordering and regrouping among smaller member states, in particularly in the north of Europe. As the EU takes steps to avoid becoming nothing more than a vehicle for Franco-German cooperation, opportunities for new minilateral groupings will emerge. The nature of the future partnership between the UK and the EU27 will, moreover, be critical in determining both parties' future strategic relevance (see Chapter Five).

One informal grouping with an uncertain future but a long-underestimated role in the forging of a transatlantic and European consensus on foreign policy is the Quint. Comprising Germany, France, Italy, the US and the UK (and including other states as particular policy focuses demand), the grouping expands on efforts by some of these states to secure common foreign-policy objectives and positions as members of the Contact Group during the Balkan wars in the 1990s. Critics see the Quint as a threat to the CFSP, while proponents argue that it can give momentum to EU policymaking, whose consensus-based nature inclines it to be more than a little stodgy, and facilitates transatlantic alignment.[54]

The Quint has certainly been useful in the past in the context of Europe's transatlantic diplomacy, in particular during times when the US has struggled with how to navigate the overlapping networks of power in Brussels. The reported frustrations of US assistant secretary of state Kurt Campbell during a visit to Brussels in spring 2012 to discuss transatlantic cooperation on the Asia pivot, for example, will be familiar to many an experienced third-party diplomat contemplating engagement with the EU.[55] When Campbell's successor Danny Russell visited Brussels in January 2014 to try his luck at navigating its networks, his informal conclusion appeared clear: efforts to direct an effective transatlantic partnership on Asia were better targeted at the informal institution of the Quint than at the confounding corridors of Brussels.[56] Long before Trump arrived in the White House and suspicions that the EU's transatlantic ally might be working to a divide-and-rule agenda had emerged, US policymakers already preferred to look to member states and sub-groupings in their efforts to engage and shape European thinking on foreign and security policies. Obama flew repeatedly to Europe but did not visit the EU institutions in Brussels until March 2014, more than five years after taking office. (He did meet EU institutional leaders on a variety of occasions before this, for example at the 2009 informal US–EU summit in Prague.)

Recent crises have put the future of this historically important strategic grouping into doubt. Fuelled in part by differences in perspective among its members on relations with Russia, the Quint was notable by its absence when crisis came to the EU's eastern neighbourhood. However, discreet meetings on Russia continue in quadrilateral format (minus Italy), with more attention also being given to China. Even as the impact of these groupings remains unclear, any format that promotes dialogue and cooperation between these powers should be welcomed by the transatlantic community at large. While bilateral and multilateral groupings such as the Quad can be expected to continue to appeal to the UK, it appears unlikely that its enthusiasm will be matched by counterparts on either side of the Atlantic.

Other states have noted the trend (which predates Lisbon) towards minilateral cooperations of convenience and sought to take advantage of it, one example being the '17 plus 1' initiative that China launched (as the '16 plus 1') in 2012 aimed at intensifying and expanding its interactions with 12 EU member states and five Balkan states. Although focused on economic cooperation, including infrastructure and high technology, the initiative has unwelcome strategic implications, not least for internal EU cohesion.

There are clear dangers inherent in the centrifugal forces encouraged by the EU's decade of crises, and the responses of and within member states to the countervailing centripetal forces. Coalitions designed to inject momentum and deliver consensus that are ad hoc can be more resource-intensive and less predictable, and tend to come with ambiguities of leadership. But they also offer opportunities for quicker, more flexible, more substantive responses in the face of crises. Sometimes, as with the emergency, informal 'coalition of the willing' summit on migration convened in advance of the June 2018 European Council meeting, these ad hoc formulations are simply the only options on the table. At other times, such as the Normandy format, they provide a fig leaf for more individual efforts. As Europe's geopolitical environment grows more complex, such formulations of convenience might be the only practical answer. If used with a clear sense of purpose and in close coordination with other institutions of governance and with the EU objectives for external action, this should be welcomed by Europe's partners on the international stage. This flexible and open approach allows for a more active engagement and so provides an opportunity for the emergence of Europe as a more visible and credible strategic actor.

Imagining influence beyond enlargement?

In the years preceding the euro crisis, there was a lively academic debate on the best future trajectory for the EU. At its most basic, this deliberation was over the relative priority that should be accorded to 'wider' (horizontal) versus 'deeper' (vertical) integration, posed misleadingly as alternatives on the grounds that the former obstructed the latter. Yet, as the crisis took hold, bringing concerns over EU cohesion and solidarity, and the nature of the EU's new geopolitical environment became clear, EU interest even in an 'enlargement-lite' engagement with its neighbours began to fade. The feeling, at times, appeared mutual.

At the outset of Juncker's term as European Commission president in 2014, there was little hiding the informal moratorium on expanding the EU's territory. When Juncker announced his priorities, he explicitly took enlargement off the table: 'Europe now needs to digest the addition of thirteen member states in the past ten years. Our citizens need a pause from enlargement so we can consolidate what has been achieved.'[57] The Union, he declared, would focus its attentions on jobs, growth, prosperity and security.

The pressure of events appeared to have determined the balance in the 'wider versus deeper' debate. Indeed, as the UK declared its decision to leave the EU, the pendulum swung even further from the concerns of absorbing new members to the challenge of preventing further departures. In January 2017, the lack of EU festivities commemorating the tenth anniversary of Bulgarian and Romanian accession said much about EU feelings over its recent rounds of enlargement.

This shift away from prioritising enlargement inculcated a tendency towards neglect. Prior to the EU–Western Balkans summit of May 2018, there had been no such meeting since 2003. It took the migration crisis, concerns over potential pockets of Islamist extremism in Bosnia and Kosovo, and apparent inroads being made by Russia and, increasingly, China to effect this change. Nevertheless, events beyond the Union's borders did serve as occasional reminders to a self-doubting EU of the ongoing appeal of membership for at least some of those still held at the gates. The 2013 Brussels Agreement between Serbia and Kosovo was brokered under the prospect of EU membership negotiations.[58] Later the same year, Ukrainians wrapped themselves in EU flags on the streets of Kiev during demonstrations against the pro-Russian president.

However, European concerns over the prospect of further enlargement were sufficiently entrenched that, two years later, an EU–Ukraine Association Agreement could only enter force after explicit guarantees were added to appease Dutch voters. Under the terms of this agreement, there would be no commitment that Ukraine could ever become a candidate country of the EU, and no obligation for the EU to provide collective-security guarantees to Ukraine. As Juncker made the case for the agreement, he argued that 'Ukraine will definitely not be able to become a member of the European Union in the next 20 to 25 years'.[59]

The lack of realistic prospects for accession brought new management challenges for the EU, both in relation to its formal candidate countries as well as with its broader neighbourhood. In the Western Balkans and in Turkey, the shift clearly dampened the appetite and ability of national governments to implement EU-related reforms. Frustration with hypocrisy mounted as EU member states, such as Hungary, appeared able to flout EU standards while candidate countries were held to higher standards.

Yet the process did not entirely stall. Serbia was granted EU candidate status in March 2012 and an Association and Stability Agreement in September 2013. The migration crisis let Serbia and Macedonia prove their value to the Union as they helped close down the Balkan route. Indeed, Serbian cooperative efforts and administrative capacities contrasted uncomfortably with those of EU member Greece. When the first two chapters on Serbian accession were finally opened in December 2015, the timing was not coincidental.

In 2017, the EU appeared belatedly to react to Russian influence and Chinese investment in the Balkans as it considered steps to reinvigorate the prospect of EU membership for all six Western Balkan states (Albania, Bosnia, Kosovo, North Macedonia, Montenegro and Serbia). In September 2017, Juncker introduced 'Perspective 2025', designed in part to accelerate accession negotiations for Serbia and Montenegro as the front runners for EU accession in the region. This was developed into an EU strategy presented, in February 2018, as a 'credible enlargement perspective for and enhanced EU engagement with the Western Balkans'. Serbian Prime Minister Ana Brnabić described its publication as a call 'to work every day from now … to become part of the European family of nations'.[60]

While this apparent reinvigoration of EU interest was welcomed, the need to keep expectations in check made it appear insincere. Referring to the declared 2025 timeline for Serbia and Montenegro to join the EU, Mogherini noted, in classic inaccessible Brussels-speak, 'it is clear for us this is not a target date, this is not a deadline, this is a perspective'.[61] In case there was any doubt, in what appeared to be a reference to the allegedly rushed accession of Bulgaria and Romania, EU Enlargement Commissioner Johannes Hahn urged the EU not to repeat 'past mistakes'.[62] Scepticism in some member states about the process remained high; in June 2018, France almost torpedoed even the prospect of accession talks for Albania and Macedonia.[63] With Serbia's chief negotiator on record as noting the increased role that EU member states are now playing in the accession talks compared to previous rounds, differences within the EU over the best strategies for extending influence are set to become more contentious.[64] With enthusiasm for EU membership varying across the region, the EU will have to be particularly judicious in its engagements in the Balkans to avoid further inflaming popular disillusionment with expectations that cannot be met.[65] Failure to manage expectations would provide fertile ground for the very powers whose room for influence the EU's Western Balkans strategy has been designed, at least in part, to contain.

Yet, for its own sake, the EU cannot bend its technical requirements for membership for strategic convenience, even as it must engage in discussions that have strategic consequences with strategic purpose. In 2018, a weak judiciary, the rule of law and organised crime were just a few of the serious concerns that continued to challenge the Western Balkans. Meanwhile the mean per capita GDP of the six Balkan countries was a mere 30% of the eurozone average.[66] Nevertheless, renewed EU attention to the Western Balkans is crucial for a neighbourhood where more needs to be done to embed political stability and structural reform (see Chapter Three).

The choices facing the EU with regard to Turkey, a nation of 80m people at the strategic crossroads of East and West and led by a government that does not recognise an EU member state (Cyprus), are particularly problematic. The opposition of some EU member states to Turkish membership has weakened constraints on President Recep Tayyip Erdogan's autocratic tendencies. His rollback of democracy and attacks on the rule of law, separation of powers and human rights have in turn eased some of the immediate dilemmas over the conduct of accession talks.

The immediate challenge for the EU is to find a credible strategy for its strongman neighbour that enables it to exert influence shorn of the prospect of accession. How can the EU credibly frame its engagement with Turkey in a way that can give the EU strategic influence, support Turkish human-rights activists and the country's liberal classes, and show the respect due a country accommodating more than 3.5m refugees, all while securing cooperation from Ankara on issues such as migration and counter-terrorism? The EU has yet to settle on an answer as to the extent to which accession mechanisms can continue to provide a useful (perhaps even the strongest) tool for helping Turkey reverse the losses it has suffered on rule of law and democracy.[67]

In the meantime, EU–Turkey relations are shifting towards a more limited format that focuses on shared interests in areas such as trade and counter-terrorism. In recent years, for example, attention has turned to upgrading the EU–Turkey customs union. Proponents argue that the original iteration of the customs union proves that modest conditionality can deliver modest results, suggesting that this formula can be revived to the benefit of both parties in ways compatible with the promotion and protection of EU values.[68] Opponents question whether the conditionality attached to the customs union has delivered anything meaningful, and wonder why the EU would reward a partner who has still not implemented the initial agreement in full, continuing to ban Cypriot ships and aircraft from Turkish ports and airspace.[69]

Today, the EU's language on accession has shifted to referencing 'the Western Balkans', implicitly excluding Turkey. Yet it is inescapable that Turkey is, in the words of analyst Kemal Kirisci, a 'necessary ally in a troubled region'.[70] Indeed, geography puts this NATO ally on the front line of many of the EU's recent and potential challenges. The EU will thus need to continue to try to highlight areas where interests converge and to leverage the co-dependencies that exist between Turkey and the Union towards a more cooperative relationship. This means returning to the basics of the relationship: common prosperity delivered through common trade, and dialogue about the shared challenges of integration and the threats that instability and illiberalism pose for the region's modernisation and growth. The conversation will not be easy, but sincere efforts to continue engagement will be fundamental to protecting what remains of Turkey's Western orientation, limiting the necessity for Ankara to turn to other strategic partners with objectives and outlooks that compete in the respect of not just Western interests but also Western values.

From internal shifts to external consequences

Europe's decade of crises has brought old debates about the purpose, cost and structure of the Union back to the surface. It has sharpened pre-existing internal tensions and introduced new ones, including several that affect the future of the EU and its member states as foreign- and security-policy actors. The EUGS reflects a recalibration of ambition and approach. The influence of the EU's bigger member states has become relatively greater, yet, paradoxically, the influence of the European Commission has also grown. Constraints of circumstances are pushing the EU to acknowledge its multi-speed and even multi-track nature as more than a temporary feature. Prospects for an emergence of a slowly tightening core will grow over time, with as-yet-unclear consequences for those who choose to remain one step removed. Many of the established patterns of EU cooperation have been damaged by the centrifugal forces unleashed by the crises, but the increasing tendency towards coalitions of the willing that has surfaced in response brings opportunities for more substantive and effective action. The EU's most successful foreign policy to date – enlargement – is largely spent and better strategies for regional influence now need to be imagined.

CHAPTER THREE

Europe, the EU and foreign affairs

The EU's Common Foreign and Security Policy is supposed to include 'all areas of foreign policy and all questions relating to the Union's security, including the progressive framing of a common defence policy that might lead to a common defence'.[1] Yet member states not only have sovereign differences over how best to respond to the threats the continent faces, they often disagree over the very nature of these threats. All too often, compromises between these perspectives are in fact deliberate obfuscations that may buy time, but also seed disappointment and frustration. Even the basic processes of decision-making, including the unanimity demanded for (almost) any action under the CFSP, serve as a drag on the institutional presence of the EU in international affairs. No EU strategy can entirely erase these innate tensions; no EU institution, even one that somehow functions perfectly, can ever wholly mitigate them. The development of a more coherent foreign and security policy is thus regularly cited by the continent's leaders as one of the biggest challenges facing Europe in the years ahead.[2]

A strong and strategic European presence in international affairs requires the full and active engagement of individual member states, confident in their sovereign roles and fully committed to the collaborations they choose to pursue. Far from undermining the EU's strategic aspirations, as is commonly asserted, these activities can, if properly harnessed and understood, drive them. Much of today's EU has, after all, been the result of inclusive bilateral cooperation between France and Germany set into an EU framework that enables smaller member states to bind themselves to larger member ones, confident that their voices and interests will be heard.

While some of the EU's smaller members remain committed to the CFSP to protect their interests on the international stage, the attitude of others is more ambivalent. With Brexit, there is the prospect that the long-standing issue of the UK's sensitivity to any and all perceived infractions of sovereignty will be resolved. But the UK, although particularly vocal, is not alone in such concerns. More than a few uncomfortable whispers can be heard in Berlin and Brussels about the 'Gaullist instincts' of some of those advising the Elysée on EU policy since Macron became president.[3] Similarly, some of the increased Italian financial and personnel commitments to defence and security operations in North Africa in the wake of the migration crisis have been notably bilateral in nature.[4]

By contrast, the EU remains the preferred medium for the expression of German national interests. This means that as Berlin engages more actively on issues from counter-terrorism to migration, so it will push the EU to do likewise. Furthermore, as its support for Macron's proposed European Security Council suggests, Berlin appreciates the advantages of a more structured approach to such issues and the opportunity this offers to bind member states more closely together.

Policy practitioners and commentators regularly reflect on the role of shared experiences and joint actions in paving the way for the development of a more common set of geopolitical and cultural perspectives. French Defence Minister Florence Parly is correct to note that 'the success of European defence does not depend on the institutions … it will come from new missions and operations'.[5] Yet if this is the only road to greater European strategic effectiveness and willingness, the scale of the task is daunting. It is doubtful, for example, whether there could ever be enough Lithuanian officers deploying in support of EU military training missions in Mali, or Portuguese officers deploying to Georgia to monitor the ceasefire agreement, to effect real convergence at the EU level of the deep-seated cultural and strategic preferences of its member states.

In the meantime, EU institutions will continue to be relegated to the sidelines of world affairs. European states will continue to differ in the details of their sovereign external engagements, particularly with regard to larger powers with deep pockets such as China. It would be difficult, for example, for any institution to close down every channel China might use to develop its influence in Europe. Such efforts include not just bilateral engagements but also initiatives such as the '17 plus 1' format that China runs with Central and Eastern European states, 12 of whom are EU members, and which the EU Commission, in common with several EU states, refuses to regard as the 'win–win' China proclaims the initiative to be. More generally, the EU's description of third parties which are too important to ignore as 'strategic partners' loses any meaning when the quality of its relations with such parties varies so widely. The concept covers close partners such as Canada, problematic partners such as Russia and potentially close partners such as Mexico.

If the EU is judged by what it fails to do, its record is doomed forever to disappoint. Too often, the pull of competing national policies and interests drains oxygen from the EU's rhetoric of strategic intent. For example, Mogherini has been involved in

UN-sponsored attempts at peacemaking on Syria, in particular by using what she has called 'the convening power of the EU',[6] yet her contribution has been consistently circumscribed by the lack of agreed EU policy positions on Assad's political future and Russia's intervention. Other Western actors, to be sure, have hardly acquitted themselves well in developing a clear and consistent strategy to curtail the horrific levels violence in Syria. And when peace is finally restored, the EU will undoubtedly be a main player in post-conflict stabilisation, supporting the country's reconstruction and rehabilitation. Similarly, it is not the fault of the EU and its member states that they have struggled to win political traction amid the breakdown of any semblance of a Middle East peace process.

The evidence suggests that forming an EU consensus at the institutional level, even on declaratory statements, is actually becoming more problematic. Member states are increasingly willing to stand alone or play blocking roles. This trend can be seen, for example, in the growing difficulty of forging joint positions condemning Chinese human-rights violations or challenging the legality and purpose of Chinese claims and activities in the South China Sea: Greece, Hungary and Poland have all played important blocking roles in this regard. In February 2019, after Venezuelan President Nicolás Maduro ignored demands for fresh elections, many EU countries recognised National Assembly President Juan Guaidó as interim president. Others, however, only issued messages of support for Guaidó, whilst Italy blocked a joint statement by the EU. Despite Mogherini's clarification that it was not in fact the EU's prerogative to recognise states, Moscow predictably jumped at the opportunity to accuse the EU and its members of mixed messaging.[7]

The deterioration of the EU's external security environment is forcing a greater mutual empathy between member states. If

Macron, for example, wishes to encourage Central and Eastern European nations to engage with his vision for 'a revision of the European architecture for defence and security' grounded in his perception that 'Europe can no longer rely on the United States for its security', then he has, at a minimum, to be more willing to engage with them on Europe's security challenges to its east.[8] But a system under external pressure does not always respond logically with internal unity of purpose. Divisiveness can be contagious. It will not be easy for Europe to respond to a world in which multilateralism and multilateral institutions appear increasingly out of favour and unfit for purpose with a full-throated defence of and further investment in such multilateralism. Can EU member states continue to use their individual and joint institutions to common purpose even as the winds of populism swirl both within and beyond its borders? Certainly the EU has a role to play in the struggle between liberalism and nationalism that is unfolding internationally, but the scale of the challenge should not be underestimated.

The goal of 'strategic autonomy' outlined in the EUGS is a high benchmark that stretches credibility. If the policy goal is, however, understood simply as the ambition to maximise the strategic choices and options for action that tomorrow's European policymakers will have available, it is less controversial and more achievable. The EU's growing agreement over this ambition both reflects and has been aided by its strategic disarray in the face of Trump's apparent worldview. It recognises that broad structural shifts have left the continent and its Union no credible alternative. Yet, even in present circumstances, EU aspirations for strategic autonomy are not necessarily or universally about losing faith in the future of the transatlantic relationship. A rupture would require more serious European investment than is currently planned, most notably with regard to defence. The seeds the EU is planting to

cultivate strategic credibility will still flourish best in partnership with its US ally and the transatlantic security alliance that
is NATO. The challenge is not to replace NATO but to reaffirm
its relevance. To achieve this, the EU states must not only do
more and spend more, but do so collectively. That will build
strategic autonomy without threatening NATO.

C is for common, cooperative or coordinated

The choice of 'common' to describe the CFSP is aspirational. Yet
it encourages misunderstandings and raises unhelpful expectations on the part of the EU's partners, whilst also constricting
the contributions some of its participants might be ready to
make in other contexts.

The growing use of informal minilateral groupings within
the Union (highlighted in the previous chapter) carries over
into EU foreign, security and defence policies. France and
Germany have, for example led the European response to the
Ukraine crisis under the Normandy format. The initial design
of the JCPOA with Iran (as well as attempts to dissuade the
Trump White House from quitting the deal) were led by France,
Germany and the UK. The EU will not survive and prosper if
its institutions become too weak, yet institutions that are too
overbearing will similarly threaten its future, encouraging
member states to work around them, leaving them as shells.

On issues of foreign, security and defence policy, EU institutions are unlikely ever truly to take centre stage. But while
the lead actors in any production may get the most attention
and may ultimately be responsible for the success or failure
of the performance, the stage manager has a crucial supporting role to play. As the EUGS puts it, 'EU foreign policy is not
a solo performance; it is an orchestra which plays from the
same score'.[9] An EU that embraces the budding minilateralism
in European foreign and security policy, coordinated through

EU institutions and the HR/VP, could play a critical role in coordinating member-state approaches and in amplifying their effects, while constraining a more dangerous trend towards unilateralism and fragmentation.

There are periodic explorations of the EU's willingness to shift to a greater use of QMV as part of this drive to increase the freedom and ability of the Union to act in international affairs and, as importantly, to protect it from attempts by third parties such as Russia and China to blunt EU effectiveness by co-opting individual member states.[10] (Decisions with specifically military and defence implications would continue to be exempt from QMV under Article 31.4 of the TEU.) Were EU member states able to find a formula that allowed them to move comfortably in this direction on issues of foreign-policy consequence, it would signal greater strategic intent on their parts. The challenge of persuading member states is, however, considerable, not least with regard to those whose preferences have already been threatened by QMV on migration. Even should modest progress on QMV in foreign policy prove possible, its use is likely to prove rather conservative, for example if a member state, or a very small grouping, does not so much outright oppose an action as feel mildly unenthusiastic about it. Meanwhile, larger states that do not wish to be overruled on their national foreign policy would not find it too difficult to prevent any undesirable vote from taking place.

For the moment, however, EU strategic influence in foreign affairs is hampered not only by the bureaucratic demands of the CFSP, including the requirement for unanimity, but also by the operational realities of the EEAS. Processes are followed, interests formulated and policies announced, but all too often the follow-through is underwhelming. The constraints here are understandable, perhaps for a few member states even desirable. Moreover, as the EEAS works to minimise the gap between its declaratory policy and implementation, it must depend on an EU toolbox that is outside its immediate control. Meanwhile, the range of tasks for which it bears some responsibility is unusually extensive, incorporating aspects covered not just in the foreign ministries of member states but also in their defence and development ministries.

The CFSP in a strongman's world

The CFSP came into being in a world where Western liberal democracy was set to become, as Francis Fukuyama famously ventured, 'the final form of human government'.[11] The EU's ambition to transform the world around it in its image can be clearly seen in the Lisbon Treaty. Through the decade of crises, however, member states instead found themselves confronted with the realities of a power-based world in which even Western actors, for all their talk of 'a rules-based order', were beginning to question whether the institutions of global governance were still fit for purpose. Political dysfunction no longer appeared to be the preserve of failed or failing states.[12] Far from working comfortably on development, security-sector reform and non-traditional security alongside the promotion of liberal democracy overseas, the CFSP and CSDP instead faced a neighbourhood of instability and illiberalism, from the murderous Assad to the revanchist Putin to the increasingly autocratic Erdogan. Uncomfortably for the CFSP, skills in transforming societies in partnership with willing liberal elites are proving to be less in demand than skills for managing crises and containing conflict.

It is little wonder that a self-doubting Union has struggled to develop an already weak CFSP. The EU has consistently strained to make its influence felt on the big strategic challenges, from China to Russia to the stability of the Middle East. There are multiple instances of member states forging ahead with foreign policies they know will meet with resistance from fellow member states, only subsequently to lobby for the EU to fall in behind them. Macron's July 2017 initiative to broker an agreement between the internationally recognised government in Libya and the eastern strongman General Khalifa Haftar, for example, was heavily criticised by an Italian government which had long viewed Haftar with suspicion, and had instead been backing a Misrata-based militia.[13] In May 2018, when Macron hosted rival militia leaders in Paris, Italy was again unhappy at being excluded as well as with the policy agreed there. Such competition for influence between member states is symptomatic not just of the challenges of coordination but also of a desire on the part of some key European players for more individual recognition on the international stage. Such divisions can have major consequences. In Libya, Franco-Italian differences, and the tensions these stoke on the ground, risk undermining counter-terrorism efforts by distracting from a common interest in keeping foreign and local terror groups from developing their footholds in the country.[14]

Similar differences have been on display with regard to countries such as Syria and Saudi Arabia. In January 2019, the Italian foreign minister departed from agreed EU policy when he suggested that his government was reviewing whether to become the first European country to renew diplomatic relations with Damascus, severed in 2011 after the regime's brutal crackdown on protests. The murder of Saudi journalist Jamal Khashoggi in the Saudi consulate in Istanbul was met by universal condemnation in Europe. Soon after his disappearance, the foreign ministers of Germany, France and the UK issued a joint statement aligning themselves with concerns expressed by Mogherini and UN Secretary-General António Manuel de Oliveira Guterres. But disagreement over the appropriate policy consequences was not helped by the differing strategic importance that France, the UK and Germany attached to Saudi Arabia and their respective levels of arms sales to Riyadh. EU institutions were also largely sidelined in the initial diplomatic exchanges that followed Russia's annexation of Crimea and the outbreak of conflict in the Donbas, with Germany and France leading crisis talks on Europe's behalf. As discussed later in the chapter, however, EU processes would prove useful in the formulation and retention of EU sanctions on Russia and the linkage between those sanctions and the implementation of the Minsk agreements.

As the list of foreign-policy divergences between the EU and the US grows, it becomes harder to hide the interests that divide among the interests that unite. The line taken by the Trump administration has often been actively hostile to European approaches on a range of issues, from the JCPOA to claims that the terms and conditions for the import into the US of European steel and aluminium constitute a national-security threat. Washington's shift of its embassy in Israel to Jerusalem was not just a point of transatlantic disagreement, it symbolised a broader divergence between EU and US interests in the region that has been under way for a while.

More generally, the US shift from leader to disrupter of established multilateral forums clearly demands a reaction from European states. There are other, equally concerned parties with whom the EU can work as it seeks to mitigate the strategic upheaval. From Canada to South Korea, Australia to Japan, the EU has partners that may be sceptical about the ability of Europe to step up its strategic game, but not about its desirability. Such countries are similarly keen to demonstrate the enduring appeal of effective multilateralism and a rules-based system against the forces of disruption.[15] Europe must consciously reinforce cooperation in areas where transatlantic interests continue to align, even as it engages more seriously in the development of crisis-management capabilities on key strategic issues where the US might choose to stand aside. Strengthening European resilience in the face of the maelstrom of destabilising developments in international affairs is identified in the EUGS as the CFSP's overarching goal.

There have been some modest cases of coordinated and coherent EU action on the world stage, beyond the transformative stories that EU enlargement policy helped script. The 2013 EU-brokered Brussels Agreement between Kosovo and Serbia and the EU-facilitated dialogue for the normalisation of bilateral relations that followed have important strategic significance in that unstable region. The prospect of EU (and NATO) integration also helped bring about the 2018 Prespa agreement between Greece and North Macedonia, with the EU, led by Mogherini, playing an active role in the negotiations. Less parochially, the EU has positioned itself at the centre of a web of partnerships on climate change with developing and developed countries alike. Its leadership in this area is still more important since the US announced its intention to withdraw from the Paris Agreement. The EU and its members collectively acted as facilitator and convenor in the final brokering of the JCPOA, and effectively became its chief guarantor. In May 2018, as Trump announced that the US would stop implementing the nuclear deal, European states worked closely together to keep the UN-sanctioned treaty from completely falling apart. This included the creation of a Special Purpose Vehicle (SPV) designed to blunt the impact of US secondary sanctions through the facilitation of financial transactions with Iran. Although this pushback against US dominance of the global financial system is limited, Europe's first SPV is unlikely to be its last.

That EU support for the JCPOA has proved insufficient to keep the US engaged should not reflect badly on the EU.

Likewise, if the deal should fall apart because of unreasonable Iranian demands, behaviours or failures (for example, to pave the way for small- and medium-sized firms in Europe to engage more easily in Iranian markets), it should also not reflect badly on the EU. That the EU cannot credibly aspire to be a great power able to determine the direction of world affairs does not prevent it from being a stabilising force that works with like-minded powers to protect the credibility of multilateralism, uphold international treaties, project stability in its neighbourhood and pursue a rules-based approach to issues of international concern.

A common sanctions policy

One area of modest European strategic influence has been in the deployment of sanctions, or 'restrictive measures', in the pursuit of its CFSP objectives. The EU has considerable authority as an international trading power. In recent years, it has also begun to improve its sometimes problematic record on implementation and sanctions enforcement. In some areas, the EU thus has both a reasonable 'stick' and 'carrot' to contribute. While some of the EU's record here is by default, with sanctions offering a convenient substitute for more direct pressure, a growing part is also by design. The EU has consciously developed its sanctions policies to meet a wider range of CFSP concerns. Meanwhile, its policy of aligning third parties, including European Economic Area (EEA) and accession-candidate countries, to its position also adds presentational and sometimes real weight to the sanctions the EU adopts.[16]

By January 2019, the EU had 43 sanctions programmes in place, confirming its position as the world's second-most-active user of restrictive measures after the US.[17] By contrast, in 1991 just six countries were under EU sanction. Since around 2010, when the EU (in coordination with the US) imposed sanctions on Iran well beyond those demanded by the UN Security Council, the EU has become notably more ambitious with its sanctions policies. In early 2011, for example, the EU adopted unusually broad economic measures against the government of Côte d'Ivoire, including banning European companies from trading through the country's harbours and from importing its cocoa crop. The same year, the EU acted autonomously and repeatedly to sanction Syria. Not only did it not wait for UN sanctions to be in place, as it had with Iran and Côte d'Ivoire, it rapidly escalated the sanctions it chose to deploy, including a ban on the import of Syrian oil and gas.[18] In July 2017, the EU became the second major actor, after the US, to start composing a framework for adopting sanctions in the face of cyber attacks.

While the EU has usually followed the United States' lead, and its measures are usually modest by comparison, it has shown itself ready to take on more of a leadership role. This can be seen in the range of sanctions it adopted against Russia after the annexation of Crimea, and in particular following the downing of Malaysia Airlines flight MH17 over eastern Ukraine in 2014. These measures have proved more extensive and more durable than many critics initially thought possible. The costs have been higher for EU states than for the US: Russia was the EU's third-largest trading partner in 2013, but only America's 23rd. The EU has navigated repeated sanctions renewals despite the discomfort of several EU member states, including Greece, Hungary and Italy, and despite Russian counter-sanctions. Merkel's push to link EU sanctions to Russia's implementation of the Minsk II agreement proved strategically smart, helping deflect tensions between EU member states over the higher tiers of sanctions in particular, as the OSCE continued to record serious ongoing violations of the ceasefire agreement.

EU sanctions (working in combination with those of the US) certainly magnified the impact of falling global oil prices on the

Russian economy and hurt Russian foreign-exchange reserves as Russia's indebted corporate sector found its access to the world's capital markets undercut. Whether this had any influence on the Kremlin's Ukraine strategy is less certain. But even in cases where the direct economic effectiveness of restrictive measures can be questioned, they may have a greater impact by virtue of economic and political signalling. Relatively limited sanctions can send a message to European (and other) companies to stay away. In Myanmar during the junta years, for example, the direct damage to the Burmese economy from EU sanctions may have been small, but the discouragement they provided to otherwise interested private Western investors was not. Sanctions also sent a political signal of support for a brutalised opposition, making then-opposition activist Aung San Suu Kyi a vocal supporter. In the wake of the killing and forced displacement from their homes of Rohingya Muslims in Myanmar's Rakhine State, in mid-2018 the EU turned again to sanctions once it became clear that quiet diplomacy with the Burmese military and Aung San Suu Kyi, now in the role of state counsellor, was failing to yield satisfactory results.

Since 1989, the EU has helped protect and defend US strategic interests through its arms embargo on China. This has been sustained in the face of considerable pressure on individual European states from Beijing, which argues that the embargo is 'outdated'.[19] There is no doubt that appeals from fellow members within the common club have played an important role in sustaining the embargo, along with the eight criteria established under the European Council's common position on exports on military technology and equipment. The US has sometimes had to apply pressure of its own, in particular in the difficult years around 2003 when the US Congress threatened to restrict US military exports and technology transfers to European countries were the arms embargo to be lifted.

These sanctions have never been formalised into a common position under the CFSP; their legal basis remains nothing more than a presidency statement. But this lack of formalised sanction has permitted some helpful flexibility, including the development of closer contact between the People's Liberation Army and the militaries of EU member states. When carefully controlled and monitored, this can build confidence as well as facilitate interactions on joint missions such as combatting piracy off the coast of Somalia under *Operation Atalanta* and cooperating on humanitarian assistance and disaster relief. More controversially, however, it also means that there is no single prescribed common list of arms embargoed for sale by EU states to China, while sales on contracts agreed before 1989 were largely able to continue uninterrupted.[20]

This points to a wider issue with EU sanctions enforcement. The EU has no equivalent to the US Office of Foreign Assets Control, the financial intelligence and enforcement agency of the US Treasury. Instead, EU member states rely on a range of different agencies for enforcement and oversight. This often chaotic situation has led, in several circumstances in several geographical areas, to sanctions-breaking behaviour. EU sanctions on Russia, for example, do not apply to Europe-based subsidiaries of Russian companies, which can make circumvention difficult to establish. In July 2017, two electricity turbines made by the German company Siemens were delivered to Crimea, even though Crimea was subject to an EU-wide ban related to the supply of energy technology. A 2016 investigation revealed at least two European retailers still active on the Crimean market through Russian subsidiaries.[21]

These flaws in policy execution are compounded by more generic issues of policy design. The more sanctions are tailored and targeted to minimise civilian costs, the more loopholes there can be for exploitation. European states have been slowly stepping up their enforcement activities in response. In April 2017, the UK moved to a US-style enforcement policy, creating an Office of Financial Sanctions Implementation able to impose civil fines for breaches of financial sanctions to the tune of £1m or 50% of the breach, whichever is greater.[22] In 2017, successful enforcement actions were brought by at least nine different EU member states across a range of sanctions regimes including North Korea, Russia, Syria and counter-terrorism measures.[23]

Differences between US and EU sanctions policies have, at times, caused considerable transatlantic tension, for example over the principle of extraterritoriality of US sanctions. In 2015, French bank BNP Paribas pleaded guilty to violating US sanctions against Cuba, Iran and Sudan and was fined US$9bn.[24] In 2019, transatlantic tensions ran notably high as the US threatened to sanction European companies involved in the Nord Stream II pipeline aimed at increasing Russian gas supplies to Europe.

US sanctions are often broader in scope than the EU's. For example, the EU forbids cooperation with Russian oil companies on new deep-water, Arctic and shale projects, but permits existing cooperative projects to continue, while US sanctions forbid existing projects and include the gas sector. In March 2017, after establishing its authority to rule on CFSP issues, the ECJ limited the scope of sanctions imposed on Russia at the bequest of the German government and Rosneft. In excluding the processing of third-party payments from 'financial assistance' sanctions, the decision marks a further divergence between EU and US sanctions practices, which usually forbid US-governed financial institutions from providing any services at all to sanctioned parties.[25] Unlike US sanctions, however, most of which tend to be open-ended, EU sanctions are adopted for limited periods not exceeding a year. Before expiry they are subject to review and either extended or dropped. This allows the EU to be quicker to respond to positive developments, transforming the stick of sanctions into the carrot of closer trading relations far more adeptly than the US system allows, as can be seen in the case of Myanmar, where the EU eased sanctions four years earlier than the US.

EU foreign policy and the unavoidables

In the next few years, demands on European foreign policy will continue to outstrip capacity. Rather than looking at where the EU struggles to add value, it is more useful to consider those areas where it does not have the luxury of failure without forfeiting any pretension to strategic relevance and endangering its survival. Two key challenges are worth highlighting in this regard.

Migration and conflict in the Sahel and North Africa

Africa's population is set to more than double by 2050, to 2.6bn, accounting for more than half the global population increase over that period.[26] In the western Sahel region (Burkina Faso, Chad, Mali, Mauritania and Niger, which together make up the five-nation G5 Sahel), already afflicted by extremes of poverty, unemployment, and food and water insecurity, the population will rise from 78m to 200m by 2050. The need for a comprehensive approach that considers security support and political partnerships alongside other aspects of development policy and stimuli for economic growth has rarely been so obvious.

As leaders from Europe and Africa prepared to meet at the fifth African Union (AU)–EU summit in November 2017, European Parliament President Antonio Tajani called for 'a radical change that puts the African continent on the top of the EU's policy agenda', reflecting growing talk back home of European engagement in Africa as a 'security belt' for the continent.[27] A similar emphasis has been appearing in the foreign policies of individual member states such as France, Germany, Italy and the UK. Macron, for example, has talked of the importance of prioritising Africa in France's economic diplomacy alongside France's ongoing defence and security contributions to the continent's stability.[28] Migration challenges are also pushing the EU to work more closely with its immediate African neighbours, for example through Turkey-style deals that aim to extend a buffer around the EU policed by willing neighbours supported and paid to manage migratory flows before they reach European shores. Berlin has been at the centre of many initiatives, for example sponsoring the 'Compact with Africa' during Germany's G20 presidency in 2017, a year that it not coincidentally declared as 'Africa Year in Germany'. In all the enthusiasm, coordination seemed at times a forgotten luxury. Three different government ministries released strategies for cooperation with Africa in 2017: the Development Ministry's 'Marshall Plan with Africa', the Finance Ministry's 'Compact with Africa' and the Ministry of Economy's 'ProAfrika' concept. The continent is mentioned 28 times in the 2018 government-coalition agreement. Developments, for example, in Egypt, Libya and Algeria are set to continue to demand European attentions for some time to come. This is because of their consequences for European security and prosperity, as well as because of the growing influence of third parties within these countries in exploiting matters in ways not conducive to European interests.

The crises of the past decade are refashioning EU relations with a continent once seen as a test bed for the CSDP, where the EU has tended to pursue missions that were relatively insubstantial or heavily restricted in their mandate. Issues of irregular migration and security are now firmly on the agendas of European states and EU institutions. That Mali was Macron's first official trip outside Europe was revealing not just of sharpening French priorities, but also about where the EU will need to follow. Indeed, in such instances, defence-policy initiatives are making their own demands on EU foreign policy. With the sacrifice of European lives and taxpayer money in the pursuit of peace and stability in Mali, for example, demands for EU actors to understand the complexities of local and national dynamics and the pressure points these afford in the management of a problematic peace deal are likely to become more acute.

Africa is already the main recipient for EU ODA, with the EU and its member states collectively spending some €20bn every year. Even as the nature of this assistance and engagement changes, the size of the challenge and the resource and financial commitments it will require is likely to grow. Negotiations over a replacement for the Cotonou Agreement with Africa, Caribbean and Pacific nations (which expires in February 2020) are set to see more of a continent-to-continent approach, bridging previous divisions between the EU's approach to North Africa through Cotonou and to sub-Saharan Africa through the Joint Africa–EU strategy. The latter will also be revamped and upgraded, with a greater focus on migration and security alongside the more established themes of growth and development. Since 2016, the EU has been developing a Migration Partnership Framework, leading to bilateral agreements on migration with a number of priority countries of origin and transit including Mali, Niger and Senegal. Other initiatives involving EU security concerns include the launch in 2015 of a Trust Fund for Africa, backed by more than €3.3bn for the Sahel, North Africa and the Horn of Africa and focused on addressing the root causes of irregular migration and managing it better.[29]

European interest in African security concerns is hardly new, but the focus has intensified and shifted to include more attention to capacity-building for conflict prevention and crisis management, most notably with regard to irregular migration. What is also new is that the migration challenge is helping restore balance to the internal disconnect between France's traditional focus on Europe's south and Germany's on Europe's east, as increasing concern over migration and terrorism is bolstering German security interests in Africa.

Only time will tell how successful the EU will be in building African resilience and projecting stability, as well as whether the EU will maintain and develop the commitments it is making. Yet the scale and persistence of the challenge, especially along the northern shores of Africa, means the EU and its member states cannot but engage. Without a serious, coordinated approach to foreign, security and defence policy, even the tens of billions of euros on development policy currently being promised will not be able sustainably to stem the flow of people. This is not to deny that Europe has benefitted from migration in the past, nor the increasing need for immigrants in the future. But it is important that the processes for migration are controlled, and are seen to be controlled, while the routes for seeking asylum under international law are protected.

Not all EU member states will prosecute this strategy to the same degree or to the same effect. Just as an EU emergency meeting on migration in June 2018 summoned only a 'coalition of the willing', much practical action will come from bilateral and minilateral initiatives and agreements. Member states are learning from experience that too strict a requirement for unanimity does little to promote unity and a lot to ensure inaction. Fortunately, that it not what is now happening. Just as thinking on development assistance has been moving towards a more blended approach, the EU and its member states are cautiously and carefully showing a willingness to countenance a more blended approach to their strategic concerns on the African continent.

Balancing in the Balkans

The second unavoidable foreign- and security-policy challenge for the EU lies in its ability collectively to manage what it describes as 'the heart of Europe' in the Western Balkans. Failure to maintain security and stability in this neighbourhood – not covered by the CFSP – would be judged by those not preoccupied by such technicalities as a catastrophic strategic failure of EU foreign and security policy. In the Balkan wars of the early 1990s, when Luxembourg foreign minister Jacques Poos fatefully and infamously declared 'the hour of Europe' to have dawned, the EU showed itself incapable of bringing an end to the violence without the intervention of the US and NATO.[30] Meanwhile, many of the factors that brought such destruction to the region remain, from the preponderance of strongmen to the promotion of identity nationalism. With a growing number of outside powers manoeuvring to increase their influence in the Balkans, for the EU to lose influence in its own backyard would mean that the Balkans would serve not just as one of the first brutal exposures of the weakness of a common foreign policy, but likely also one of the last. There would be little credibility left to salvage.

Much has changed since the 2003 European Council's Thessaloniki agenda, which offered new European partnerships to the Western Balkans while confirming the prospect of EU membership. China had yet to become even a marginal consideration in the region's geopolitics; Beijing's Belt and Road Initiative, with its strategic targeting of countries such as Serbia, had yet to be conceived. Russian engagement with the region was largely restricted to energy diplomacy. Turkey was a biddable accession candidate and the US was an active partner, engaging with the EU to stop inter-ethnic violence in Macedonia from escalating into war in 2001.

The European Commission's new enlargement strategy, published in 2018, came in the context of growing frustration within the six countries of the Western Balkans over the pace of progress, and EU concerns that such frustrations provided fertile ground for the growing influence of external actors including China and Russia, but also Iran, Saudi Arabia and Turkey. Intended to revive the enlargement process and encourage the necessary reforms, for the first time an indicative membership date (of 2025) was suggested as a credible target for Serbia and Kosovo, the two countries most advanced in this process. Even as the strategy was being launched, however, grumblings could be heard in more than a few EU capitals about the political sensitivities of managing the prospect, let alone the reality, of further enlargement, especially when concerns over borders, the movement of people, and ethnic and cultural nationalism were increasingly sensitive in domestic policy discourse. Yet the strategic pull of EU membership can provide an important stabilising role in a region that too often struggles to maintain even a slow pace of integration.

Crudely put, the debate within the EU boiled down to the merits of a 'yes but' versus a 'no if only' approach to the membership prospects of the Western Balkans. The 'yes but' approach begins by confirming the desirability of accession, before slowly rolling out policy chapters laden with lists of conditions and reforms that need to be carried out first. This positive approach risks raising unrealistic regional expectations but gives the EU greater strategic traction and minimises the dangers that it will be marginalised in its own backyard. The 'no if only' posture puts greater emphasis on the conditions that first need to be met before membership can credibly be countenanced. Proponents argue that the 'yes but' approach risks setting up a Turkey-style counter-productive dynamic where the EU might never be able to make good on its offer, or even be interested in so doing.

The narrow triumph of the 'yes but' approach, shown by the July 2018 launch of a screening process aimed at permitting accession talks with Albania and North Macedonia to begin by June 2019, was a strategic move that recognised the contest for influence building on the EU's borders. It did not reflect an increased belief by more sceptical EU member states in the added value Balkan countries could offer the EU. After all, while countries such as Romania remain strongly supportive of Balkan accession, its compatibility with the more ambitious elements of Macron's 'more with fewer' agenda is less clear. Nor is it difficult to find officials in Berlin concerned at the domestic politics of managing migration from the Western Balkans propelled by EU membership. Five EU member states continue not even to recognise Kosovo as an independent country, further complicating the path towards enlargement.

Accession by the Western Balkan states could import to the EU the very disruptive influences that a more credible path to enlargement is intended to close down. One criterion for accession of candidate members is alignment with the EU's external relations with third parties. Yet the close relationships of some Western Balkan states with Russia has undermined their interest in aligning with EU sanctions. Montenegro and Albania (the two NATO members in the region) have done so, but Serbia has not. Indeed, Belgrade's engagement with Moscow has, if anything, become closer and more active since 2014. Its ties with China have likewise grown. This has broad implications for European and EU unity. It is difficult to see how further EU enlargement could occur without rewriting the voting rules on issues of foreign and security policy to limit the power of veto of individual member states.

Whether or not EU member states ultimately decide that their pronounced openness to further enlargement is sincere, with the US less engaged and other powers more likely to see the region as one where they can take action with limited consequences, Europe will need to find ways to manage these geopolitical tensions in its immediate backyard.

The changing imperatives of foreign policy

As the tools and targets of foreign policy evolve, so too will estimates of Europe's strategic impact, both potential and realised. As traditional geopolitical pressures return to centre stage, the instruments that define a country's defence and security capabilities and vulnerabilities are diversifying. Europe's future ability to protect and defend itself will be determined not just by its defence and diplomatic capabilities, but increasingly by other capabilities, including technological ones. Developments in areas such as artificial intelligence (AI) and quantum computing will change the nature and even meaning of geopolitical competition and conflict. New dependencies are already being forged. Most of the AI-powered hardware and software solutions needed to run the industries of the future are currently manufactured outside of Europe.[31]

One area of growing concern is investment security. Foreign investment in an obscure high-tech company in a little-known European town can now affect European foreign and security policy to an unprecedented degree. A series of complex derivative transactions can result in the emergence of a foreign investor as the single-biggest shareholder of a key European company, as evidenced for example by Li Shufu's surprise emergence as the largest individual shareholder of Daimler, with technology and security ramifications. Issues of this nature are likely to increase in both number and severity.

Concerns have been growing about the strategic implications of some foreign investments in Europe since the financial crisis. These tend to focus on China in particular: between 2008 and 2015 Chinese investments in the EU increased from approximately €2bn to €20bn.[32] Such concerns have also been raised by the advent of China's Belt and Road Initiative, its ambitions for a 'community of common destiny in cyber-space' and its 'Made in China 2025' strategy for transforming the country into a high-tech 'manufacturing superpower'.[33] The strategic significance of this latter ambition is a useful reminder of the changing nature of great-power competition and influence. Based on the US Industrial Internet Strategy and extensive study of Germany's 'Industry 4.0', which focuses on the efficiency and productivity savings that can come from the combination of advanced technology and the internet, China's strategy is aimed not just at joining but dominating the market in critical high-tech industries. This includes the pursuit of technology substitution that, if officially espoused rather than unofficially pushed through internal or informal interactions, would violate World Trade Organization (WTO) rules.[34] These state-sponsored policies are having a notable impact on European countries from Germany to Ireland, and the Czech Republic to Hungary.[35] China's strategy, moreover, does not just include its promotion of foreign acquisitions, but also coercive technology transfer and the promotion of commercial espionage, including cyber espionage.[36] China is using similar methods in the pursuit of its ambitions in AI; the AI strategy developed by the European Commission falls considerably short of the necessary mark in its response.[37]

EU member states are only just starting to consider the scale and nature of the challenge posed by these initiatives. The concerns, at first wrongly seen as evidence of a protectionist backlash, are more strategic, even if they are vulnerable to abuse by protectionist lobbies.[38] Prompted by US intelligence and information sharing, for example, in October 2016 Germany withdrew approval for a €670m takeover of chip manufacturer Aixtron and its US subsidiaries by Chinese group Fujian Grand

Chip. Concerned by the impact on US subsidiaries, Obama blocked the move on the grounds of 'credible evidence' that the investors 'might take action that threatens to impair the national security of the United States'.[39]

Germany saw a tenfold increase in Chinese foreign direct investment (FDI) between 2015 and 2016 alone. The takeover by a Chinese appliance manufacturer in early 2016 of troubled German robotics maker Kuka united politicians concerned about the loss of technology, trade unions concerned about job losses and business groups frustrated by the lack of reciprocal investment access in China. The deal focused European minds on the lack of individual and collective screening mechanisms for foreign investments in and between EU member states: only 12 member states had their own screening mechanisms to address investments from the perspective of security or public order. In September 2017, the European Commission proposed a framework for screening FDI inflows into the EU on the grounds of security. It attempts to balance the EU's position as one of the regions most open to FDI with concerns that this openness should not contribute to the inadvertent undermining of EU security.[40] In particular, the commission noted, 'state owned enterprises taking over EU companies with key technologies for strategic reasons' require 'careful analysis and appropriate action'.[41] The framework agreed in November 2018 to increase intra-EU cooperation on screening did not attempt to harmonise existing screening mechanisms of individual member states, or to replace them with an overarching EU-wide mechanism. The agreement did, however, set up a coordination group between member states and the European Commission to 'help identify joint strategic concerns and solutions'. Member states can take individual actions to revise their screening mechanisms, as Germany and Italy did in July and October 2017 respectively.

Even if still notably insufficient, the agreement, involving as it does not just investments with direct defence implications, but also investments in other areas, including media, technology and even real estate, is nevertheless a sign of Europe's growing appreciation of the comprehensive nature of foreign, security and defence policy. Moreover, given the opposition even this modest framework faced from countries such as Cyprus, Greece and Malta, its creation is further testament that the EU is something more than a lowest-common-denominator grouping. Individual member states might be able to block or water down EU declarations, but for issues with real strategic import, such as the EU's embargo on arms sales to China, sanctions or concerns of investment security, an EU framework can provide genuine strategic value.

Meanwhile, even the baseline of greater transparency and information sharing on investments that present a genuinely plausible threat to national security (as opposed to cover for the promotion of more protectionist industrialist policies) is a welcome development. The development of more formal cooperation between member states and the commission on this matter is a first step along the way to greater convergence and harmonisation between national regimes. While the EU is unlikely ever to end up with something as tightly controlled as the Committee on Foreign Investments in the United States, there are clear lessons to be learned from the model.[42] There are also perhaps more applicable lessons to be taken from the experience of Australia's Foreign Review Board that scrutinises foreign investments into a country that has been the world's second-largest recipient of Chinese investment (after the US) since 2007.[43]

Significantly, this is not an area where the European Commission is in danger of getting ahead of member states; its engagement followed specific instructions from the European

Council, pushed by some of the larger member states.[44] The balance between member states supportive of a formal transfer of FDI screening powers to the commission and those determined to protect member-state sovereignty in this area is admittedly difficult to strike. Yet decisive action is needed in short order, as the time frame for Made in China 2025 underlines.

Identifying key technologies that involve national security is never easy, and the ability to do so will remain dependent on the resources of member states, including their intelligence agencies and their partners. The difficulties are further complicated by the lack of subtlety the Trump administration is showing in confronting the national-security implications of Chinese high-tech mercantilism.[45] The divisiveness of the president's approach is particularly galling, given that many of Washington's European allies, both in government and in the private sector, share the administration's underlying concerns, if not always how it chooses to address them.

Weaknesses in the EU's response should not be glossed over. The recovering economies of Southern Europe and the growing economies of much of Central and Eastern Europe have much to gain in the short term from Chinese FDI, including in their high-tech sectors. The technology-transfer agreements that tend to accompany such deals are often all too easily written off as the price that needs to be paid. As concepts of national security evolve, however, these areas of growing defence and security concern might prove better suited to EU strengths than the sharper end of defence cooperation. Effective action in this area will be grounded in the very processes and rules in whose design the EU is often criticised for specialising.

The future of European foreign and security policy

Against this backdrop, and with the apparent waning of enthusiasm for multilateralist approaches on the part of Europe's chief ally, the inadequacy of European foreign policy appears at first glance to be starker than ever. But expectations for the CFSP are, all too often, unrealistic, and the fact that other actors are similarly struggling to get to grips with more complex and multifaceted security issues is often conveniently ignored. As noted elsewhere, EU foreign policy must be judged, at least in part, by what it is able to effect, rather than what it is not. The challenge is not only to do more with the CFSP and CSDP, it is also to use the resources that the EU has for external action more coherently, linking more effectively the EU's work on development policy, technical assistance and trade with its objectives for its neighbourhood and for foreign and security policy.

Member states are increasingly unable to deny that effective domestic policies on concerns such as irregular migration are likely to require more active and coordinated foreign policies. Migration agreements and readmission arrangements will not be easily sustained, and will commit EU member states to broader partnerships in key regions that focus not just on development or on good governance but also on the provision of peace and security in these lands. A more coordinated and cooperative network of European foreign and security policies will need to emerge. Such efforts will depend primarily upon individual members, but EU institutions will have an important role to play in corralling and representing these states. Cooperation will come in many forms: multilateral and institutional, bilateral, informal, and sometimes multilateral but based on national legislation. Many of the ambitions for European global strategy and influence will go unfulfilled, and the mechanisms for achieving them unrealised. The limitations and frustrations of European foreign engagement will continue to be easier to cite than the triumphs. But already-established and yet-to-be-imagined formats can lend Europe serious strategic weight in international affairs. The first signs of a European strategic awakening might finally be starting to emerge.

CHAPTER FOUR

Europe, the EU, security and defence

European efforts to develop a common security and defence policy have, like parallel efforts with regard to foreign policy, fallen far short of the mark. When the 1998 Franco-British St Malo Agreement was heralded as a transformational moment in European defence, the way ahead was already clear: 'the EU must have the capacity for autonomous action, backed up by credible military forces, the means to decide to use them, and a readiness to do so, in order to respond to international crises ... where NATO as a whole is not engaged'.[1] Some 20 years later, it is difficult not to reflect on the paucity of progress. As he made the case in 2015 for greater European defence cooperation, Jean-Claude Juncker colourfully suggested that 'a bunch of chickens looks like a combat formation compared to the foreign and security policy of the European Union'.[2]

The lack of progress is easy to understand, if not to accept. Sensitivities of sovereignty are most acute on issues of security and defence, and there are fundamental differences between EU member states in their strategic cultures and approaches to such issues, just as there are in foreign policy. Nuclear-armed France, for example, continues to cultivate an interventionist approach (with occasional tinges of 'France first'), ready to stand alone if necessary. By contrast, Germany prefers the comfort of acting within broader coalitions and, even then, ideally in supporting roles. Domestic constraints on German defence policy, though loosening, remain significant.[3]

Even where common positions and actions can be agreed, years of underinvestment in European militaries and a rising demand for their services mean that, all too often, key capabilities are unavailable for lack of spare parts or trained operators, while those that are available are outdated or unsuited to the operational terrain where they are required. The sorry state of Germany's armed forces attracts particular attention in this regard, even though the situation mirrors that of many smaller European militaries. The long list of complaints covers air, sea and land services alike. In October 2017, for example, after Germany's only operational submarine was involved in an accident off the coast of Norway, the entire German fleet of six 212A-type submarines was declared out of commission. In February 2018, only 105 of the Bundeswehr's 244 combat tanks were operational.[4] As a report from Germany's Parliamentary Commissioner for the Armed Forces Hans-Peter Bartels noted, 'the material readiness of the Bundeswehr is a catastrophe. This situation came about because we spent 25 years cutting the defence budget ... we thought everything could be solved through negotiations, agreements, co-operation and partnerships.'[5]

France, meanwhile, has struggled to muster the air transport needed to support its otherwise impressive record of interventions in sub-Saharan Africa. Paris may be able to deploy some 4,000 troops to the region, but it depends on other capitals for logistical supply. Even before any budget squeeze that might result from Brexit, the UK faces a recruitment crisis, with all three military branches 'running to stand still'.[6] A former commander of the UK's Joint Forces Command told the UK Commons Defence Committee in 2017 that the army was 'twenty years out of date', the RAF was 'holding together a bunch of very good equipment but really at the edge of their engineering and support capacity' and the Royal Navy was 'structurally under-funded'.[7]

However, as finance ministries across Europe are fond of noting, not all of the deficits in defence capability can be conveniently attributed to budget cuts. Procurement processes also need to be addressed. That the Bundeswehr was running short of long johns in 2017, for example, is perhaps better attributed to problems in the management of the supply chain than to lack of financing.[8]

EU defence policy is not, to be sure, really about defence, or at least territorial defence. The 'strategic autonomy' for which the EUGS calls is more immediately concerned with crisis-management capabilities, linked to the three priorities the strategy sets out: the ability to respond to external conflicts and crises, to build the capacities of partners, and to protect Europe and its citizens.[9] Despite turmoil in transatlantic relations and concern over a post-American order, there will be no credible alternative to NATO on matters of territorial defence, war fighting and conventional deterrence for the foreseeable future. The fact that Russia's armed forces number more than 1m, whilst each of the three largest European militaries number just over 200,000, is a reminder of the scale of the imbalances that Europe will face, even before Russia's military modernisation is taken into account. Fears over US dependability currently relate primarily to support for crisis-management operations rather than European territorial defence. The budget for the US Defense Department's European Deterrence Initiative has seen year-on-year increases from US$3.4bn in FY2017 to US$4.8bn in 2018 and US$6.5bn in 2019.[10]

This chapter considers developments in the CSDP following the EUGS as well as European bilateral and multilateral defence and security cooperation outside the EU legal framework. The majority of developments in the CSDP by early 2019 concern military structures, instruments and ambitions, but similar efforts with regard to the civilian CSDP are also under way. In November 2018, a Civilian CSDP Compact put forward a new framework for civilian crisis management focusing on the development of EU capabilities. Full delivery of the compact is expected by summer 2023 at the latest.[11] In theory this will improve EU engagement on issues such as rule of law and policing, with civilian CSDP given a clearer role in the broader external response to challenges such as irregular migration, hybrid threats, terrorism and organised crime. In time, this should lead to more policy and operational synergies with other non-CSDP instruments such as the commission's Directorate General for International Cooperation and Development (DEVCO) on security-sector reform, or the European Union Network and Information Security Agency (ENISA) on cyber security, or Frontex on border security.

New momentum … but to what effect?

The European Commission has been as clear on EU ambitions to ensure, for example, that the EU force catalogue has a 'full-spectrum of land, air, space and maritime capabilities' as it has been unclear on how to achieve them.[12] But the emerging consensus among EU policymakers is that the Union must play a role, for the sake of its own credibility if nothing else, in delivering a 'Europe that protects, empowers, and defends' (the title of the commission's 2017 Work Programme).

Four days after the UK's Brexit vote, the French and German foreign ministers released the first of two papers arguing that the time was ripe for the EU again to try to move towards 'a comprehensive, realistic and credible Defence in the European Union'. The paper called for 'concrete action plans on the short term' to support CSDP military operations, develop European military capabilities and sponsor European defence cooperation.[13] In the months that followed, the EU (and NATO) agreed a three-pronged defence 'winter package'.

Firstly, a Security and Defence Implementation Plan (SDIP) proposed by the EEAS outlined 13 specific policy actions to enhance defence cooperation in the EU. These included a voluntary Coordinated Annual Review on Defence (CARD) to synchronise defence planning cycles and capability plans in member states, and the proposal to activate PESCO in defence. The latter attracted particular excitement within EU institutions; Mogherini labelled PESCO's launch 'a historic day for European Defence'.[14] Countries could now cooperate more closely on defence within the legal architecture of the EU and in ways potentially more binding than alternative routes, for example the EDA or NATO's Framework Nation Concept.

The second prong, a Defence Action Plan proposed by the European Commission, introduced the commission as a significant sponsor of European defence integration, including through the establishment of the EDF. Alongside a 'financial toolbox' focused on support for small and medium-sized enterprises in particular, a 'research window' (with a projected annual budget of €500m from 2020) will support collaborative research in defence technology in priority areas identified by member states. A linked 'capability window' (with a budget of some €1bn a year from 2020) will also offer co-financing and commission support for the joint development and procurement of defence projects involving at least three companies from two member states. This funding is intended to be an incentive for a fivefold multiplying of national-level financing. If this happens, EU states will collectively be investing a further €5bn per year on defence capabilities from 2020. While this is hardly a revolutionary amount, it would turn the EU (and with it the commission) into a serious actor in the area of European defence research and development, particularly in contrast to NATO's modest role in this area and its more short- to medium-term focus.

The final element of the winter package, an EU–NATO declaration, sought to re-energise long-standing efforts at closer coordination. Time-specific measures for closer coopera- tion on capabilities and shared threats were listed, including promoting ties on issues of cyber-defence research and tech- nology innovation.

Institutions alone do not automatically add value. European defence, as Macron noted in his Sorbonne speech in 2017, cannot simply be about the establishment of new institutions. Are the latest moves simply examples of framework prolifera- tion? Or might they actually help the EU respond to external conflicts and crises? By late 2017, officials in Brussels were suggesting that more had been achieved in the field of security and defence in the previous ten months than in the previous ten years. Yet the question is not how far these common poli- cies have come, but whether any of the progress has strategic consequence, making EU citizens more secure and bolstering the EU's relevance in international affairs. The initial signs are mixed. There are, however, four initiatives under way at the EU institutional level with the potential to make a substantive difference to European pretensions on security and defence: closer EU–NATO cooperation, CARD, PESCO and the EDF. Although unlikely to be transformational, these initiatives point to the development of more positive political dynamics in European capitals in support of genuinely deeper defence partnerships and consolidation.

Closer EU–NATO cooperation

Closer practical cooperation between the EU and NATO could make a substantive difference to both organisations. NATO's 2016 Joint Declaration in Warsaw highlighted seven areas for closer cooperation, but the 42 action items agreed across these seven priority areas under the winter package provide a clear road map for tangible action. Subsequent reviews have added to these action points; by June 2018, 74 areas for intensifying cooperation had been identified. One area in particular where there has previously been poor coordination or even institutional competition is capacity-building. As both NATO and the EU look to increase their work with international partners under this heading, effective cooperation here will become even more important.

While relations between non-NATO Cyprus and non-EU Turkey remain fraught, there will be limits on the possibilities for formalising some of the increased interactions. Nevertheless, progress reports suggest the mainstreaming of closer cooperation as a daily practice across key policy areas.[15] In the Central Mediterranean, for example, NATO's *Operation Sea Guardian* and the EU's NAVFOR MED *Operation Sophia* share daily situation reports and have begun to evolve a pattern of tactical information sharing beyond simple deconfliction of sailing intentions and operations schedules. NATO cooperation with Frontex on both the tactical and operational level has also improved, with support for reconnaissance, monitoring and surveillance operations aimed at stemming irregular migration. A joint EU–NATO declaration in July 2018 recognised EU defence efforts to increase transatlantic burden sharing and expanded cooperation in areas such as military mobility, counter-terrorism and chemical, biological, radiological and nuclear threats.

How far this cooperation can ultimately go will depend as much on the willingness of member states of the two institutions to address long-standing political constraints as it will on the evolution in attitudes and practices within and between NATO and the EU.

Coordinated Annual Review on Defence

The objective of CARD – 'to develop a more structured way to deliver identified capabilities based on greater transparency, political visibility, and commitment from Member States' – should help redress the complaint during the euro crisis by a former director of the EDA that 'what is worrying is not so much the scale of cuts as the way they have been made: strictly on a national basis, without any attempt at consultation or coordination within either NATO or the EU, and with no regard to the overall defence capability which will result from the sum of these national decisions'.[16]

The CARD process will be overseen by the EDA and begin its first formal run with the member states that opt into the process in autumn 2019, following trial runs involving all member states from 2017. The information collated will feed into the EDA's Capability Development Plan and the results delivered to a steering board of national defence ministers. The review's operational utility should be enhanced by the financial support for capability development provided by the EDF as well as by a Cooperative Financial Mechanism structured around two pillars, one intergovernmental and one involving the European Investment Bank. These initiatives should increase European support for defence-technology research and development (R&D) and joint acquisition projects, including by the provision of loans to enable governments to participate. The intent is to make it easier for member states to align their spending and procurement cycles.

What impact CARD can have in the face of the substantive and structural problem of state sovereignty, and whether it can persuade governments to change deep-seated and not entirely irrational behaviours, remains to be seen. Its initial ambition is limited to information sharing. Participants are expected to dedicate 20% of defence spending to equipment procurement, with 35% of this spent collaboratively. Spending on defence research and technology is expected to be a minimum of 2% of defence spending, with 20% of this spent collaboratively. As long as these benchmarks are voluntary and non-binding, however, the danger of disappointment is obvious, as the experience of NATO's 2% target demonstrates. Similarly, member-state compliance with equivalent efforts to coordinate economic policy across the EU has generally been underwhelming. Voluntary contributions and collective-defence benchmarks agreed by EDA member states in 2007 had little impact on subsequent investment decisions, in part because the intergovernmental EDA lacks the ability to offer economic incentives or to impose consequences on member states for non-compliance.

The review will also have to be compatible with, and add value to, the well-developed NATO Defence Policy Planning (NDPP) process. Non-EU NATO allies might reasonably question the need for a separate mechanism, not least since there are already tensions between the EDA's Capability Development Plan and the NDPP. There are, however, important differences that mean CARD has the potential to add value, despite the overlap. As CARD, unlike the NDPP, has no aspirations for force generation, it can work to a longer time frame than the NATO process, which operates on a four-year cycle and focuses on planning periods up to 20 years. The political level of ambition to which NATO members subscribe is, moreover, driven by NATO requirements rather than more comprehensive defence plans and requirements of EU member states, of which NATO is but one part. This different focus and time frame mean that plugging CARD into NDPP effectively will not be straightforward. But integrated into other mechanisms, CARD should at least present a clearer picture of the EU's collective capability requirements, which can in turn boost the political vision and commitments of participating member states.[17]

Permanent Structured Cooperation

Described by Juncker as 'the Sleeping Beauty of the Lisbon Treaty', there is a clear risk that the now-awakened PESCO may prove prone to narcolepsy. With 25 EU member states (Denmark, Malta and the UK remain on the sidelines) participating under Berlin's broad-tent approach, PESCO's activation has proved less divisive internally than many feared. This is not necessarily a good thing if it means PESCO focuses on softer defence capabilities better suited to promoting European cooperation, rather than delivering much-needed new capabilities at the hard end of the defence spectrum.

After two rounds of formal initiatives in March and November 2018, each involving 17 projects, the most engaged member states are Italy (involved in 21, leading seven), France (involved in 21, leading six), Germany (involved in 13, leading seven), Spain (involved in 18, leading one) and Greece (involved in 14, leading five). Of the heavy hitters in European defence, it appears only Poland, involved in seven projects and leading none, is still to be won over.[18]

A lack of high-end capability projects (for example, development of a new main battle tank or a sixth-generation fighter) in the first tranche of 17 projects formally adopted in March 2018 suggests that bilateral or trilateral cooperation is a better way to deliver those sorts of projects. It is revealing, moreover, that some of the most significant capability projects attracted the smallest numbers of participants. One of the most popular of the first batch of PESCO projects, for example, was the

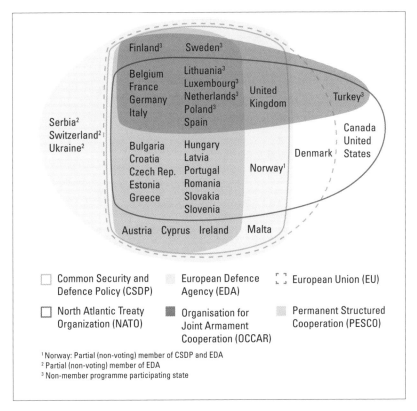

Figure 3. **Principal European and Western defence arrangements**

creation of a Centre of Excellence for EU Training Missions, led by Germany and supported by Austria, Belgium, Cyprus, the Czech Republic, France, Ireland, Italy, Luxembourg, the Netherlands, Romania, Spain and Sweden. In contrast, the project to develop and build a prototype interoperable European Armoured Infantry Fighting Vehicle/Amphibious Assault Vehicle/Light Armoured Vehicle is led by Italy, with Greece and Slovakia participating. The Indirect Fire Support (EuroArtillery) project to develop a mobile precision artillery platform is led by Slovakia and joined by Italy. France, notably, has taken the lead on only two of the first 17 projects, but both have clear operational focus: the European secure software-defined-radio to facilitate interoperability on joint operations,

Table 1. **Examples of PESCO projects, 2018**

Project	Description	Participating countries
TRAINING, FACILITIES		
European Union Training Mission Competence Centre (EU TMCC)	Improve numbers, expertise and interoperability of trainers for EU Training Missions.	Austria, Belgium, Czech Republic, France, Germany, Ireland, Italy, Luxembourg, Netherlands, Portugal, Romania, Spain, Sweden
Helicopter Hot and High Training (H3 Training)	Specialised tactics training for military and civil aircrews in a 'Hot and High' environment.	Greece, Italy, Romania
LAND, FORMATION, SYSTEMS		
Armoured Infantry Fighting Vehicle/Amphibious Assault Vehicle/Light Armoured Vehicle	Develop vehicle to support fast deployment manoeuvre, reconnaissance, combat support, logistics support, command and control, and medical support.	Greece, Italy, Slovakia
Indirect Fire Support (EuroArtillery)	Develop a mobile precision artillery platform to help EU combat-capability requirements in military operations.	Italy, Slovakia
Integrated Unmanned Ground System (UGS)	Develop a Modular Unmanned Ground System that is multi-mission capable, with cyber-secure autonomous navigation and early warning (EW)-resilient Command & Control interface.	Belgium, Czech Republic, Estonia, Finland, France, Hungary, Latvia, Netherlands, Poland, Spain
EU Beyond Line of Sight (BLOS) Land Battlefield Missile Systems	Develop a new-generation medium-range BLOS Land Battlefield missile-systems family to provide, amongst other things, autonomous target designation capability.	Belgium, Cyprus, France
Maritime (semi-) Autonomous Systems for Mine Countermeasures (MAS MCM)	Develop a mix of (semi-) autonomous underwater, surface and aerial technologies for maritime mine countermeasures.	Belgium, Greece, Latvia, Netherlands, Poland, Portugal, Romania
Harbour & Maritime Surveillance and Protection (HARMSPRO)	Develop an integrated system of maritime sensors, software and platforms (surface, underwater and aerial vehicles) to fuse and process data to help detect and identify a range of maritime threats in a specified maritime environment from harbours to littoral waters.	Greece, Italy, Poland, Portugal
Upgrade of Maritime Surveillance	Integrate land-based surveillance systems, maritime and air platforms to provide real-time information to support a timely and effective response.	Bulgaria, Croatia, Cyprus, Greece, Ireland, Italy, Spain
Deployable Modular Underwater Intervention Capability Package (DIVEPACK)	Develop an interoperable specialised modular asset for full-spectrum defensive underwater intervention operations in expeditionary settings.	Bulgaria, France, Greece
European Medium Altitude Long Endurance Remotely Piloted Aircraft Systems – MALE RPAS (Eurodrone)	Develop the common use in dedicated areas such as logistics and training of the next-generation of MALE RPAS.	Czech Republic, France, Germany, Italy, Spain
European Attack Helicopters *Tiger* Mark III	To upgrade the *Tiger* detection, aggression and communication capabilities to develop a modernised and life-time-extended European attack helicopter.	France, Germany, Spain

Table 1. **Examples of PESCO projects, 2018**

Project	Description	Participating countries
Counter-Unmanned Aerial System (C-UAS)	Develop a system of systems with command and control (C2)-dedicated architecture, integrated and interoperable with C2 info-structure to counter the threat by mini and micro UAS. Able to deploy in operational theatres as well as in homeland defence, security and dual-use tasks.	Czech Republic, Italy
CYBER, C4ISR*		
European Secure Software defined Radio (ESSOR)	Develop common technologies for European military radios to guarantee interoperability of EU forces and to provide a secure military-communications system.	Belgium, Finland, France, Germany, Italy, Netherlands, Poland, Portugal, Spain
Cyber Threats and Incident Response Information Sharing Platform.	Develop a networked member-state platform aimed at strengthening national cyber-defence capabilities.	Austria, Cyprus, Greece, Hungary, Italy, Portugal, Spain,
Cyber Rapid Response Teams and Mutual Assistance in Cyber Security	Teams to detect, recognise and mitigate cyber threats, to develop cyber resilience and collective response to cyber incidents.	Croatia, Estonia, Finland, France, Lithuania, Netherlands, Poland, Romania, Spain
Strategic Command and Control (C2) System for CSDP Missions and Operations	Improve C2 systems of EU missions and operations at the strategic level, including through the integration of information systems and logistics systems.	France, Germany, Italy, Portugal, Spain
European High Atmosphere Airship Platform (EHAAP)-Persistent Intelligence, Surveillance and Reconnaissance (ISR) Capability	Balloon-based ISR platform to provide persistence in area of operations and high degree of freedom of movement.	France, Italy
Electronic Warfare Capability and Interoperability Programme for Future JISR Cooperation.	Unify EW approaches and procedures towards the establishment of a joint EW standing force.	Czech Republic, Germany
ENABLING, JOINT		
European Medical Command	Provide an enduring medical capability to support missions and operations, with a rapidly deployable capability for basic primary care.	Czech Republic, France, Germany, Italy, Netherlands, Romania, Slovakia, Spain, Sweden
Military Mobility	Support member states in simplifying and standardising cross-border military transport procedures to enhance speed of movement of military forces across Europe.	Austria, Belgium, Bulgaria, Croatia, Cyprus, Czech Republic, Estonia, Finland, France, Germany, Greece, Hungary, Italy, Latvia, Lithuania, Luxembourg, Netherlands, Poland, Portugal, Romania, Slovakia, Slovenia, Spain, Sweden
EU Radio Navigation Solution (EURAS)	Promote development of EU military positioning, navigation and timing capabilities.	Belgium, France, Germany, Italy, Spain
European Military Space Surveillance Awareness Network (EU-SSA-N)	Develop an autonomous EU military SSA capability.	France, Italy

*Command, Control, Communications, Computers, Intelligence, Surveillance and Reconnaissance

Source: The European Council and the Council of the European Union

and a project to integrate energy management into operational planning while seeking to ensure a steady energy supply during missions. There are more strategic projects in the second batch of 17 projects adopted in November 2018, such as an upgrade to the *Tiger* attack helicopter and a high-altitude intelligence and reconnaissance capability, alongside other projects of questionable value. A joint EU intelligence centre, operated on an extremely modest budget and run by two of the more Russia-friendly member states, Greece and Cyprus, is unlikely to be strategically significant.

Although advances in EU coordination on softer issues such as the development of a common medical command might be helpful, they will not be transformational. The risk is that PESCO will be just one more story of underwhelming EU incrementalism. The extra funding available under the EDF for PESCO projects, for example, is unlikely to be sufficient to overcome some of the sovereign sensitivities that dissuade states from meaningful cooperation. There is also a risk that Germany's political investment in PESCO comes at the expense of its engagement with other initiatives for more flexible forms of defence cooperation. This gamble will pay off if PESCO can contribute meaningfully to European capabilities. But if it does not, it risks increasing the frustration of some of Berlin's European partners with regard to both German defence policy and prospects for a more robust EU defence policy. Such a dynamic would likely push France, for example, to focus even more on defence activities outside the established structures of the EU.[19]

The European Defence Fund

When the new funding stream begins to flow in full from 2020, the EDF will represent a significant expansion in power for the European Commission, which will become the fourth-largest sponsor of defence research in Europe (after the UK, France and Germany). The impact on current defence projects is likely to be minimal, with most intergovernmental cooperation continuing to be either bilateral or through other institutions, such as NATO and the Organisation for Joint Armament Cooperation (OCCAR). Like the initiatives discussed above, as a stand-alone measure the EDF will be far from transformational. The sums involved may be impressive by EU standards, but they are a long way from being game changers.

As with other recent European defence initiatives, some parts of the Trump administration are lukewarm towards the EDF. The US ambassador to NATO has warned that the EDF should not become a 'protectionist vehicle' for the EU.[20] The risk is that US concerns, expressed in 1998 in US secretary of state Madeleine Albright's 'three Ds' (no delinking of European efforts from NATO, no duplication of existing processes and no discrimination against non-EU alliance states) will be reawakened.[21] An EDF that promotes a 'buy European' approach, disadvantaging US defence industries in the European market, would be a source of further transatlantic tension. European arguments that support for their defence-industrial base and the further development of European global competitiveness in the arms trade would be a valuable contribution to US political goals by helping to deliver security abroad (if not jobs in the US) would be unlikely to be well received, in particular by the Trump administration.[22]

The importance of interlinking

The effect of these new frameworks on the real world of defence industry and defence planning will be determined not just by their substance but by how effectively they are interlinked. The commission and its EDF will need to work closely and effectively with the EDA, not least as the latter acts as the secretariat for CARD. The EDA, which has observer status within NATO's Framework Nation Concept, will also need to monitor the implementation of PESCO to ensure cohesion with parallel NATO initiatives. As noted above, CARD will need to be integrated not only with the EDA's Capability Development Plan, but also NATO's NDPP. Turf wars over decision-making between the assorted actors and institutions involved are likely to be an issue, especially for those member states concerned about the limits of the European Commission's mandate.

Funding for the CSDP, like CFSP funding, is modest given the scale of the challenge. Even after what the commission touts as an impressive-sounding 22-fold increase in EU defence funding in 2021–27, spending within this seven-year period is still set to be just €27.5bn, or €3.83bn per year. This will include €13bn dedicated to the EDF and €6.5bn earmarked to support strategic transport infrastructure. Even spent with perfect efficiency, this will only buy so much additional defence and security capability. A new off-budget European Peace Facility, with a suggested 2021–27 budget of €10.5bn, will allow the EU to take on the common costs of CSDP military operations. One challenge is that commission money is regarded by many of its recipients as expensive money. The terms and conditions of EDF funding cannot be so onerous that it becomes more a symbol of EU commitment to defence cooperation than an active catalyst of such cooperation. The primary purpose of European defence integration must be to make Europe more secure, not to showcase that the EU is alive and well despite Brexit, or to further an integrationist agenda for ideological reasons.

These figures are a reminder that the balance of authority and responsibility for action on defence issues rests clearly at the level of individual European states. While the commission is focusing more on defence technology and industry cooperation, EU member states remain firmly in charge of core business, such as force generation and operations. There is little desire on the part of member states to upset the existing balance, even with regard to capability development. The EDA, for example, may have enjoyed a 5% increase in its modest budget in 2018, but it has hardly been given a central role in the latest initiatives. There is little support in most member states, moreover, for a more substantive budget increase for the agency.

Defence cooperation, including capability development, remains deeply political. There is a reason that the majority of concrete proposals put forward by defence professionals in recent years have gone nowhere, including for example the 300 recommendations offered by the 28 defence chiefs in 2011. The EU's decade of crises did not remove the structural factors working against EU strategic cohesion. Many of the factors that have limited, for example, the potential for OCCAR (established in 1996 to improve efficiency in capability developments and cut costs), remain firmly in place. Nevertheless, collectively implemented and smoothly integrated, the sum effect of these latest individual initiatives in EU defence should be more than their individual parts.

Beyond the winter package

The EU has pushed forward with assorted other initiatives alongside the highlights discussed above. In June 2017, for example, a permanent headquarters for EU military operations was finally approved. Called the Military Planning and Conduct Capability (MPCC) thanks to political sensitivities over the use of 'headquarters', it was mandated to cover only non-executive CSDP missions.[23] But ambitions for a more fully fledged EU civilian–military headquarters are already well established. Sooner rather than later, the MPCC, the EU Civilian Planning and Conduct Capability and the EU's Crisis Management and

Planning Directorate are likely to be combined under such an umbrella. Useful though such a reform might prove, however, it is unlikely to do anything, in itself, to bolster the EU's strategic presence or strategic will.

The winter package is not the only point of progress in collaborative ventures on European defence outside the NATO umbrella. In 2017, for example, a European Tactical Airlift Centre (ETAC), conceived by the EDA and jointly owned by ten EU member states and Norway, was opened in Zaragoza, Spain. Military mobility is one area with real strategic implications. If forces cannot rapidly be deployed or maintained in a time of crisis, the deterrent they are supposed to provide loses credibility, and the utility of early crisis-management capabilities is diminished. Minimising physical, legal and regulatory barriers to the movement of troops and military equipment across Europe is important for both the EU and NATO. (This is sometimes referred to as a 'military Schengen', but the commission rejects this language, as implementation lies firmly at the level of member states.) Since the CSDP cannot presently operate within EU territories, work in this area is, from a strictly EU perspective, about speeding up the processes for deployment.

Improvement in this area will be mostly down to member-state governments and local authorities. Yet there is a clear role for EU institutions, for example with the commission effort to reduce the fragmentation of European airspace through the Single European Sky initiative. A Dutch-led project on military mobility has proved the most popular of the 17 initial PESCO projects, with 24 of the 25 PESCO countries signing up (France opted for observer status). On the basis of recommendations from an EDA working group, the commission unveiled in March 2018 an Action Plan on Military Mobility aimed at supporting both NATO and EU interests. The 11-page plan lays out a vast work programme spanning military requirements, transport infrastructure and regulatory and procedural issues. Coordinating across agencies, between member states and with parallel NATO efforts will be challenging, yet the contribution of such measures to more credible and mobile European defence capabilities is clear.

One area where the EU might have to do more of its thinking alone (rather than in conjunction with the US) concerns its approach to Europe's defence-industrial base. At the moment, European consolidation strategies are confused and uncoordinated. In 2012, the opportunity to create a European aerospace and defence giant was sacrificed to German government concerns about domestic job losses and reservations about investing in the defence industry. There is little to suggest that Berlin's calculations have since changed. In September 2017, France and Italy made cautious moves towards consolidating Europe's notoriously fragmented shipbuilding industry, with Paris and Rome agreeing a deal on joint ownership of STX France.[24] The same month, the UK's National Shipbuilding Strategy replaced a strategy of consolidation with one that encouraged competition among domestic shipyards in bidding for the contract to build the new Type-31e frigate.[25] The EU's single market for defence is a work in progress, with limited impact on Europe's defence-industrial base to date. As the commission attempts to tighten the implementation of EU rules on public procurement in defence and security markets, member-state governments have repeatedly used the TFEU effectively to exempt substantive portions of their defence sectors on the basis of 'the essential interests of [their] security'.[26]

A related question involves the arms-export policies of individual European states and the complications these present for collaborative defence projects. Germany's 2018 coalition agreement, for example, includes a commitment to work towards an update of the EU Common Position on arms exports (the only legally binding region-wide arrangement on conventional arms exports). This could involve a supervisory body with sanctions mechanisms for non-compliant member states, and could include steps such as post-shipment controls. The clash of interests that followed Germany's ban on arms exports to Saudi Arabia after the murder of Jamal Khashoggi, and the consequences for Germany's partners, confirmed considerable French interests in the creation of such rules, perhaps along the lines of the Schmidt–Debré principle of 1972 which makes decisions on export destinations for joint-venture products the sole responsibility of the country of final assembly. Germany's suspension of sales to Riyadh includes, for example, four *Cobra* radar systems built by a consortium including Thales, Airbus and Lockheed Martin. The January 2019 Aachen Treaty duly committed France and Germany to work towards developing a common approach to arms exports on joint projects. While Berlin subjects Paris's global export ambitions to the shifting political sensitivities of the German arms-export debate, there will be limits on the interest from Paris in further high-end Franco-German defence-technology cooperation. Resolving these tensions will be critical to the ambitions of both nations jointly to build a Future Combat Aircraft System.

Serious political engagement and collective leadership will be needed to forge the conditions for a truly European defence-industrial base; even then, it will take decades to emerge. EU institutions will have an important role, but so too will a myriad of non-EU institutional bodies that set standards and regulations, such as the European Committee for Standardisation and the European Committee for Electrotechnical Standardisation, both of which operate in the defence and security sectors.

Beyond EU structures

The most meaningful cooperation will likely take place outside EU frameworks. As with CFSP, smaller groupings are the preferred model for cooperation between member states. Anglo-French cooperation under the Lancaster House treaties (signed in 2010 under the pressures of the financial crisis) is a good example. The two agreements expanded bilateral cooperation in such areas as capabilities, industry, operations and intelligence. Indeed, France's 2017 Strategic Review of Defence and National Security called pragmatically for the country to seek the 'optimal combination of different formats of European cooperation'. While this could in theory lead to a situation in which EU-sponsored formats such as PESCO compete for precious attention and resources with minilateral groupings outside the purview of the EU, it does not have to. A more cooperative, mutually reinforcing framework is possible, in which EU institutions provide coherence, strategic input and support for more minilateral groupings.

In more formal legal terms, there is a constitutional protection that should encourage EU member states to feel comfortable with such small-group cooperation. The duty of 'sincere cooperation' that binds EU member states to cooperate with EU institutions and the EEAS to support the consistency of EU external actions should be the basis for the activities of any emerging core groupings on defence and security topics.[27]

There are, as previously noted, considerable implications for the EU if members who are willing and able to act decide to do so not just outside the EU but in disregard of it. But initiatives taken outside the complex and demanding EU framework should not in themselves be taken as evidence of such disregard or competition. Patience with the EU's old habits on defence and security is, to be sure, running very thin in some capitals, particularly Paris and Rome. However, even if France and Italy

Table 2. **Selected instances of German bilateral military cooperation from 2014**

Partner	Service	Action implemented/planned	Year	Aim
Netherlands	Army	• Association of Dutch Airmobile Brigade to German Rapid Response Forces Division • Association of Dutch 43rd Mechanised Brigade to German 1st Armoured Division • Association of German 414th Armoured Battalion to Dutch 43rd Mechanised Brigade • Integration of one Dutch company, using German equipment, into German 414th Armoured Battalion	2014 2016	• Interoperability • Preserving capability through Dutch access to German main battle tanks
	Navy	• Association of German Sea Bataillon to Dutch Navy • Provision of German access to Dutch *Karel Doorman* Joint Support Ships	2018	• Development of amphibious capability • Pooled use of resources • Interoperability through joint training and development of operating procedures
	Air Force	• Project Apollo • Association of German Surface to Air Missile Group 61 to Dutch Ground-Based Air Defence Command • Development of operating procedures, creation of binational Air and Missile Defence Academy • Development of binational short-range air-defence task force • Assessment of potential for joint procurement • Creation of binational command and control capability	2018 Ongoing Ongoing Ongoing Ongoing	• Ability to provide operational air- and missile-defence task force • Harmonisation of requirements to enable future synergies in acquisition • (TF supposed to be operational by 2023) Protect the VJTF from short- and very short-range threats
Czech Republic	Army	• Association of Czech 4th Rapid Deployment Brigade with German 10th Armoured Division	Ongoing	• Interoperability • Training and exercise opportunities
Romania	Army	• Association of Romanian 81st Mechanised Brigade with German Rapid Response Forces Division	Ongoing	• Interoperability • Training and exercise opportunities
Lithuania	Army	• Affiliation of Lithuanian Iron Wolf Brigade with a German panzer division; Lithuanian officers assigned to the 1st and 10th Armoured Division	Agreement signed 21 Oct 2018	• Increase cooperation and improve processes and interoperability; prepare Lithuanian brigade to cooperate as part of a division; opportunities for extensive training cooperation • improve interoperability with German-led eFP Battalion
Poland	Army	• 'Cross-attachment' - between the German 41st Armoured Brigade and the Polish 34th Armoured Cavalry Brigade. Association of a German battalion (414 Armoured Batallion) to the Polish brigade and vice versa. In 2018 the affiliation was transferred from the 34th to the 10th Armoured Cavalry Brigade	Planned: operational by 2021 (originally: 2020)	• Increase interoperability; exercise opportunities and training; collective deployment

Source: IISS, *The Military Balance 2018*

are increasingly inclined to take action alone or in small groups, the EU effectively gets dragged along in their wake. As high-intensity deployments such as France's *Operation Barkhane* in the Sahel or Italian operations in what it calls 'the expanded Mediterranean' take their toll on the resources of the states involved, demands on partners inevitably follow. As the EU is discovering, events have an irritating habit of shaping policy. What France and Italy choose to do in defence and security terms in North Africa has repercussions for European and EU defence and security engagement.

A European Intervention Initiative

French frustrations can be seen in Macron's formulation of a European Intervention Initiative (EII) as first proposed in his September 2017 Sorbonne speech. Despite subsequent calls from the European Parliament and Germany to develop this initiative under PESCO, Paris sees little advantage in integrating its initiative into a framework over whose design it retains some fundamental reservations. From the French perspective, part of the advantage of operating as a smaller, more flexible group outside EU structures is precisely to be able to respond collaboratively and ambitiously to time-sensitive deployments in a way that EU structures can make rather difficult. Furthermore, by avoiding the complications of EU rules for interactions with third parties, an EII outside EU structures provides an opportunity to keep post-Brexit UK and CSDP non-member Denmark engaged in European military cooperation.

In June 2018, nine nations (including the UK and Denmark) signed a Letter of Intent on the development of the EII. (Finland joined the group in November.) Many will have had their doubts about the details to which they were signing up; participation appears to be fuelled as much by fear of being left out (or at least fear of not appearing to be willing) as by enthusiasm for the project. London, for example, was initially concerned that the initiative might one day develop into an intervention force which Paris might want to blur with the developing Anglo-French Combined Joint Expeditionary Force due to become fully operational by 2020. By the time of the first meeting of EII defence ministers in Paris in 2018, however, things had started to become clearer. The EII would, in effect, be a military-to-military workshop, helping its members anticipate crises and scenario plan for them. It should not compete with other existing formats.

Macron's grand ambitions face a modest start, with progress likely to be more incremental than the original architect intended. A common intervention force supported by a common defence budget and a common doctrine realistically lies some way off, well beyond the beginning of the next decade as Macron initially proposed. Transforming the EII, in the medium term, into some sort of flexible and responsive common operational club, working to spearhead European operational readiness and able to carry out interventions of the type that France has traditionally commanded in Africa, would be both difficult and rewarding. The EII could yet become an operationally focused example of what might have been with the capability-focused initiatives under PESCO (until, as Paris sees it, those efforts were diluted by Berlin's over-prioritisation of the principle of inclusivity).

There is a risk that the EII will emerge as a supplemental mechanism to further French national aims and ambitions. Similar initiatives, moreover, have been tried before, such as the Eurocorps launched with Franco-German sponsorship in 1992. Envisaged as a tool for European defence, the force has unintentionally become a symbol for all that is problematic in mobilising substantive European cooperation on operations. If the EII is to fulfil anything like its potential, lessons from such mediocre ventures, as well as from more successful efforts such as the UK-led Allied Rapid Reaction Corps (involving staff from 14 countries), will have to be applied.

The Europeanisation of member-state armed forces

A Franco-German brigade has existed for more than 30 years. Other multinational corps are dotted around Europe, including a Danish–German–Polish corps (NATO's Multinational North-East Corps) based in Szczecin. This slow Europeanisation of the armed forces of many EU member states has, in recent years, accelerated through multiple bilateral and multinational associations as a result of both carrot (efficiency savings) and stick (requirements-led policymaking). Germany has led the way with its Framework Nation Concept (adopted by NATO in 2014), promoting more systematic cooperation between the Bundeswehr and other European forces. The Anglo-French Combined Joint Expeditionary Force referred to above comprises land, naval and air elements able to carry out expeditionary operations and to provide peacekeeping, disaster-relief or humanitarian assistance. More modest initiatives include the association of German Surface-to-Air Missile Group 61 to the Dutch Ground-Based Air Defence Command and the association of the Dutch 32rd Mechanised Brigade to the German 1st Armoured Division. Germany has similar agreements with the Czech Republic (the association of the Czech 4th Rapid Deployment Brigade with the German 10th Armoured Division) and Romania (the association of the Romanian 81st Mechanised Brigade with the German Rapid Response Forces Division) (see Table 2).[28]

As the experience of the Franco-German brigade highlights, multinational forces do not, in themselves, take forward broader efforts at harmonisation. Moves branded as advances in integration are often little more than associations, with member states preserving sovereignty over the actions of their troops within the units to which they become attached. Such moves are, moreover, as often driven by politics or the pressures of force deficits as they are by grand operational visions or commitments. This dynamic helps explain why talk of an 'EU army' or even a 'European army' undermines and distracts from a more sensible debate on issues such as interoperability and specialisation. It also glosses over the fact that the EU Battlegroups, which reached full operational capacity in 2008, had as of early 2019 yet to be deployed even once, and ignores the practical operational limits that are imposed by joint decision-making on deployments. However, given the crises that have mushroomed on and beyond the EU's borders in these unstable years, the fact that the 'ideal crisis' for EU Battlegroups has not yet appeared does not bode well for their utility. Instead, the deployment of battlegroups has been repeatedly considered and rejected by the EU, including but not limited to the Democratic Republic of the Congo (2006 and 2008), Sudan (2010), Libya (2011) and the Central African Republic (2013).

The EU Battlegroups have, as a result, been subject to regular tinkering. In June 2017, for example, it was agreed that deployment costs should henceforth be considered as 'common costs', meaning that they would no longer be borne on a national basis. The reduction in the overall deployment burden was, however, modest, with approximately 80% of the total cost still not covered, meaning that some of the smaller EU member states in particular will likely remain reluctant to seek out larger roles in battlegroup formation. The move did not, moreover, address the more fundamental challenge of securing political will for deployments.

Increasing defence spending

The increases in national defence spending in Europe since 2015 (see Chapter One) have to cover not just the growing demands of operations and equipment maintenance, but also the considerable costs of military-modernisation programmes that have been too long delayed. Even with the recent increases, in early 2019 only 13 European NATO states were on course to meet the 2% GDP target for defence spending by 2024.[29]

In February 2018, Macron reversed almost a decade of defence-spending cuts, approving a rise of €1.7bn per annum until 2022, followed by €3bn per annum until 2025. With the bulk of the increase due after the end of Macron's five-year term, however, the degree to which it will, in his defence minister's words, both 'repair' and 'renew', will depend upon the degree to which the increases are actually sustained.[30] The UK's Defence Equipment Plan for 2017–27 already looks, to many informed observers, entirely unrealistic, with the UK House of Commons' Public Accounts Committee suggesting that the Ministry of Defence (MoD) could find itself falling up to £21bn short of the £180bn it says it needs.[31] Germany has set out its plans to increase defence spending by 80% between 2014 and 2024, bringing annual spending up to €60bn by the end of the period, but doubts remain over its intention to reach even its self-determined readjusted target of 1.5% of GDP on defence spending by 2024.[32] In order to reach the 2% target, Berlin would need to be spending in the region of €80bn per year on defence by 2024, compared to €37bn in 2017.[33]

Other European countries are increasing defence spending with more certain impact, albeit from a more modest base. Romania, for example, saw a nominal rise in its defence budget from 2016 to 2017 of some 46%, with further increases planned up to 2020.[34] In 2019, Lithuania is set to join the small club of European members honouring their NATO 2% commitment, a considerable turnaround from five years ago, when Vilnius was perceived as one of the most flagrant free-riders in European defence, spending under 1% of GDP. (In contrast to Romania, however, spending is rising not just on equipment but also on personnel, following the 2015 reintroduction of selective military conscription, seven years after it was abolished.) In October 2017, Poland passed a law committing to spend 2.5% of GDP on defence by 2030, and setting out steps to double the size of its armed forces.

Some countries are finding ways to make their defence contributions felt despite inadequate spending levels. Italy spent just 1.13% of GDP on defence in 2017, yet its operational record was far more impressive, with some 5,000 troops deployed overseas that year, taking part in as many military missions as Germany and twice as many as Spain.[35] Indeed, in the first four months of 2018, Rome committed troops to five new or enlarged African missions. In April 2018 Italy took on responsibility (in conjunction with Greece) for policing the skies of Montenegro, bringing the number of current or planned missions involving Italian troops to 24.[36] While the arrival in office of a government backed by the far right undoubtedly complicated Italy's engagements here, with Interior Minister Salvini threatening, for example, the future of *Operation Sophia* unless other EU states opened their ports to its migrant-rescue ships, other engagements have continued more smoothly. Indeed, in early 2019, Italy had almost 6,000 personnel engaged in missions and operations across 23 different countries, including CSDP missions such as EUTM Somalia and EUNAVFOR Med.[37]

Nevertheless, European defence budgets are unlikely to rise fast enough to ease transatlantic tensions, not least as Trump has already called the 2% commitment 'insufficient'.[38] Europe's increases should also be viewed in the context of rising defence budgets globally, most notably in Asia, as well as the qualitative increase and quantitative spread of asymmetrical capabilities.

CSDP missions and operations

In early 2019, the EU was running ten civilian and six military CSDP missions and operations, involving more than 4,000 European civilians and military officers across three continents, pursuing goals such as maritime security off the Horn of Africa, security in the Sahel, the rule of law and capacity-building in the Balkans and security-sector reform in Ukraine. In 2017, as part of its efforts to project stability in neighbouring regions, the EU supplied security-related equipment such as cameras, software and evidence kits worth more than €8.4m, helped draft almost 200 laws on issues such as security-sector reform and money laundering, prosecuted or adjudicated at 39 criminal trials and monitored 290 criminal cases on issues such as war crimes.[39] More than 45 non-EU states have participated in CSDP missions since 2003.

Three CSDP missions in particular are worth exploring in more detail for the different aspects and prospects for European and EU military engagement they display. The first, Mali, involves a European state taking the lead and corralling others to follow. The second, in Bosnia, is an example of EU–NATO cooperation. The third, EUNAVFOR Somalia, is an example of EU collective engagement. Cases such as these demonstrate the EU's near-unrivalled ability and experience in mixing civilian and military instruments. This comprehensive approach across the conflict cycle from prevention to management, resolution and stabilisation, has set the standard for similar approaches adopted by others. Even as many CSDP missions are small in scale and some struggle even against modest targets, they often have advantages that other deployment formats, such as NATO, are unable to match, and where they experience problems, these are usually not unique to European operations.

Mali

In March 2012, a coup in Bamako helped open the door for Tuareg separatists and militant Islamist groups to expand the territory under their control in Northern Mali. By October, the European Council was citing the crisis in Mali as an 'immediate threat' to Europe. Plans were made to send military instructors to train the Malian army, although member states were anxious to avoid troops being drawn into combat.[40] In early January, Mali's interim president, Dioncounda Traoré, sought French military assistance. Inside a day, deploying what a subsequent RAND assessment called a 'model expeditionary force', France began its largest military operation since the end of the Algerian war.[41] *Operation Serval* showcased France's impressive military capabilities, deploying airpower, special forces and ground troops to reverse the rebel advance and reduce their ranks. Other European states contributed strategic airlift, air-to-air refuelling, logistics and intelligence. UK support included two RAF C17 transport aircraft and a *Sentinel* R1 surveillance aircraft.

In July 2014 *Operation Serval* became *Operation Barkhane*, with a mandate to conduct counter-terrorism across the Sahel. As of early 2019, some 4,500 French personnel were conducting joint air and ground operations alongside G5 Sahel counter-terrorism forces against terrorist insurgents. Germany sent elements of the Franco-German brigade to bolster the EU training mission in Mali. Supplementing the UK contribution, since August 2018 three RAF *Chinook* heavy-lift helicopters, operated by some 90 troops, have provided 'niche logistical support' for French troops.[42] The EU now has three CSDP missions in the region: a civilian capacity-building mission supporting the Nigerien internal security forces (EUCAP Sahel Niger), a civilian capacity-building mission in Mali in support, amongst other things, of security-sector reform (EUCAP Sahel Mali), and a military training mission in Mali (EUTM Mali).

As part of an €8bn package of financial assistance to the region, the EU has committed to finance the construction of a new headquarters for the G5 Sahel forces.[43] France's European partners have also contributed to the UN's MINUSMA stabilisation mission that operates alongside *Barkhane* and the G5. The Netherlands, for example, has provided troops and equipment to MINUSMA since 2014 (although these will be withdrawn in May 2019). The Bundeswehr has been upgrading Niger's military capabilities, building an officer-training school and expanding the military section of Niamey airport. Germany has also provided in-theatre support in the form of its C-160s. Other important contributions have been made by EU member states including Belgium, Denmark, Spain and Sweden, as well as by non-EU member states, most obviously the US.

French intervention and multilateral support may have saved Mali from falling further under the control of Islamist extremists, but deep problems of governance continue as do concerns over the competence and behaviour of local forces in what one expert has described as a 'complex, multi-dimensional security crisis of interlinked micro conflicts'.[44] The region will be a major European security concern for some time to come. The initial intervention may have been another case of European military action outside the EU, yet EU engagement now can help pull together the various military, political, economic and development strands. Military efforts alone will not resolve the issues that led to the Tuareg/Islamist insurgency.

The Balkans

Operation Althea, which took over from NATO's Stabilisation Force in Bosnia-Herzegovina in December 2004, is the only CSDP operation so far to deploy under the EU's Berlin Plus agreement with NATO. (This means it uses NATO staff, communications and support, and falls under NATO's operational command.) In an unusual division of roles, since 2004 EU forces have been responsible for providing a safe and secure environment, while NATO has taken the lead on security-sector reform. *Operation Althea* provides a reassuring security presence in a divided country, although its mission has been refocused several times. Some member states would prefer to bring the mission to an end, but those most engaged in the operation point to the situation on the ground as good reason to stay. That Bosnia has made questionable political progress, and that latent inter-ethnic tensions remain, should not reflect badly on the operation. Moreover, the EU has been instrumental in helping to build one of the country's only functioning national institutions – its armed forces.

Elsewhere in the Balkans, the rule-of-law mission EULEX Kosovo is the EU's largest civilian mission (by both budget and staff). Its impact has been bolstered by other EU policies, including those concerned with enlargement. The prospect of visa liberalisation, for example, is an important incentive for local cooperation, although it is in danger of backfiring due to popular frustrations over slow progress. Despite confirmation by the European Commission in July 2018 that Kosovo had met the required benchmarks, opposition by some national governments appears to have put council approval on something of a go-slow.

EUNAVFOR Somalia

The EU has conducted counter-piracy operations off the coast of Somalia since 2008. *Operation Atalanta* typically involves some 600 personnel, one to three surface combat vessels and one to two maritime-patrol and reconnaissance aircraft at a given time. Unlike the 33-nation Combined Maritime Forces, which is focused on maritime security, counter-terrorism and counter-piracy in the Indian Ocean, *Atalanta* is permitted to function within Somalia's territorial waters. This broad multi-national effort (there was also a NATO mission that ended in November 2016) brought piracy down from a peak of 736 hostages and 32 captured ships in October 2011, to zero in October 2016.[45] Indeed, between 2012 and February 2017 there was not a single successful hijack of a commercial ship by Somali pirates.[46] The dramatic drop-off in attacks owes much to EU efforts to ensure captured pirates are prosecuted in courts in the Seychelles and imprisoned in Somalia. This has involved considerable political engagement (including by the UK), and played to EU strengths. *Atalanta*'s ability to operate in Somali territorial waters lets it engage with local coastal communities and help with local capacity-building.[47] EU security engagement has also won local support through the provision of significant development assistance to Somalia, alongside financial support for the AU mission there.[48]

Atalanta is one of three CSDP missions in Somalia. The EU Training Mission (EUTM) in Somalia has met with more mixed success, in part because the emerging Somali military architecture is still fragile and in part because the troops have been trying to train and fight al-Shabaab militants at the same time. EUCAP Somalia, a civilian mission aimed at developing Somali counter-piracy capability, is the least convincing of the three, suffering at times from inadequate resourcing.

New threats and opportunities

EU defence policy may, in reality, largely be EU crisis-management policy, but EU security policy is exactly what it says. Security is moving up the EU agenda, as the appointment in 2016 of a new Commissioner for the Security Union shows. As euroscepticism merges with issues of European identity, nurtured by migration pressures and physical-security concerns, the EU's credibility in the eyes of its own member states and citizens will increasingly become intertwined with its ability to deliver in this area.

While the CSDP will not be the primary instrument for addressing internal-security challenges, many CSDP missions are linked to such core European concerns. Migration, for example, is an issue in operations from *Operation Althea* in the Balkans, to EUNAVFOR MED in the Mediterranean, to local capacity-building and training in operations such as EUTM Mali and EUCAP Sahel Niger. There is also a growing (if not always explicit) connection to EU counter-terrorism efforts, for example advising host-country police forces and judiciaries using CSDP civilian expertise.[49] Some European Commission officials, moreover, are starting to explore the possibilities contained within the mutual solidarity clause (Article 222) of the Lisbon Treaty, which provides, they argue, a potential legal basis to allow CSDP operations on EU territory in support of front-line member states which find themselves victims not just of terrorist attacks but other major disasters, potentially including hybrid attacks.[50]

As the issue of hybrid warfare – the blending of traditional and irregular warfare with cyber and information operations and unconventional methods – has come to the fore, EU institutions have been tasked with forging credible responses. Hybrid threats have been a particular focus of EU–NATO cooperation; the mission of the European Centre of Excellence for Countering Hybrid Threats, for example, includes the development of doctrine, conduct of training and arrangement of exercises aimed at enhancing the capabilities of individual member states as well as their interoperability. EU member states are collectively beginning to think about ways to push back against state-sponsored disinformation. The EEAS East StratCom

Task Force has, since November 2015, for example, produced weekly fact-checks of Russian disinformation campaigns, identifying more than 3,800 individual cases by spring 2018 and disseminating its findings in 18 languages, including Russian.[51] This effort is, of course, modest in comparison to the Russian government's troll factories. Moreover, the EEAS task force operates under a far more limited mandate than its NATO counterpart, the NATO Strategic Communications Centre of Excellence.

In December 2018, the commission identified Europe's eastern and southern neighbourhoods and the Western Balkans as the three priority regions for combatting the spread of disinformation online beyond the EU. Its action plan allocated more resources for the detection of disinformation and pushed for a more coordinated continental response, including the establishment of a Rapid Alert System between EU institutions and member states to provide alerts on disinformation in real time.

Countering radicalisation is another area where the EU's role in security provision is growing. Europol works on the rapid removal of illegal terrorist content from the internet, the EU Internet Forum promotes counter-narratives to terrorist propaganda and works with tech companies, the commission and Europol to support civil-society measures to protect against radicalisation, and more than 3,000 experts in an EU-mandated Radicalisation Awareness Network review and disseminate best practices and support those engaged in counter-narratives. The EU and its member states contribute financially and intellectually to a growing network of global and regional initiatives designed to counter and prevent violent extremism. The 2016 European Strategic Communications Network, which works to stem the flow of foreign fighters, grew out of an 18-month Belgian–British Syria Strategic Communications Advisory Team financed by the commission.

As old foes prosecute old agendas through new means, hybrid threats could herald a change in the long-established narrative about the utility of the EU for security and defence. A more networked threat is best met with a more networked response. The EU does not need to own every initiative at every level to make a net contribution to European security. The task is not to do more in more areas; it is to do the important areas well. The world of hybrid threats has the potential to be one such area.

CHAPTER FIVE

Determining Europe's strategic prospects

Many issues unrelated to defence and security, both within Europe's borders and beyond, will help determine the continent's strategic future. Just as the EU appears to be showing signs of greater seriousness in its foreign-, security- and defence-policy pretensions, ironically, forces elsewhere could tear it apart. The future development of the eurozone, for example, will have implications for the cohesion of European foreign policy. An economically strong and stable eurozone would not automatically translate into an EU with a greater presence in international affairs, but it would give such ambitions greater credibility. The break-up of the eurozone, on the other hand, would likely destroy any prospects for greater European cohesion on the international stage. Serious questions also hang over the sustainability of Europe's social model, which appears increasingly unaffordable in light of falling birth rates and rising life expectancy. Yet anything more than a piecemeal approach to tackling the challenge threatens to tear at the very social fabric such reforms would be intended to secure.

Beyond defence and security

Two issues not directly related to European defence and security are particularly germane to Europe's broader prospects as a strategic actor. The first may be the most critical internal issue facing the EU, while the second may be its most critical external challenge.

Populism, disillusionment and the 'democratic deficit'

Much has been written about the EU's 'democratic deficit', but the phrase's alliteration is more convincing than its substance. The EU has, to be sure, largely been an elite construction, easily comprehensible neither to its citizens nor its partners, but its complexities reflect the intricacy involved in managing a broad union of disparate sovereign states. Some EU structures are, moreover, almost deliberately convoluted, designed more to nurture peace and compromise on a fractured continent than to maximise efficiency. The formula of one commissioner per member state, for example, nurtures inclusivity even if it does little for efficiency or effectiveness. Likewise, Europe might well 'be easier to understand' if, as Juncker suggested in his 2017 State of the Union, 'one Captain were steering the ship' through the amalgamation of the commission and council presidencies, but such long-standing federalist ideas go squarely against the zeitgeist and are unlikely to be approved by member states.[1]

This is not to say that there are no issues around the legitimacy and accountability of the EU's democratic structures. The euro crisis, in particular, brought existing challenges into sharper focus as national parliaments found their fiscal sovereignty constrained, while the supervisory authority of the ECB and the European Commission were enhanced. Asymmetries in power and influence between member states were intensified; dynamics within the Bundestag, for example, increasingly influenced the dynamics in debtor-state parliaments.[2] In 2012,

Van Rompuy included strengthening democratic legitimacy and accountability as one of four 'building blocks' needed for a genuine economic and monetary union.[3] A 2015 report by the five EU presidents argued that EU institutions and political credibility were being undermined by a crisis-engendered atmosphere of late-night meetings and rushed decisions, which had sometimes led to 'far reaching decisions' being taken inter-governmentally to circumvent opposition.[4]

The complexities of the system also give considerable power to a few insiders, not all of whom are elected. Perhaps the most obvious recent example is the disproportionate influence of Juncker's first chief of staff, Martin Selmayr, in 2014–18, when complaints about the 'Selmayr Commission' could be heard in the corridors of Brussels. Selmayr's subsequent manoeuvring to become secretary-general of the EC (following an opaque double promotion and closed-door machinations) testified as much to the vulnerability of the EU bureaucracy to insider manipulation, as to Selmayr's undoubted bureaucratic skills.

The controversial *Spitzenkandidat* process, used for the first time in Juncker's appointment in 2014, may marginally increase the visibility of the consequences of voters' political choices, but it could also inadvertently undercut the confidence of elected national leaders in the stewardship of EU institutions. As the European Parliament, the only directly elected EU institution, pushes to increase its policymaking role, it confronts a presentational problem: it appears to be at least as interested in expanding its own authority and budget as it is in supervising and checking the power of the executive. The problem is not so much one of democracy but of legitimacy.

Is this so-called 'democratic deficit', then, really a front-line issue for the EU? Compared with other complex international organisations, the EU is far from undemocratic. The challenge is more one of performance deficit, which can be addressed through a clearer set of priorities and working practices that focus on delivering concrete outcomes rather than declaring lofty ambitions. Representation, transparency and accountability are at least as much of a problem for individual member states as they are for the Union. In more than a few instances, in fact, standards within EU institutions are higher than within their national counterparts. Where standards fall short, too, it is sometimes with good reason. Meetings of the European Council, for example, are held mainly behind closed doors; the EU ombudsman has complained that this risks fostering a 'blame Brussels' culture.[5] But it also reduces political showboating for domestic audiences, instead focusing minds on outcomes which are then communicated in a transparent and timely manner. Brussels may be one of the lobbying capitals of the world, but monitoring has increased in recent years, for example through the introduction of an EU Transparency Register, while civil-society scrutiny remains impressive.

Popular suspicion of the EU's 'undemocratic' supranational authorities can be exaggerated. 'Brussels bashing' may have become an art form in London, but it has long been a hobby of governments on the continent. EU institutions can, on occasion, through a process of abstention, be left to execute unpopular decisions, while the approval of member states for those decisions is conveniently ignored.[6] Meanwhile, the Lisbon Treaty introduced a control mechanism giving national parliaments greater scrutiny of the application of the principle of subsidiarity, which is intended to ensure that EU institutions only act in areas where they can deliver more than EU countries acting alone. The so-called 'orange card', when half of the member-state parliaments force the EU to review a legislative proposal, has yet to be used, while 'yellow cards', which require one-third of national parliaments to object, have been used three times to 2018, two of which were on issues of employment and industrial relations.[7]

A related internal challenge, not unique to Europe, is the rise of illiberalism.[8] Popular distrust in established institutions is embedded in political systems across the West. A rise of populism, nationalism and nativism is putting pressure on some of the EU's core values such as an independent judiciary and a free press. Norbert Röttgen, chair of the Bundestag's Foreign Affairs Committee, has described the resulting 'state egotism' as going 'right to the foundations of the European idea'.[9] In Hungary, Orbán has openly declared the end of Europe's post-war liberal consensus as he oversees a troubling democratic decline.[10] Austria appears intent on protecting a 'European identity' that more outward-looking European states have long rejected as both impossible and self-limiting. It does not bode well for the future of the EU when member states hold outside partners to higher standards than they demand of colleagues within the fold. As Michael Ignatieff, rector of the Central European University, has warned, if the EU cannot find a way to disrupt the emerging split between liberal democracies in the EU's west and a possible trend towards single-party states in its east, the prospect that it will ultimately break apart is considerably enhanced.[11]

The forces of illiberalism and nativism have been nurtured by the debate on migration and asylum reform. The extent of the meltdown could be seen in Europe's handling of what should have been a fairly inoffensive UN migration compact.[12] Although 152 countries around the world approved the deal in December 2018, the Czech Republic, Hungary and Poland joined the US and Israel in voting against it. Austria, Bulgaria, Italy, Latvia and Romania joined seven other countries in abstaining. Austria's abstention while holding the EU presidency sparked particular anger in many quarters of the EU.

These forces are explicitly anti-establishment and often opposed to the EU. Their impact is felt both directly, as previously fringe parties or newly established parties enter the political mainstream, and indirectly, through the policies and politics of the centre-ground parties they threaten. Often fuelled by Russian financial and cyber support, this nativist shift is conducive to Russian interests in part because it brings to positions of political authority those less likely to view Putin as an autocrat than as a model for national revival, self-confidence and patriotism.[13]

Anti-mainstream movements across Europe have been enabled by Trump's victory in the US. Just as Trump rails against Washington, nationalist forces within the EU rail against Brussels. Trump's early outreach to Orbán and his July 2017 Warsaw visit, his first as president to an EU member state, boosted governments that the EU was simultaneously accusing of assaulting independent democratic institutions. Commenting on Trump's America First agenda, Orbán said that 'we have received permission from, if you like, the highest position in the world so we can now also put ourselves in first place'.[14] The leaders of the far right in the Netherlands fêted Trump's victory as a 'Patriotic Spring' that should inspire Europe. The co-chairs of Germany's far-right AfD informed the new president that they would be 'a natural ally at his side'.[15] Later that year the party captured 12.6% of the vote in the federal elections, entering the Bundestag for the first time with 94 seats and becoming the largest party in opposition. In Italy's March 2018 election, the far-right Lega Nord, a party modelled along Trumpist lines and with a leader who was, at least until 2017, a vocal supporter of Trump, saw its vote jump from 4% to 18%. In 2008, Italy's establishment parties shared some 80.5% of the vote between them; by 2018, this had fallen to just 36.5%. More than one in five Italians voted for one of three anti-European populist groups.[16]

The development of euroscepticism from a constitutional complaint into an agenda deeply intertwined with concerns of identity and security is a serious challenge for Europe and the EU. Key to containing the attractions of populists who rail against the system will be the system's ability to deliver prosperity and security for its citizens. If it is to survive, the EU will need to present itself not just as an agent of the positive forces of globalisation, but also as a protector from its more problematic aspects. Although this would not resolve issues of identity politics, it would help check their spread.

Changing US strategic perspectives

Europe and the US do not always walk in lockstep. American resentment over European defence deficiencies ran deep during the Balkan bloodbath of the early 1990s, and the early 2000s were marked by unprecedented European resistance, led by France and Germany, to the US invasion of Iraq under President George W. Bush. More recent examples include the WikiLeaks fallout over the extent of US espionage against its European allies and differences on whether to participate in the China-led Asian Infrastructure Investment Bank. Transatlantic tensions during the Trump administration are, in some ways, a continuation of this historical pattern. Trump is not the first US president to berate European powers for their failure to live up to their NATO commitments, and is unlikely to be the last.

In the past, however, such differences were largely discussed behind closed doors. Trump's sharper public tone and more abrupt approach have brought them into the open and elevated disputes to a near-existential level. The result is a weakening of both partners and their efforts to promote and protect their interests on the international stage. Moreover, there is nothing familiar about a US president who appears not to view safeguarding European unity as conducive to US strategic interests, or who one day labels the EU a 'foe' and the next describes Putin as a 'good competitor'.[17] Casting doubt on Washington's commitment to its European security guarantee, as Trump did when he publicly failed to endorse Article 5 of the NATO Treaty at the 2017 summit in Brussels, undermines NATO members' confidence in the Alliance.[18] While the White House press secretary may dismiss reports of Trump's interest in withdrawing from NATO as 'meaningless', the mere suspicion damages the credibility of the Alliance from the viewpoint of potential adversaries.[19]

Geography and geopolitics dictate that Europe faces a different set of immediate strategic priorities than does its ally. The US was, for example, far less affected by the migration crisis. The US, with a population of some 320m, announced it would welcome 85,000 refugees from around the world; Germany, with one-fourth the population, took in nearly ten times as many. Many sympathetic American supporters of the EU do not instinctively understand the sense of crisis engendered in the EU by Brexit. Trump's decision to withdraw from the Iran nuclear deal threatens to nurture wider tensions in the transatlantic relationship, in particular as European nations struggle to keep the agreement alive. The deal was, after all, orchestrated and underwritten by European powers who highlighted it as a major contribution on a front-line, 'hard security' concern of international standing.

That the EU now has a partner which is positively dissatisfied with some aspects of their bilateral relationship and dismissive of others is significant not just for US–Europe relations or European strategic aspirations, but also for the struggle to project Western influence and protect Western values more broadly. If it no longer views the US as a reliable partner, Europe must at least remember that the US remains the continent's most important one. Ways to defend what common understanding can be protected, and to build new empathies and ties where possible, must be found. At the same time, European states will need to resist the reciprocal temptation to make their own perspectives on the transatlantic relationship more transactional.

Two key variables

Europe's ability to defend, secure and promote its collective interests internationally depends on many factors it cannot control. But of the factors that lie within the control of the continent and its nation-states, two key ones stand out: Germany's strategic maturation and the future of UK–EU relations.

Germany's strategic maturation

The EU's decade of crises has made German power more visible. There was nothing reluctant about Germany's self-appointment as enforcer-in-chief during the euro crisis, when it was promoting a narrative, in the words of one US commentator, 'of Southern fiscal sinners and Northern budgetary saints'.[20] As Wolfgang Kauder, leader of the Christian Democratic Union (CDU) parliamentary group, boasted at his party's 2011 conference, 'suddenly Europe is speaking German'.[21]

Berlin has become more comfortable with taking a leadership role within the EU. Merkel's announcement of an 'open door' policy for Syrian refugees might be criticised for being misguided, but it can hardly be described as a lack of leadership. *Time* magazine called it a 'bold, fraught, immensely empathetic act of leadership' that risked the stability of Germany's own government.[22] Berlin is also more comfortable with pushing policies at the EU level that are nakedly aligned with German national interests. Germany's unwavering promotion of its prescription for the management of the euro crisis, for example, helped kick-start a boom in the country's housing market and contributed to its ability to balance its budget, thanks to its reputation as a safe haven in an otherwise uncertain economic environment.[23]

The challenge is to extend this readiness to shoulder greater responsibility beyond the eurozone and into European foreign and security policy, preparing if not to lead alone at least to lead in partnership. As the continent's two nuclear powers and permanent members of the UN Security Council, France and the UK have traditionally played the front-line role in shaping the EU's profile in defence and security, whilst accounting for the bulk of European power projection on the international stage. When Timothy Garton Ash called Germany Europe's 'indispensable power' in 2011, he noted that this applied only to the European economy and its single currency.[24] This was just three months after Germany sided with China and Russia, rather than its US, French and British allies, when it abstained on the UNSC resolution authorising military intervention in Libya. To many of Germany's partners, this appeared to set Berlin apart as an unreliable ally; former German defence minister Volker Rühe labelled the move 'a serious mistake of historic dimensions'.[25]

Most attributed Berlin's positioning on Libya more to popular passivity than to a calculated strategy to align German interests with influential emerging powers. Some feared that Germany's internalisation of its role in past world wars ran so deep as to forever undercut its ability to act, to Europe's detriment. As Polish foreign minister Radoslaw Sikorski put it later that year, 'I fear German power less than I am beginning to fear German inactivity'.[26] Even prior to Russia's annexation of Crimea, however, Germany's foreign-policy establishment was gearing up for a push to recognise the country's 'new power' and 'new responsibilities'.[27] At the 2014 Munich Security Conference, just before Russia's invasion, the German president, foreign minister and defence minister lined up in turn to declare their common conclusion: Berlin should do more to contribute to the security that for decades had been guaranteed by others. In short, 'Germany should make a more substantial contribution, and it should make it earlier and more decisively'.[28]

Germany had already shown a greater inclination to exercise influence in some areas, including the negotiations that concluded with the JCPOA, its contributions to peacekeeping in the Balkans (in particular in Kosovo) and its engagement in Afghanistan, where it contributed to the International Security Assistance Force (ISAF) (2001–14) and then to *Resolute Support* (ongoing since 2015). But it was Crimea that crystallised the need for a more serious and comprehensive German response. It shredded what remained of the establishment's delusions that all disputes could ultimately be solved through dialogue and negotiations. 'We are', Merkel argued in 2016, 'experiencing that peace and security are not a matter of course, even in Europe'.[29] It was not realistic to think that Germany might be able to insulate itself from geopolitics and the strategic influences that substantive hard-power capabilities proffer. A country that persisted in putting disproportionate weight on its commercial and economic engagements when assessing national interests would, in time, be unable adequately to protect its own security.

Russia's actions in Crimea and eastern Ukraine prompted a difficult debate within the German political establishment and the wider public, with sympathies split across party lines. Many in Merkel's centre-right CDU criticised her response, while many within the centre-left Social Democratic Party (SPD) were more understanding of the tougher line within the spectrum of European reactions that she came personally to represent. In this instance, at least, Merkel did what the rhetoric had promised, stepping into a leadership vacuum and stepping up Germany's crisis diplomacy. Berlin soon took effective responsibility for the four-party Normandy format, and Merkel was influential in bringing together the increasing array of substantive European sanctions. Germany also agreed (following foreign lobbying) to lead one of the four battalions of the Very High Readiness Joint Task Force (VJTF) created at the 2014 NATO summit to enhance the existing NATO Response Force, which began NATO's reorientation towards its more traditional platform of collective defence. Germany's persistent efforts to press ahead with the Nord Stream II pipeline project to increase its supplies of Russian gas (favoured by domestic economists and energy experts but rarely by foreign-policy advisers) stands, however, as a counter-example to this narrative. Many of Germany's European partners, as well as the US, have serious misgivings about the strategic effects of the project and have made their opposition known, only to find themselves ignored.

In September 2014, Germany also began to train and equip a light-infantry brigade of Kurdish Peshmerga to fight ISIS in Northern Iraq. Although this was a big moment in Germany's strategic maturation, the effort was modest; Germany was a contributor to a mission but not yet a definer of it. When France invoked the mutual-defence clause of the Lisbon Treaty after the 2015 ISIS attacks in Paris, Germany responded by offering a frigate to the French carrier group in the Eastern Mediterranean, deploying *Tornado* jets to help with reconnaissance and sending a further 650 soldiers to participate in UN peacekeeping in Mali even as it extended its engagement into the more risky north of the country. It continued to provide two *Transall* C-160 aircraft to support French activities in the Sahel. That Paris was distinctly underwhelmed by the scale of this response does not detract from the relative shift in outlook and willingness to engage militarily; only five years earlier, president Horst Koehler had been forced to resign for daring to suggest on a radio programme that military force could be useful for protecting trade routes.

The 2016 White Paper on German Security Policy and the Future of the Bundeswehr was as clear about the need to do more within Europe as it was on the importance of the transatlantic alliance. There was no hint of the EUGS goal of 'strategic autonomy' but rather a clear statement of fact: 'only together with the United States can Europe effectively defend itself against the threats of the 21st century and guarantee a credible form of deterrence'.[30] The 'two pillars' of Germany's foreign, security and defence policy would therefore be 'a strong and resolute North Atlantic Alliance' and a 'united and resilient European Union'.[31] The White Paper's declaration of the country's 'long-term goal of a Common European Security and Defence Union', however, showed the integrationist impulses that help, or are necessary to, propel European defence cooperation in Germany. Such parallel agendas are not always a net positive for the substance of European defence. They also set Germany apart from other major European powers, most obviously France, whose tendency towards cooperation is undermined rather than fuelled by such strategically confusing subtexts.

While the 'new responsibility' discourse has embedded itself in the thinking of the German foreign-policy establishment writ large, it has yet fully to infiltrate the broader domestic debate, constraining the reluctant and relative upturn in political appetite for the deployment of German troops on active operations abroad. Although Germany dispatched a small group of military medics to Cambodia as early as 1992, most of the 60 or so operations in which it has been involved since have been presented through the prism of humanitarian operations. Although by January 2018, 3,584 German soldiers were deployed on more than a dozen missions and operations abroad, Berlin's preference for logistical, reconnaissance and medical tasks remained. As German troops deployed in 2014 to support French forces in their stabilisation of the Central African Republic following the March 2013 coup, the focus of Germany's contribution was on air transport and a medical-evacuation plane, as well as troops to help guard the mission's headquarters. German soldiers were given no mandate for combat.

Intensive lobbying by allies is often still needed to secure German military deployments overseas. France had to work hard to encourage Germany to increase its contingent of train-ers in Iraq from 50 to 150 soldiers in early 2016. US and Polish interests will also have been at the forefront of German minds when Berlin agreed to lead one of the VJTF battalions. French and US pressure has been important in encouraging Germany to become more active in out-of-area operations, most notably in the Middle East. This dynamic is fuelled in part by Berlin's interest in mitigating transatlantic frustrations with the coun-try's relatively low level of defence spending as well as its desire to maintain cohesion within NATO. The return of Russian aggression in Ukraine and the revival of the Bundeswehr's traditions in territorial defence this has prompted have helped soothe popular opposition to some of these developments. Deterrence is less domestically controversial than out-of-area deployments, not least because, if deterrence works, deploy-ments on active operations become less likely.

As circumstances now require Germany (and others) to learn to multitask, however, Germany's response to the increas-ing level of activity is likely to remain centred around training, logistics and reconnaissance roles in missions and operations overseas. Mali is a good example: Germany is the lead troop contributor amongst European nations and, as of November 2018, the only one to make the list of top ten troop-contributing nations.[32] Germany has deployed four NH-90 medium-class military helicopters and four *Tiger* attack helicopters in support of the UN operation and the EU training mission, performing a range of transport, rescue and surveillance tasks, yet these helicopters were only deployed after considerable debate in the Bundestag and a waiver from the German military permitting them to operate in higher temperatures. Similarly, the deployment to Mali of troops from the Franco-German brigade from 2014 was emblematic of the two countries' ongoing cultural and command differences. While German troops deployed in support of the UN and EU missions, French soldiers from the same brigade were sent to fight in the French-led anti-insurgency *Operation Barkhane* (which was excluded from the Bundestag's deployment mandate).

Germany's preference for support tasks does not, to be sure, mean that German soldiers are not fighting and dying abroad. As of July 2018, some 420 German soldiers had lost their lives in service since the turn of the century.[33] Indeed, with German troops comprising the third-largest contingent in ISAF, taking responsibility for Regional Command North, there was no way for Germany to deny that the military engagement in Afghanistan was as much a war as a peacekeeping and reconstruction mission. Afghanistan was transformative for the German military. In July 2009, in what the *Frankfurter Allgemeine Zeitung* called a 'fundamental transition' from 'defensive to offensive', 300 German soldiers joined the Afghan Army and National Police in a firefight that led to the deaths of 20 Taliban fighters and the arrest of more.[34] In the wake of Afghanistan, the Bundeswehr could no longer be described as little more than 'an aggressive camping organisation', as one British officer is supposed jokingly to have once referred to it.[35]

Some sectors of Germany's foreign-policy establishment have, cautiously, begun to speak more publicly about the rationale for strengthening the country's foreign and security policy.[36] Political considerations, however, too often lead politicians to play to voters' most pacifist instincts rather than to try to challenge and redirect these instincts in line with the changing international environment. For example, during the 2017 federal election campaign, the SPD questioned the logic of the NATO defence-spending target, warning against plunging Germany into a 'new arms race'.[37] At the 2017 Munich Security Conference, German foreign minister Sigmar Gabriel, his eyes on the upcoming election, queried the direct link between increased defence spending and increased security. However, at the same conference one year later, with the elections now over, he lectured on the importance of increased defence spending, warning his fellow Europeans that 'it is going to be dammed hard for us as the only vegetarians in a world of carnivores'.[38]

If these are indeed times when 'Europeans have to take our fate in our own hands', as Merkel claimed in 2017, then there needs to be increased public political discussion about what this strategic aim might actually entail. All too often, popular domestic defence debates instead wander down pointless and distracting avenues, such as the pursuit of a German nuclear weapon or the merits of an EU army.[39] In this regard, the debate over the reliability of the transatlantic alliance will at least raise public awareness of the issues at stake. Such discussions are important because simply spending more money to accrue more capability is not in itself sufficient. Germany's body politic will need not just to sign off on increasing defence spending but also to develop the political will to deploy its new-found capabilities as part of a stabilising force in international affairs and in the defence and security interests of the continent.

Germany's defence budget increased by 32% between late 2013 and late 2018.[40] The country's defence minister has committed to increase defence spending to 1.5% of GDP by 2024, yet even this appears domestically politically contentious. This belated course correction is unlikely to impress allies, especially the US. In 2016, Defense Minister Ursula von der Leyen estimated that the Bundeswehr would need to invest €130bn through the year 2030 to reach its goals. In 2017, investment amounted to only around €5.25bn, just over half the average annual figure required.[41]

The course of incremental boosts in defence spending upon which Germany now appears set will take time to have effect.[42] If the Bundeswehr is to meet the ambitions set out in the 2016 White Paper (and the concept paper that followed), this trend will need to be sustained through further increases. In the meantime, Germany's defence-capabilities deficit will continue to plague the country's ability to follow through satisfactorily on the slow change towards more strategic thinking under way across much of its establishment.

The timelines for delivery of the capability initiatives aimed at addressing Germany's readiness problems are long, but a road map has been drawn. Under a NATO initiative aimed at improving the Alliance's collective-defence capabilities in the long term, for example, Germany has committed to raising, by 2032, three divisions collectively boasting eight to ten armoured brigades ready to deploy in combat operations within 90 days. This would clearly change the dynamics of European defence, not least because it would see as many as 19 smaller NATO countries plug in aspects of their capabilities to the Bundeswehr under the Framework Nations Concept, making Germany a leading power. As noted in Chapter Four, a modest but meaningful 'Europeanisation' of Germany's armed forces is already under way. The Netherlands has affiliated some two-thirds of its land-forces brigades to German divisions. Germany supports submarine sales, for example to Norway, with proposals for clusters of cooperation on international training and exercises on submarine warfare under the auspices of the German Navy. Since 2016, Germany has repeatedly announced increases in the size of its armed forces, which should, if problems with vacancies can be fixed, reach 198,000 by 2024, from a low of 165,000 in June 2015.[43]

Cultural and structural constraints on greater German defence activity include the need for every overseas deployment to be approved by the Bundestag, a stricter process than required in many other EU member states, including France. Between 1991 and August 2016, the Bundestag held 149 votes to approve military engagement. By contrast, over the same period France's Assemblée National held just seven, and the British Parliament only six.[44] While Bundestag approval has always, so far, been forthcoming, the requirement still introduces uncertainty about the utility of German troops in multinational units, at least at the outset of operations.

As Germany gears up to do more, there is a risk that it will fetishise processes rather than focus on outcomes. For example, as explored in Chapter Four, Germany has taken a leading role in the design and activation of PESCO. But this lead will need to be sustained from establishment through to execution. The four projects Germany has chosen to lead from the first tranche are worthy, if unexciting and institutionally focused: a European Medical Command, a network of logistics hubs in Europe and other logistical support for operations, an EU Training Mission Competence Centre and a flagship project to improve EU crisis management through the development of an EU Crisis Response Operation Core. By contrast, ambitions for Franco-German bilateral defence cooperation are more exciting, in particular with regard to collaborative commitments in defence aerospace. Yet history shows that delivery on these ambitions is far from assured.[45]

Short of a truly global security crisis, Berlin will fail to meet its NATO targets just as surely as it will continue to deflect pressure to increase defence spending more radically by pointing to its record on development spending and the inefficiencies that follow from increasing defence budgets too quickly. Von der Leyen encapsulated this viewpoint when, in early 2018, she rhetorically questioned the purpose of liberating residents of Mosul only for them to die of starvation.[46] Within Germany, there has been some effort to shift the framing of the debate on 'inputs' to a 3% GDP target for spending on defence, crisis diplomacy and development assistance, combining the NATO commitment with a UN-endorsed threshold for development programmes of 0.7% of GDP. Such a move would require careful consideration of its net effect. With Germany having finally reached the 0.7% development target for the first time in 2017 (44 years after the initial pledge was made), moving to a more holistic target could certainly provide domestic cover for increased defence spending.[47] The risk, however, is that such a shift would facilitate a strategically naive belief that Germany's contributions to international security can be broadly confined to 'diplomacy, humanitarian aid and development cooperation'.[48]

German leadership in Europe can never be hegemonic. Given its outsized power and influence, and its problematic history, German leadership is not generally about deciding the course and calling on others to follow. Its approach must be subtler, guiding and encouraging progress as the continent's balancer. If it is able, over time, to assume a more serious European presence, it will be as a collaborative, patient, corralling partner that is ready to make long-term investments in a stable centre-ground platform of defence and security politics, policies, capabilities and operations. The country knows it must lead or risk there being no substantive EU agenda, but it also knows it can only lead where others are prepared to follow. This makes the equilibrium that the Franco-German partnership can provide all the more critical. To feel comfortable leading, Germany needs partners; its military is not designed to act alone. France has repeatedly showed itself willing and able to act alone, but willing and capable continental partners will give it the incentive to cultivate more cohesive European responses. The nature of German leadership will play a key role in determining the credibility of the continent as a defence and security actor as well as the credibility of the European project writ large, in which German national interests are so intimately entangled.

The future of UK–EU relations

The UK's prospective departure will have myriad consequences for the EU's internal processes and functions, as well as its external engagements and profile. The referendum result did initially give some momentum to areas of European defence cooperation where the UK has been accused of standing in the way of progress (the most obvious being the emergence of a nascent EU operational headquarters in the guise of the MPCC). Such small victories, however, cannot disguise the fact that the management of Brexit and the building of a new UK–EU relationship is an exercise in damage limitation, however events develop. After all, the EU faces losing a permanent member of the UN Security Council, a nuclear power, and one of its top two spenders on defence and defence procurement. The UK was one of the few EU member states inclined to invest in defence and security both to the Union's east and south. It has repeatedly proven it is willing to deploy its capabilities overseas. It is committed to maintaining full-spectrum security and defence capabilities, and has substantive value to add to the EU's collective capabilities in strategic enablers such as transport and intelligence.

At least in some aspects, however, the prospective loss is more theoretical than real. In 2017, fewer than 100 UK troops were serving in EU missions, and the UK has accounted for just 2.3% of total member-state contributions to CSDP to date.[49] Many of the UK's particular strengths in high-end war fighting have been largely unavailable to or not required by the EU. Moreover, as UK politicians are quick to note, the UK may be leaving the EU but it is not leaving Europe. The mechanisms of its defence and security partnerships with the continent are changing, but they are open for reinvention.

The extent to which the prospect of Brexit will affect the authority of the EU and Europe's cohesiveness in international affairs will depend on how the EU27 handles the foreign-, security- and defence-policy aspects of its relationship with the UK. Many in the EU27 have become accustomed to thinking of Brexit as primarily a political challenge, whose management should not be permitted to pose a risk to the integrity of the EU. In this context, it is reasonable that economic interests should be relegated to second place. It is less reasonable, however, for defence considerations to be handled as second-order concerns. Protecting the integrity of the single market and the 'four freedoms' does not require pushing a willing defence and security ally into the mid-Atlantic through inflexible frameworks for third-party cooperation designed for countries such as Norway or Turkey. At the 2018 Munich Security Conference, Theresa May outlined the clear contributions the UK is able and willing to make towards an effective EU foreign policy, increased security provision for EU citizens and improved defence capabilities.[50] While there are obvious limits to many aspects of May's wish list, the EU's ability to meet the ambitions set out in the EUGS and SDIP will be severely challenged by any form of Brexit that fails to limit the fallout on EU27–UK security and defence relations.

Management of the Brexit process and its aftermath will also affect the EU's defence-technological and -industrial base, which has benefitted from the free flow of goods, data and people as well as from intellectual-property mechanisms between the EU27 and the UK.[51] In theory, at least, the fewer the borders, the more competitive and efficient this base will be. Any changes will affect not just multinational companies such as Airbus, MBDA, Leonardo and Thales, but also smaller UK and EU27 firms involved in the supply chains of collaborative defence projects. As of early 2019, how the EU would square, on the one hand, its interests in continuing access to UK military expertise and capabilities and the UK's reciprocal interests in being able to plug in to EU operations and capability-development programmes, and on the other, the need for the costs of the UK's decision to leave to be fully visible to other fractious parties within the EU, was unclear. Although this uncertainty included the precise nature of the UK's relationship with the EDA, the intergovernmental (non-EU) nature of the Letter of Intent Group and OCCAR should at least ensure the UK's continued participation in these bodies. The former dates back to a 2000 treaty between France, Germany, Italy, Spain, Sweden and the UK aimed at improving the political and legal framework for industrial restructuring in pursuit of a more competitive defence-industrial base. The latter organisation, which promotes armaments cooperation between Belgium, France, Germany, Italy, Spain and the UK, includes an administrative arrangement that allows it to implement projects that originate in the EDA.

It is notable that the CFSP has been of only secondary concern in the management of Brexit and the future of EU27–UK relations when compared with the issue of security and defence cooperation.[52] But one concern that does fall under the umbrella of the CFSP is the future of sanctions coordination. The absence of the UK from internal discussions on EU sanctions, including measures such as arms embargos, could significantly alter the balance of debate, given the UK's traditional vociferous support of restrictive measures, for example with regard to China, Iran and Russia. Since, as a UK House of Lords European Union Committee report on the issue notes, 'the most effective sanctions regimes are designed and applied alongside international partners', it will be important to find mechanisms that permit such a coordinated approach to continue in the future.[53] But one of the putative benefits of Brexit has been the opportunity for the UK to craft a new foreign policy as 'Global Britain'. If this means the development of a foreign policy independent from rather than parallel to the EU, sanctions policies could begin to diverge, adversely affecting Europe's strategic impact (as well as companies attempting to do business in both the UK and the EU27).[54]

With regard to the CSDP, on the other hand, Brexit is likely to have greater impact on security arrangements than on defence arrangements.[55] This is, in part, because security policy is more highly regulated and the role of EU institutions better established. There are, moreover, few if any alternative credible frameworks to the security mechanisms provided for through Europol (including the European Counter Terrorism Centre and the European Cybercrime Centre), the European Arrest Warrant and other EU criminal-justice measures. There are, in contrast, several non-EU mechanisms already in existence to facilitate cooperation on defence-industrial issues.

Any loss in inputs, for example to EU databases, thus risks translating into a net loss in outputs. To limit this loss, mechanisms for securing and improving intelligence and information sharing between the EU27 and a post-Brexit UK will be of the highest priority. Current mechanisms for exchanging security information include data pooling by the Schengen Information System II, Passenger Name Record data sharing, Eurojust, the EU Intelligence and Situation Centre and many others. Achieving accommodations that are both politically acceptable to the EU27 and also serve the best security interests of Europe will not be easy.[56]

In areas such as hybrid warfare, cyber security and countering violent extremism where the UK has particular security capabilities, the EU27 has an interest in ensuring that the UK continues to regard the EU as a natural docking point alongside its partners in the Five Eyes intelligence community. Indeed, this mutual interest in security cooperation is shown by the fact that, prior to the June 2016 UK vote to leave the Union, EU member states were the largest market for UK security exports.[57]

The UK has, on more than a few occasions, put forward capabilities or fulfilled a function that has provided qualitative benefits to the CSDP, and some of this is not readily substitutable by many (or sometimes even any) other member states. Examples range from early UK leadership in *Operation Althea* (important in winning US confidence for the transition from a NATO-led to an EU-led operation), to the use of UK diplomatic and intelligence networks on the ground in African countries where other EU members did not have the access a CSDP operation suddenly required.[58] UK military expertise and experience has also informed the design and development of many CSDP missions.

In the area of defence capabilities, the UK's contribution to the EU's profile is more dramatic. An IISS–DGAP study found that the UK enjoys around 25% of the key enabling capacities and 20% of all military capabilities within the EU, including

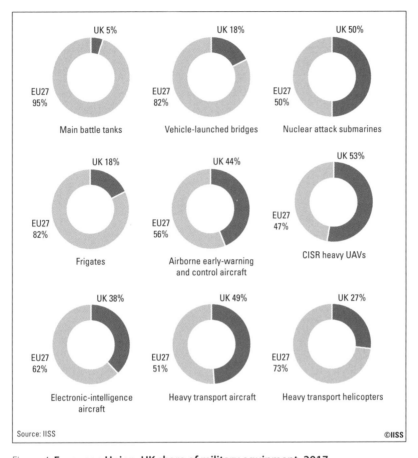

Source: IISS   ©IISS

Figure 4. **European Union: UK share of military equipment, 2017**

53% of the EU's overall equipment holding for combat intelligence, surveillance and reconnaissance heavy unmanned aerial vehicles (UAVs).[59] The situation is even worse than the numbers imply. Capability is about more than an inventory list, it is also about the political will to use it – something the UK has repeatedly demonstrated. The UK also provides some 21% of EU28 defence spending and around 40% of the continent's total R&D spending.[60]

Even the process of reaching agreement on inclusive arrangements for UK participation in EU defence projects and funds following any UK departure from the EU will do some damage. Uncertainty is not conducive to collaboration; there is anecdotal evidence of self-censoring in applications for EU funding by putative collaborations between EU27 and UK industries and research institutes. Moreover, a move by the EU towards 'buy European' measures exclusively defined, whether the inadvertent result of an overly active regulatory environment focused on ensuring security of supplies or a deliberate and targeted attempt to exclude UK industries, would affect not just those industries but the European defence and technology industrial base writ large. Meanwhile, a UK outside the EU would, of course, also be freer to link defence procurements to the UK's prosperity agenda.

The UK, rather than the EU27, will absorb the bulk of the impact of Brexit. But any diminution of the UK as a defence and security actor is also a loss for Europe. The effect of Brexit on sterling exchange rates has already begun to impact over-committed UK defence budgets and over-optimistic defence aspirations. A weak pound may be good for defence exports, but it is also increasing the costs of defence-equipment imports. The 2016 Defence Equipment Plan includes procurement commitments, most notably from the US (including F35s, *Apaches* and P8s) that should boost UK capabilities that could in turn conceivably still be put at the EU's disposal. Yet in 2017 the UK National Audit Office was already concluding that 'the risks to the affordability of the Ministry of Defence Equipment Plan are greater than at any time since reporting began in 2012'.[61] Slower economic growth may assist the UK government in meeting its commitment to spend 2% of GDP on defence, but it jeopardises the prospect of securing the increases in defence spending the UK's military requires.

Nevertheless, to 2019 the MoD's core budget has proved largely exempt from government cuts. Real-terms defence spending is set to rise through 2021, alongside a more noticeable hike in expenditure on real-terms procurement spending. The UK will remain one of the continent's most capable military powers, likely magnifying the significance of EU27 decisions on the terms and conditions for third-party access to CSDP operations as well as on capability developments, including under PESCO. The risk for the EU is that decisions that might appear to make short-term political sense do not align with the types of structures and partnerships likely to make the best longer-term sense for European defence.

The prospective departure of the UK will increase the relative weight of French and German perspectives in EU positioning on international affairs. This will push Paris and Berlin into a still closer defence partnership, despite instinctive differences that mean they will also be keen to bring trusted third parties into collaborations. There is obvious room for countries such as Italy, Poland and Spain to play greater roles in the formulation and projection of European security and defence policy.

The recent push to improve EU–NATO security and defence cooperation becomes even more important with Brexit.[62] NATO's relative inability to influence the R&D trajectories of its members has been indirectly highlighted by the financial and regulatory encouragement to which the EU has now committed. The prospective departure of the UK, which has been an important advocate for the primacy of NATO interests, is likely to leave NATO with even less influence on the trajectory of EU defence and security developments just when it might reasonably wish for more, in particular with regard to capability development.

The expected departure of a strongly Atlanticist member will also affect the EU's relations with Washington. After Brexit, the spending contribution made by EU member states in support of NATO objectives will sink still further.[63] The leaders of three of the four forward-deployed multinational battalion-sized battlegroups stationed in Poland and the Baltic states will be from outside the EU. Brexit could thus both magnify and embolden US expressions of dissatisfaction with EU defence commitments under NATO. The nature of the future EU27–UK defence and security partnership will affect US perspectives on EU defence cooperation from CSDP to the EDF to PESCO.

There are some modest positive indirect consequences for the EU from Brexit. In November 2016, with the removal of the traditional UK veto, the EDA received its first budget increase in six years. Similarly, the UK has previously discouraged the EDA from working more on issues of hard defence (instead preferring a focus on lower-intensity capabilities to ensure deconfliction with NATO programmes). The UK and Germany have been discussing improving bilateral defence cooperation for years; it is ironic that Brexit will likely force some substance finally to develop around these good intentions. More than a few French defence industries will be looking with relish at the opportunities Brexit affords them, for example as they seek to replace UK-based Surrey Satellite Technology Ltd as the prime contractor for payload electronics for the *Galileo* satellite navigation system.

The *Galileo* project is a prime example of the price of strategically myopic behaviour in pursuit of short-term opportunities for national development. In setting the terms and conditions for future UK participation in *Galileo*, the EU effectively left London with little alternative but to announce its withdrawal from the development of the system. As a consequence, there may be a delay in *Galileo* becoming operational, the EU will lose critical cryptographic knowledge, and a proposed sovereign UK alternative will mean a deliberate duplication of European efforts with negative resource consequences for other areas of space research, such as secure space communications, from which alternative UK investments Europe could otherwise also have benefitted. The prospect, moreover, of leading European forces operating to different satellite navigation systems will unnecessarily complicate joint operations (and joint platform development) in the future.

Much of the debate on the future EU27–UK defence and security partnership is likely to involve processes and structures for engagement. After leaving the EU, the UK will ideally like to secure observer status at, or at least some formal mechanism for contact with, the EU's Political and Security Committee, the body responsible for the CFSP and CSDP. Yet failure to secure formal new institutional arrangements will not necessarily mean failure to protect close EU27–UK relations. London's close relationship with Washington on security and defence issues does not require the UK to be an observer at the US National Security Council; it rests on a web of intensive contacts, including in intelligence sharing, and on a network of dialogues and secondments across ranks and institutions.

The UK has been clear that continuing close cooperation with the EU's foreign-, security- and defence-policy institutions as well as with its European partners is in its interest. An outcome that respects EU cohesion while keeping the UK as the EU's closest partner on issues of foreign and security cooperation should not be beyond the continent's collective strategic imagination. In the meantime, the management of Brexit is likely to nurture greater engagement by the continent's key powers in bilateral, trilateral and minilateral groupings, in formats that are both exclusively continental and more international (such as the Small Group on Syria).

The irony is that the EU has always sought to promote close political relationships in Europe. It would be a tragedy if the continent's leaders now forsook that vision, even towards a partner that had spurned them. Europe would be a lesser force for it. The EU has enough problematic neighbours to its east and to its south, and now, in different ways, to its west. It could surely do with a genuinely close strategic ally and partner to its north. That the development of European security and defence cooperation will be roped off from political disputes over the nature of the broader future relationship, however, cannot be taken for granted. Any potential defence and security benefits from the EU's new initiatives outlined in the previous chapters would be dramatically overshadowed by a failure of the EU27 to treat Brexit as a strategic problem that will shape the future of the continent.

CONCLUSION

Although some of the crises Europe has faced over the past decade have been managed, none have been fully resolved. Yet the real story of the European Union is sometimes lost in the cacophony of doomsaying. Others besides the EU under-estimated the dark side of globalisation, and are suffering populist convulsions as a result. The multiple presidents of the EU can be confusing, but the divisive and extremely partisan politics in the US perhaps puts EU consensus-driven behav-iour in a more favourable light. Meetings between the EU and the Association of Southeast Asian Nations (ASEAN) can have even EU officials despairing at the bureaucratic processes and divided interests they face. The trends that we see now are not necessarily linear. Structural challenges may render Europe's social-welfare system unsustainable, but 'social Europe' is a key component of Europe's soft power. The continent remains, after all, one of the most prosperous and most equal regions of the world.

Europe's slide towards the strategic sidelines in world affairs is not preordained. Investor flight from emerging markets in early 2014, for example, was a reminder, that it is far from predetermined that this will be the 'Asia-Pacific century'. Europe's self-doubt in this regard is in danger of becoming a self-fulfilling prophecy. For example, a 'hard landing' in China would certainly put the challenges that Europe is facing into perspective.

Such modest optimism should not be mistaken for complacency. The problems are well known and widely discussed. But much of Europe's fate as a strategic actor lies in its own hands, determined not so much by its relative economic performance as by its ability to develop a more collaborative strategic outlook and to translate this outlook into action. The EU has a key role to play in Europe's strategic future. A weak and crisis-beset EU will be a poor champion for European interests and values abroad, but an outward-looking EU, with a stable and sustainable eurozone at its heart, would have an obvious and urgent role in upholding the prospects for 'effective multilateralism' as well as in supporting the liberal international order as it comes under increasing challenge.

The development of EU foreign and security policy to date has been process heavy and characterised by missteps. Grand pronouncements such as the Headline Goals for defence capabilities have too often gone unfulfilled. But processes and platforms to help European states move beyond their historical underachievement in foreign-, security- and defence-policy cooperation are being moved into position. As crises unfold and overlap, from the instability in Europe's neighbourhoods to doubts over the credibility of the transatlantic alliance, the political will to do so is growing stronger. Vision and reality remain a long way apart. But Europe has responded positively to crisis before and it could do so again.

The form and function of the EU's structures continue to evolve, and hard choices with regard to the balance of responsibilities and interplay between the EU and its member states in foreign, security and defence policy remain to be made if the Union is to survive and prosper as a strategic actor. Moves towards more variable geometry or a system of QMV in foreign affairs could, for example, have a dramatic impact. Yet the development of a more effective and influential core group of actors that does not risk the loyalties of those on the periphery will not be easy. There are, to be sure, interesting precedents such as the Schengen Agreement, a treaty initially concluded between just five member states, separate from the EU treaties but designed to deliver a goal enshrined within them.

Democracies may respond slowly to all but the most immediate crises, but they are, at least in theory, supposed to respond. One challenge is that, whilst events may be pushing European establishments towards new strategic engagements, in many cases the general public still lags behind. Merkel may, for example, personally have supported the airstrikes on Syrian government targets conducted by France, the UK and the US in response to Assad's use of chemical weapons in Douma, but domestic realities meant Germany did not participate. Polling showed that approximately 60% of the German public opposed such military action. Most European governments will need to display greater leadership to bring their reluctant publics on board.

Even in the most optimistic scenario, the EU will not in the next few decades transform into a great power able to determine the structure, substance and direction of world affairs. But it can realistically aspire to be able to influence developments substantially, helping to project stability in its own neighbourhood. As it develops its capabilities in foreign and security policy, moreover, the EU can also credibly become a more heavyweight partner for other proponents of the liberal international order, including democracy activists, open governments and market economies worldwide.

Indicators of progress

As argued above, reasons for cautious and moderate optimism with regard to Europe's strategic future are emerging amidst ongoing disappointment and missed opportunities. These include examples of modest successes, an end to 'all or nothing' EU engagement, the rise of common initiatives such as PESCO with more flexible parameters of cooperation, and the changing nature of leadership.

Examples of modest successes

Not all of Europe's exploits in foreign, security and defence affairs have been weak. Few, for example, in the Malian city of Gao would view the French forces that liberated them from the Islamists in this light. French frustrations over the contributions of fellow Europeans to its actions in Mali have certainly run high at times, but contributions did increase. In early 2018, for example, with the Bundestag approving up to 1,100 German troops for MINUSMA (widely held to be the UN's most dangerous peacekeeping mission) and up to 350 for the EUTM, more German troops were posted to Mali than to any other overseas theatre. Smaller sub-groupings of EU member states have repeatedly engaged in strategically relevant initiatives, even if the results have tended to be more tactical than strategic. These include the E3 initiative on Iran as well as Franco-German efforts under the Normandy format that partially succeeded in shifting hostilities in Ukraine from all-out war to a more limited conflict.

Institutionally, the EU has also made some valuable contributions to stability and security on the international stage, for example through *Operation Atalanta*'s anti-piracy effort off the coast of Africa. Closer to home, *Operation Sophia* has pushed back against people-smuggling in the Mediterranean. The EU has also been a partner on issues of peace and security in some esoteric conflicts around the world, such as the Philippine province of Mindanao, which the European Commission's Department for Humanitarian Aid in August 2018 called a 'forgotten crisis'.[1] Here the EU has, for a decade, provided persistent and extended support for the peace process.

In the Balkans, the EU helped broker the 2015 Przino agreement among the main political parties in Macedonia, as a result of which a pro-Western government, promising NATO and EU integration, was formed in 2017. In 2018, Montenegro became a member of NATO, while Greece and the newly renamed Republic of North Macedonia signed the Prespa agreement settling their long-running dispute over the latter's name. In February 2019 North Macedonia signed an accession agreement to become NATO's 30th member.

European powers played key roles in preparing the ground for the Paris Climate Accords. The European Commission also funds and supports a global network of CBRN (chemical, biological, radiological and nuclear) Risk Mitigation Centres of Excellence and their accompanying regional secretariats.[2] Their work includes mitigating natural and accidental risks as well as deliberate CBRN use. But if Syria's repeated violations of the norms of international warfare, or Russia's extraordinary use of a nerve agent in the attempted assassination of one of its former spies in the UK in March 2018, are indicative of what lies ahead, there may yet be an increasing need for Europe's world-class collective expertise in CBRN risk mitigation.

Events are forcing further upgrades to other aspects of the EU's international security engagements. As the EU seeks to bolster its role in providing security to its citizens, for example, it is increasingly pulled into external as well as internal security issues. Its efforts to manage migration have included making deals with partners in its neighbourhood and beyond, covering a gamut of issues from developing better intelligence and oversight of key smuggling routes to arrangements on readmission. Their common denominator is that they will be expensive for the EU to secure and maintain. Some of these experiences will, however, help establish the EU's authority in the management of an international security concern that will only become more common globally.

Another area where Europe is the home of some of the world's leading expertise, and is increasing both its capabilities and its international cooperation, is cyber security. While key strategic capabilities (and therefore partnerships) will continue to be found at nation-state level, the EU has also been developing its role.[3] The proposed EU-wide certification scheme for IT products, services and processes is designed further to develop the EU's presence in the cyber-security marketplace. A new European cyber-security agency appears to be on the cards, built on the existing ENISA. Progress here will be important for the EU's efforts to develop its single digital market, alongside the more existential aspects involving the stability and security of the EU and its member states.

The EU, by its very nature, is a cumbersome and clumsy actor on the international stage, but it is wrong to think of it as operating a 'lowest common denominator' sort of approach to policymaking. If that were so, the EU's approaches to China or Russia would be rather different. Member states do not march in harmony, but they are regularly influenced in their behaviours by the agendas and interests of fellow members. The resulting compromises may not be the most forward-leaning on issues of defence and security in particular, but they are compromises that raise the floor, if not the ceiling. The EU is adding value for its members, and by extension its continent and its allies. There have even been times where the EU's lack of a singular identity and obvious military might has been an advantage. What might be understood as the EU's more post-modern profile has helped it play a supporting role in Western defence and security concerns in geopolitically sensitive parts of the world from Georgia to the Middle East.

The days of acting together or not at all could be ending

European actors appear to be becoming less ideological and more pragmatic with regard to the institutional options and formats through which they pursue their foreign-, security- and defence-policy interests. An EU presence on foreign and security policy is not sustainable if *every* European contribution in this regard takes place outside the EU framework, but a shift in this direction (including close defence and security cooperation with the UK after its prospective departure from the Union) should enhance the continent's strategic effect.

Following years of stalled discussions, since 2014 European nations have united behind a push to streamline NATO–EU relations, including welcoming NATO's expansion from collective defence into areas such as capacity-building and crisis management (especially in Europe's southern neighbourhood). This is, for example, shown by the EU's July 2017 decision to allocate €2m to NATO's Building Integrity Programme. The UK's prospective departure from the EU, which will increase the importance of close EU–NATO cooperation, is likely to strengthen interests in European defence cooperation beyond EU structures.

The EU's mechanism for structured cooperation, PESCO, is intended to facilitate closer defence integration. Its inclusive start has inadvertently undermined some of the momentum its activation was intended to generate. Whether it succeeds will depend on its substance, but evaluations of its success will need to focus not on its impact on the EU's broader internal integration efforts, but on substantive contribution to the continent's strategic capabilities. Using this metric, the logic for a strategically driven evolution of the possibility for more mean-ingful third-party defence and security partnerships with the EU should be clear.

Berlin, in particular, is rightly worried about the limits of 'unity in diversity', and anxious that the introduction of yet more variable geometry in pursuit of EU effectiveness should not inadvertently risk the very existence of the Union. It should also, however, be conscious of the risks involved in changing nothing. More of the same sets a path to obscurity for the EU in international security.

The EUGS notion of 'principled pragmatism' suggests that, for all its self-identification as a values-based organisation, the EU is unlikely to remain immune from a broader trend towards a more transactional politics. Such an approach will have rami-fications for the way the EU operates on the international stage. Indeed, a greater propensity towards flexibility in the terms and conditions of the EU's international engagements could even improve third-party perceptions of the EU as a pragmatic and effective international actor.

If, however, the EU is to maintain its credibility with partners abroad, it must also demonstrate some principles alongside its pragmatism with respect to its own member states. Within the continent, there must be a limit to the pride taken in diver-sity when such diversity infringes on core European values. Autocratic developments and violations of the rule of law in Hungary, in particular, pose one such challenge to EU integ-rity and identity. In September 2018, the European Parliament for the first time activated TEU Article 7 proceedings against Hungary, which, in the unlikely event of unanimous European Council agreement, could mean the suspension of Budapest's voting rights. In such exceptional instances, EU member states might also need to muster the courage of their convictions and link the internal distribution of EU funds to EU values despite fears that similar measures might someday be enforced against them for lesser infringements.

Common initiatives build common interests

European states are expanding their web of diplomatic and military secondments and engagements. For example, Macron's European Intervention Initiative, unbound by the constraints of the EU, creates an interesting opportunity to lock in the operational experience in particular of a post-Brexit UK. It holds out the prospect of a converging European defence identity beyond the question of EU membership and without the different internal tensions with which both the EU and NATO find themselves burdened.

In theory, at least, European defence capabilities should be bolstered by full implementation and careful coordination of other new initiatives such as PESCO, CARD and the EDF. The first of these is particularly significant for the development of German defence and security policy, as higher defence spending channelled through PESCO can be presented to those traditionally unenthusiastic about such engagements as measures that promote 'more Europe', in a way impossible with unilateral or minilateral defence spending or spending under NATO auspices.

The nature of leadership is changing

Merkel may be criticised for lacking a grand strategic vision, yet holding the EU together through the crisis years has not been easy. There may be no counterparts to Monnet, Schuman or Adenauer on the scene today. The Franco-German relationship may never again look like it did under Mitterrand and Kohl. But the world has changed, and the EU project cannot depend on exceptional leaders. The requirement now is not so much political vision as political will. As populist leaders employ sharper and more divisive rhetoric, post-nationalist projects will survive not by adopting the narrative and style of their critics but through their enduring appeal.

A more 'alpha-male' leadership style may have superficial appeal as a short-term boost to EU credibility. But it is not a form of leadership that necessarily helps the EU's longer-term prospects. Leadership of a club is different from leadership of a unitary state. Germany knows that it cannot lead alone. Macron's grand rhetoric may feel refreshing, but even the recent modest uptick in Franco-German cooperation is causing some pushback by other member states concerned that their interests will be forgotten in deals between big powers.

It is not just the nature of leadership that is changing, but the themes on which such efforts rest. Developments in technology, for example, are generating new requirements for norm setting. The way these are managed will determine the future regulatory environment for everything from data protection to the use of lethal autonomous weapons systems. If the EU sets global standards on data management, and the rights and responsibilities of technology companies in this area, it would have a strategic role in international security. It would also increase its geo-economic power in ways likely to facilitate the development of a greater sense of purpose and investment in geopolitical issues.

Looking to the future

If Europe and the EU are to address the crises they have only contained while managing ongoing structural shifts, they will need to improve upon the speed and substance of these changes. This will involve paying particular attention to issues such as action versus rhetoric, regional priorities, security cooperation, the gap between defence ambitions and capabilities, strategic communications, and cultivating partnerships.

Say less, do more

European actors have a tendency towards hyperbole that can raise expectations counterproductively. Repeatedly asking for credit from partners for things that the EU is going to do, rather than things that it has actually done, is not sustainable. A failure meaningfully to follow through on the majority of the 34 PESCO projects rolled out by early 2019 will bring into question the credibility of future projects. Follow-through on EU defence plans more broadly will be important for the EU's overall credibility. Leaders of EU institutions and national governments must be careful, moreover, not to overplay the exceptionalism of the EU's 'comprehensive approach' in international affairs.[4]

The concept that security and development go hand in hand, and that institutions across governments using different tools to resolve related problems need to work closely together, might have sounded innovative, for example, in 1996 when the European Commission discussed approaches to conflict prevention, peacebuilding and stability in Africa. This ambition, if not always the reality, is now a widespread feature of modern policymaking, informing (with differences in language) not just EU policy and but that of most individual European states or organisations such as NATO. European powers need to worry less about establishing their own 'brand' of crisis-management theory, and more about establishing their own credibility in crisis-management practice.

One way to bolster Europe's strategic presence in foreign affairs is through the greater use of joint visits on single, critical issues. If mismatched hierarchical sensitivities can be avoided, this should ideally involve not just EU member states but EU institutional leaders as well. There are bilateral examples of such cooperation at the foreign-minister level, notably between France and Germany, but the EU would do better in promoting the areas where its interests are united if this coordination could, on occasion, take place among national leaders. This could, for example, be a visit by the leaders of the E3 plus the HR/VP to Washington specifically to discuss relations with Iran. Or it could be some form of joint visit to China specifically on issues of market access and intellectual-property rights. Although national leaders generally travel in order to discuss a range of issues, which complicates coordination, it ought not to be impossible for issues of the utmost strategic importance. In this respect, Macron's invitation in March 2019 to Merkel and Juncker to join him in Paris for his meeting with visiting Chinese President Xi Jinping was a welcome start.

Finally, the EU must do more than promote multilateralism for its own sake. Multilateral institutions cannot be the sole arbiters of when action is required. The use of force in support of the rule of law and enforcement of international order cannot gain legitimacy only through the UN Security Council, given the reality that some permanent members have proved themselves repeatedly willing to use their veto. European states must become more comfortable with other justifications for action, including military action. Such a shift is already happening with regard to EU restrictive measures, with autonomous sanctions becoming more popular in recent years. The challenge is finding acceptable and effective ways for EU members not just to talk but to act together at the harder end of the foreign- and security-policy spectrum.

Setting priorities

Some parts of the world will always matter more to the EU than others. Fundamental questions of stability and security linger in the Balkans, for example, while the influence of third-party powers grows. Europe cannot afford to fail (again) in the management of its own backyard. It is not easy to craft and sustain a strategy that can leverage the EU's influence to stabilising effect while remaining grounded in realistic assessments of EU accession options and timelines. Yet if Europe does not want to be frozen out of its own neighbourhood, it has no alternative but to develop more satisfactory and consistent engagements with the countries of the Western Balkans. Similarly, demographic and migratory pressures will continue to make North Africa a priority for European engagement. The actions of individual member states, notably France and Italy, and increasingly of coalitions of the willing, are creating path dependencies for EU institutions and its other member states in this strategic area.

Elsewhere, the EU will have to find a way to stop Turkey drifting too far away from the West, and shepherd European unity on Russia while working with a difficult but vulnerable partner in Kiev and thinking about how to deter and if necessary react to any move Putin might be tempted to make in Belarus. It needs to carve out credible policies of engagement with a pro-European Georgia and to recognise the regression in its relations with Moldova. It will need to coordinate Europe's responses to China, in particular as Beijing extends its interests on the continent, most notably in Central and Eastern Europe.

Whilst only a handful of European states are substantively engaged with developments in Asia, the nature and scale of the multiple and overlapping international security concerns emanating from the region will ensure its place on the EU's foreign-policy agenda, albeit not as a first-order priority. France and the UK have led the way in upgrading their security and defence presence in the region. In 2017 France conducted at least five ship visits to the region, alongside repeated freedom-of-navigation operations through the South China Sea, often with officers from other European navies on board. In 2018 the UK (having sent no ships to the region since 2013) sent an antisubmarine-warfare frigate to help enforce sanctions on North Korea, an amphibious-assault ship to participate in exercises by members of the Five Powers Defence Agreement (Australia, Malaysia, New Zealand, Singapore and the UK) as well as with the Japan Maritime Self-Defense Force, and a Type-23 frigate to participate in joint exercises with regional partners. There was also a joint Anglo-French freedom-of-navigation operation through the Spratly Islands in the South China Sea.

Although the EU is not one of the primary actors in Asia, it has been consciously trying to develop the security aspects of its cooperation with the region.[5] It has focused in particular on Southeast Asian nations and ASEAN, and on matters of non-traditional security, developing new collaborative initiatives in areas such as humanitarian assistance and disaster relief, maritime security and countering violent extremism. Such contributions are often individually dismissed, particularly as regional powers such as Japan and Australia are also bolstering their own more significant partnerships in the region. But the supportive engagements the EU is in the process of developing in the region could, slowly and from a low base, make a strategic contribution. The EU's potential role in areas such as cyberspace, space and the deep sea, where it has particular expertise, could be significant. Even within this region, however, prioritisation is required. The EU–Japan action plan of 2001–11 covered more than one hundred areas for cooperation. The Strategic Partnership Agreement signed in 2018 covered a more sensible but still large 40 areas. Without clear prioritisation, EU engagement across the broader region is more likely to achieve piecemeal progress than develop into substantive strategic contributions.

As EU institutional engagement evolves, most notably in Southeast Asia, the EU will need to avoid becoming preoccupied with its exclusion from the East Asia Summit (which brings members of ASEAN together with Australia, China, India, Japan, New Zealand, Russia, South Korea and the US). This exclusion appears to highlight EU irrelevance in the affairs of the hemisphere. In a world where 'showing up' counts for a lot, not even being invited is a major blow. The solution is to concentrate on developing a consistent and reliable record of action that defies misguided over-simplifications that, for example, the EU cannot be a useful partner in the management and containment of maritime security concerns in Asia because its members cannot agree a strong diplomatic statement on the South China Sea.

This is a demanding, and not exhaustive, list of priorities. But substantive powers tend to face such demands. A 'whole of EU' approach does not mean every actor in the EU must do everything. Clusters of member states can take the lead on foreign-policy issues according to their respective priorities, working collaboratively, acting on behalf of the EU and representing agreed EU positions. Whilst any such further empowerment of minilateral coalitions will create challenges of coherence, if well supervised by the EU's central institutions, they would amplify EU engagement in international affairs.

Step up further on security

Europe is one of the world's richest regions, in close proximity to one of the poorest, to some of the fastest-growing populations and to some of the most unstable trouble spots. With an external border of 50,000km (80% maritime and 20% land), and free and unrestricted movement of peoples, goods, services and capital between 26 of its countries, the continent has extraordinary additional security requirements beyond those carried by individual states. These privileges are only sustainable with common rules for controlling the zone's external borders, supported by close judicial and police cooperation that permits not just the sharing of information but also, ultimately, the sharing of the burdens of operating an effective immigration and asylum system. After all, European security cooperation will only be as effective as Europe's individual agencies and ministries working on security are at cooperating within, at and beyond their borders.

The member states of the EU have made substantive (but insufficient) progress in working together to promote their security, both within and outside the legal framework of the EU. Efforts include the EU's law-enforcement agency Europol, the simplified cross-border judicial surrender procedure provided for in the European Arrest Warrant, and the large-scale information system supporting external border controls and law-enforcement cooperation that is the Schengen Information System. The 2005 Prüm Convention, much of which was adopted into EU law in 2008, acts as a laboratory for the exchange of all DNA, fingerprint and vehicle data. A new European Border and Coast Guard Agency has been established (with, however, limited powers and insufficient resources). Such partnerships and institutions are likely to evolve and multiply, including, for example and over time, agreement on an EU Agency for Asylum. In the meantime, however, especially with regard to asylum and migration, there are continuing tensions as member states seek to protect their sovereignty, even as many privately recognise EU-level rules and institutions are likely to be critical for guaranteeing effect.

The onus will be on the EU to find the mechanisms to engage with non-EU European states to the collective security benefit of all. From cooperation on Justice and Home Affairs, to international policing and counter-terrorism efforts, the EU and its member states will want to do everything possible to keep their citizens safe. When it comes to dealing with a post-Brexit UK, it would be preferable if the understandable desire to point out the privileges of EU membership from which the UK voted to walk away could be reserved for areas that are not matters of life and death. This might involve legal as well as attitudinal changes.

Shed remaining defence delusions

There is a substantial and ongoing disparity between present European defence capabilities and the declared level of ambition in key EU policy documents. An IISS–DGAP study looked at the EU's likely performance in five illustrative scenarios both in 2018 and 2020, taking into account equipment procurements: peace enforcement in the Caucasus; stabilisation and capacity-building in Somalia; conflict prevention around the Red Sea and the Indian Ocean; humanitarian assistance in Bangladesh; and rescue and evacuation in South Africa. Even taking UK contributions into account, only the latter two did not generate any shortfalls. Stripped of UK contributions, it is unclear whether any of the operations could be successfully carried out. As soon as the scenarios begin to overlap – for example, a peace-enforcement scenario with a rescue and evacuation operation – serious shortfalls arise across all domains. While procurement projects already in the pipeline should yield improvements in the maritime and air domains by 2030, these are insufficient to meet the identified shortfalls.[6]

Upgrading Europe's capabilities is a long-term project. While NATO can continue to provide a credible defence posture, particularly on Europe's eastern border, European leaders need to find a political path to give greater priority to defence spending and especially to capability investment and development. Initiatives to nurture this are under way, and the upturn in European defence spending, whether or not under the NATO umbrella, will in time make itself felt through more strictly European capabilities. There is a need in the next

few years to keep the UK defence establishment and industry intimately involved with EU initiatives, in order to retain
UK capabilities and experience as part of broader European
defence cooperation. Even then the scale of the task is daunting.

Sort out strategic communications

The EU struggles to promote a clear understanding of
the nature of its defence and security ambitions. Talk of a
'European army' is particularly unhelpful. The phrase is not
only misguided and unrealistic in its ambition, it also sets the
EU up to fail, inviting ridicule of the EU's more credible inter-
national-security ambitions. Differences in approach continue
to undermine European efforts at strategic communications; all
too often, EU Foreign Affairs Council conclusions appear to be
aimed as much at projecting influence within the EU's internal
bureaucracy as projecting influence externally.

Divergences in member states' perceptions of their own
interests are an inevitable part of the fabric of European cooperation, but the communications around these divergences
could be more carefully managed, at least at the EU institutional level. A notable failure in this regard was the disarray
in EU diplomatic messaging around the April 2018 airstrikes
that the France, the UK and the US jointly conducted in Syria.
Council President Donald Tusk took to his Twitter feed with
a firm declaration that the EU would stand 'with its allies on
the side of justice'; airstrikes, he argued, made it clear to the
aggressors in Syria that the human tragedy they were induc-
ing had costs even for themselves. Only hours later, HR/VP
Mogherini took to Twitter with a markedly more lukewarm
endorsement of 'all efforts aimed at the prevention of use of
chemical weapons' while choosing to reiterate a mantra that
Russian military engagement was already proving highly

questionable – that there 'can be no other solution to the Syrian conflict than political'.[7]

Cultivate partnerships

Europe and the EU are not alone in their desire to demonstrate that multilateralism can still be an effective way of doing business. Indeed, for small and mid-sized powers, multilateralism can protect sovereignty rather than infringe on it. Other actors remain open to partnership in upholding the values on which both the EU and the wider liberal order is founded. The US may be Europe's most powerful partner in the Western world, but it is far from the only one. From Australia to Canada to Japan, more diplomatic effort is needed to strengthen these partnerships, including in international security. This should ideally include the cultivation of the ongoing close cooperation between the E3, which offers obvious potential for strategic leadership even with the political complications of Brexit.[8]

Meanwhile, Europe's partnership with the US will need careful attention as the EU works to develop its own 'autonomous' capabilities. Such activities will have to be framed in ways that support transatlanticists in the US administration who seek to explain why continued US investment in European defence and security benefits US interests. Europe can send the message that it intends to diminish (to mutual benefit) its outsourcing of security to the US without challenging the narrative of dependable allies committed to common goals, including the most effective security alliance in history.

Despite uncertainty over the trajectory of US foreign policy, it is as the closest ally of the US that Europe, and by extension the EU, can maximise its strategic influence in international affairs. This will include geo-economic and geopolitical cooperation. The putative Transatlantic Trade and Investment Partnership (TTIP) may have fallen away, but the strategic logic for a wide-ranging and substantive US–EU trade agreement remains compelling. Moves in this direction would have a substantive impact on baseline assessments of the EU's strategic weight. In the meantime, in April 2019 the European Council gave the European Commission the mandate to start formal negotiations on two agreements (one on conformity assessment and one on eliminating tariffs on industrial products). This is still to be welcomed, even if the step was driven more by the EU's desire to manage transatlantic tensions than on shared transatlantic ambitions for a more ambitious, wide-ranging and standard-setting future free-trade agreement.

Franco-German relations as weather vane

If there is one single dynamic that will be critical for determining the EU's future strategic profile in international security, it is the development of Franco-German defence and security cooperation. France and the UK will largely continue to do as they wish and as they can – whether within EU structures or without. Even Italy is increasingly going it alone in North Africa. Meanwhile, geopolitical pressures on Central and Eastern European states mean that, for all the trouble in transatlantic relations, they are likely to continue to lean as heavily as possible on NATO. Of the larger EU powers, only Germany has the capabilities, the apparent inclination and importantly the mindset to effect and sustain meaningful momentum on international security and defence cooperation under an EU umbrella, while remaining committed to NATO.

Germany is an important balancer in the European debate between those (such as France) inclined to view the continent's search for 'strategic autonomy' independently from the US, and those who support increasing European capabilities more clearly within the framework of NATO. The extent to which a compromise emerges between the fundamentally differ-

ent outlooks and strategic cultures entrenched in Paris and
Berlin is critical (as seen, for example, in the rhetorical debate
about an intergovernmental 'Europe de la defénce' versus a
more federalist 'European army'). Franco-German leadership
alone is no longer enough to assure progress, but its absence
substantively diminishes its prospects. An effective compromise would provide a centre around which other European
states can coalesce.

There are serious short-term constraints on such developments, most obviously in terms of Germany's capabilities and
domestic politics. The Bundeswehr is in a perilous state. As
von der Leyen has warned, 'You cannot catch up in two years,
25 years of cuts'.[9] Fast-tracking those projects best suited to
delivering quick and visible results would help alleviate allied
scrutiny, most notably from the US, but fixing Germany's readiness problem and operational credibility will require not just
money but also perseverance and patience. Nor will a greater
willingness to engage in defence and security capacity-building
– helping others to help themselves – be sufficient. Germany
will need to show that it is politically willing and able to lead
in partnership with France and its other European partners. On
occasion, moreover, forces will also need to operate in circumstances where there is no reliable partner to be found. Taking
'more responsibility' will have to mean more than training
others how to do likewise.

The degree and nature of any Franco-German compromise
will also be important for European defence-industrial cooperation. Bringing perspectives on arms exports, for example,
into closer alignment will not be easy, but it will be critical. At
a minimum, Berlin's positioning on arms exports will need to
become more predictable if partners, most notably in Paris, are
to invest more systematically and substantively in the development of joint capabilities that require an export market to

make them financially viable. (In general terms, German arms exports to EU and NATO members, along with six other countries, require justification *not* to proceed. By contrast, exports to countries beyond this first grouping require justification *to* proceed.) The Middle East and North Africa will be increasingly important markets for European arms exports. Instability and authoritarian governments in these areas will continue to stoke Germany's political debate over arms exports, and affect the calculations of Germany's partners as they consider the degree to which they are willing to outsource to Berlin decisions on where they can and cannot sell military equipment. Follow-through on the 2019 Treaty of Aachen promise to develop a common approach to weapons exports on joint projects will be critical for the progress of key programmes, most notably the Future Combat Aircraft System, a future main battle tank and a future combat drone. Aachen also sets up a bilateral defence and security council to oversee its defence commitments, slated to 'convene regularly at the highest level', that might in time emerge as a useful vehicle for setting broader European trends on critical issues of defence and security policy.

Evolve or perish

Europe's strategic environment is bleak, but this reality is, belatedly, propelling greater European interest, investment and engagement on issues of foreign, security and defence policy. The open question is whether Europe and the EU can make enough progress to deflect the accusations of 'too little, too late' that have dogged the continent since at least the euro crisis.

Intergovernmentalism and incrementalism are likely to remain the order of the day. Over time, however, efforts to develop more effective EU foreign and security policies are likely to yield some success. This may see the emergence of a

core of more active member states which, in turn, will intro-
duce a new set of dynamics and tensions to the EU project.
These efforts are likely to be stimulated by long-term trends
and challenges such as migration and hybrid warfare, which
require particular coordination between state (and non-state)
actors.

The EU will at least attempt to stand for the defence of the
liberal order even as others are wavering, and as its own institutions face illiberal challenges from within. In contrast, but not
paradoxically, it will also behave more modestly and flexibly
in order to secure the deals that the security and interests of its
citizens demand. Member states will continue to take centre
stage, but as the web of interactions between them becomes
denser, the EU's central institutions have a role to play in the
stage management of those interactions. Where more decisive action is required, Europe will continue to operate under
the umbrella of broader partnerships with other international
security organisations or actors. But it will need also to be able
to stand alone.

As Europe's foreign, security and defence policies continue
to evolve, it will still be able to fall back on other sources of global
influence. Even if its relative geo-economic power is declining,
its absolute position remains strong. The EU is still the world's
largest trading bloc, and the largest trading partner for some 80
countries around the world. In 2016, the EU had more Fortune
500 companies than India, Russia and the US combined, and
13 of the world's top 25 most competitive national economies
were still to be found on the European continent.[10] The euro
remains a credible international currency and, at least for
some, even a dominant reserve currency in waiting. Europe
still needs to address problems, such as underinvestment in
R&D by public and private actors and the relative paucity of
risk-taking venture capital, which threaten innovation, espe-

cially in security and defence technologies.[11] Nevertheless, the EU's geo-economic profile is a strategic strength.

The EU faces tough challenges that might yet tear it apart. As it negotiates its next seven-year budget, the individual interests of nation-states will be on full and uncomfortable display. From 2019 to at least 2024, the European Parliament will include anti-establishment politicians in unprecedented numbers. But in foreign, security and defence policy, where the EU has long underperformed, positive changes are visible. These will not be revolutionary, but they should start to make the continent more secure and more able to project influence, at least in its immediate neighbourhood. By itself, this is unlikely to be sufficient to uphold multilateralism and the established international order, but in partnership with others, Europe can play a key role in marshalling resistance to and bolstering resilience against those intent on tearing these down.

Any final judgement on Europe and the EU's profile in foreign, security and defence policy must acknowledge the evolving character of strategic competition and conflict and its likely future nature. In their rise to strategic prominence, powers such as China have been refreshing and expanding the tools that can be used in strategic competition and, if necessary, conflict. Powers are increasingly willing and able to leverage their economic interactions and investments to strategic effect, as China's Belt and Road Initiative demonstrates. The EU's 'connectivity strategy' announced in September 2018 partly in response to China's initiative may be vague, but the challenge it recognises is not. As the EU attempts to engage more substantively here, it will draw on its experiences in enhancing connectivity between its own member states and within its neighbourhood.

The standards by which strategic influence will be judged in future might be better suited to European capabilities and sensitivities than the more exclusive focus on traditional military capabilities of previous years. Demand is likely to grow, for example, for civilian crisis-management skills such as policing, where the EU has much credibility and looks to increase its attentions further, in particular with regard to civilian capacities under the CSDP. But in these changing circumstances, open societies can be particularly vulnerable to pressure and manipulation by hostile interests. If the EU cannot step up its security cooperation in particular, some of its biggest strengths, for example its openness to international trade and investment and the degree to which it has adopted digital technology, threaten to become some of its greatest weaknesses.

That crises can be opportunities is already part of the EU's short history. Yet opportunities must be seized. Stagnation and a slide into strategic irrelevance are an entirely possible ending for one of the most extraordinary experiments in supranational government and intergovernmental cooperation in history. This past decade of crises has been brutal for Europe and its Union. Strategies that have kept the EU together in the past will not necessarily keep it together in the future. The EU will have to change in order to survive. For years it has indulged itself in the illusion that soft power and strong partners are sufficient to defend the continent's security and interests. Those most invested in that outlook now accept that the world has moved on, and that Europe must follow.

NOTES

Introduction

1 'Europe Must Not Become a "Plaything" of Great Powers, says Macron in Berlin', France24, 18 November 2018, https://www.france24.com/en/20181118-live-macron-german-parliament-bundestag-merkel-france-germany-eu.

2 European External Action Service, 'Shared Vision, Common Action: A Stronger Europe – A Global Strategy for the European Union's Common Foreign and Security Policy', June 2016, available at http://europa.eu/globalstrategy/en.

3 Richard Dobbs et al., *Urban World: Cities and the Rise of the Consuming Class* (Brussels, San Francisco and Shanghai: McKinsey Global Institute, June 2012), p. 17.

4 Stefan Lehne, 'Merkel and Macron Need to Talk about EU Foreign Policy', Carnegie Strategic Europe blog, 14 December 2017, https://carnegieeurope.eu/strategiceurope/75017.

5 Dan Steinbock, 'The Global Economic Balance of Power is Shifting', World Economic Forum, 20 September 2017, https://www.weforum.org/agenda/2017/09/the-global-economic-balance-of-power-is-shifting.

6 Moody's Investor Service, 'Moody's: Aging Will Reduce Economic Growth Worldwide in the Next Two Decades', press release, 6 August 2014, https://www.moodys.com/research/Moodys-Aging-will-reduce-economic-growth-worldwide-in-the-next--PR_305951.

7 *Ibid.*

8 For one survey of these challenges, see John West, *Asian Century ... on a Knife Edge: A 360 Degree Analysis of Asia's Recent Economic Development* (Basingstoke: Palgrave Macmillan, 2018).

9 See, for example, Kishore Mahbubani, 'The Case Against the West: America and Europe in the Asian Century', *Foreign Affairs*, vol. 87, no. 3, May–June 2008, pp. 111–24.

10 'President Trump Remarks at Rally in Fargo, North Dakota', C-Span, 27 June 2018, https://www.c-span.org/video/?447664-1/president-trump-delivers-remarks-fargo-north-dakota. He argued that the EU had been repeatedly raiding the US 'piggybank'.

11 'Presidential Candidate Donald Trump Rally in Raleigh, North Carolina',

C-Span, 7 November 2016, https://www.c-span.org/video/?418210-1/donald-trump-campaigns-raleigh-north-carolina.

12 For the consolidated texts of the TEU and TFEU, see https://eur-lex.europa.eu/legal-content/EN/TXT/?uri=CELEX:12016ME/TXT.

13 See, for example, 'European Foreign Policy Scorecard 2012', European Council on Foreign Relations, https://www.ecfr.eu/page/-/ECFR_SCORECARD_2012_WEB.pdf.

14 European Political Strategy Centre, 'Strong Europe, Better World', 22 January 2019, available at https://ec.europa.eu/epsc/publications/other-publications/strong-europe-better-world_en.

15 See, for example, the EU's 2017 External Investment Plan and its fact sheet on Africa, available at https://ec.europa.eu/commission/sites/beta-political/files/soteu2018-factsheet-africa-europe_en.pdf. The plan aims to see an EU contribution of €4.1 billion leverage up to €44bn by 2020.

16 Ministry of Foreign Affairs of Japan, 'National Security Strategy 2013', p. 27, available at https://www.cas.go.jp/jp/siryou/131217anzenhoshou/nss-e.pdf.

17 Jean-Claude Juncker, 'State of the Union 2018: The Hour of European Sovereignty', 12 September 2018, available at https://ec.europa.eu/commission/sites/beta-political/files/soteu2018-speech_en_0.pdf.

18 The complete objectives of the EU's external actions are laid out in the TEU. This includes the statement, in Article 3.1, that 'The Union's aim is to promote peace, its values, and the well-being of its peoples'. The full programme for the EU's external actions, where 'the Union shall define and pursue common policies', is laid out in Article 21.

19 TEU, Article 21.2(c).

20 Björn Fägersten, 'The Ukraine Crisis has Highlighted the Flaws in the EU's Technocratic Approach to Foreign Policy', LSE European Politics and Policy (EUROPP) blog, 8 May 2014, available at http://eprints.lse.ac.uk/71978/.

21 Gideon Rachman, 'Mid-sized Powers Must Unite to Preserve the World Order', *Financial Times*, 28 May 2018, https://www.ft.com/content/546ca388-625d-11e8-90c2-9563a0613e56.

22 Annett Meiritz, Anna Reimann and Severin Weiland, 'A Trans-Atlantic Turning Point: What was Merkel Thinking?', *Spiegel*, 29 May 2017, https://www.spiegel.de/international/germany/merkel-and-trump-a-trans-atlantic-turning-point-a-1149757.html.

23 Max de Haldevang, 'Being the Anti-Trump is the Must Have Look at This Week's UN General Assembly', *Quartz*, 20 September 2017, https://qz.com/1082972/unga-2017-federica-mogherini-outlined-the-european-unions-values-to-set-it-apart-from-the-us-under-trump/.

Chapter One

1 Gilles Grin, 'Shaping Europe: The Path to European Integration according to Jean Monnet', Jean Monnet Foundation for Europe, Debates and Documents Collection, issue 7, March 2017. For GDP and population figures, see https://www.ecb.europa.eu/press/key/date/2017/html/ecb.sp170504.en.html.

2 Jean Monnet, 'L'Europe et la nécessité', *Archives de la Fondation Jean Monnet pour l'Europe*, May 1974.

3 François Duchêne, 'The European Community and the Uncertainties of Interdependence', in Max Kohnstamm and Wolfgang Hager (eds), *A Nation Writ Large? Foreign-Policy Problems before the European Community* (London: Palgrave Macmillan, 1973), p. 19. Duchêne later became a director of the IISS.

4 Hedley Bull, 'Civilian Power Europe: A Contradiction in Terms?', *Journal of Common Market Studies*, vol. 21, no. 2, December 1982, p. 151.

5 John McWilliam, House of Commons Debate, 10 April 2002, Hansard HC series 5, vol. 383, col. 24WH (10 April 2002), https://publications.parliament.uk/pa/cm200102/cmhansrd/vo020410/halltext/20410h02.htm.

6 Donna G. Star, 'An Analysis of European Political Cooperation During the Persian Gulf Crisis', *Penn State International Law Review*, vol. 10, no. 3, art. 4, 1992, p. 452.

7 Quoted by Craig Whitney, 'Gulf Fighting Shatters Europeans' Fragile Unity', *New York Times*, 25 January 1991, https://www.nytimes.com/1991/01/25/world/war-in-the-gulf-europe-gulf-fighting-shatters-europeans-fragile-unity.html.

8 For more on the Petersberg tasks, see http://eur-lex.europa.eu/summary/glossary/petersberg_tasks.html. The Petersberg tasks were named after the hotel in Bonn where they were signed. The original tasks can be found in the Petersberg Declaration of the Western European Union, Council of Ministers, Bonn, 19 June 1992, ch. II, para. 4.6. The updated Petersberg tasks are set out in Article 17.2 of the TEU.

9 Cologne European Council, Presidency Conclusions, Annex III, available at http://ue.eu.int/en/info/eurocouncil/.

10 See, for example, Jan Zielonka, *Explaining Euro-Paralysis: Why Europe is Unable to Act in International Politics* (Basingstoke: Macmillan, 1998), p. 229.

11 For discussion, see Helene Sjursen, 'Missed Opportunity or Eternal Fantasy? The Idea of a European Security and Defence Policy', in John Peterson and Helene Sjursen (eds), *A Common Foreign Policy for Europe? Competing Visions of CFSP* (London: Routledge, 1998), pp. 95–112.

12 For more information, see the Civilian Headline Goal for 2008, https://eur-lex.europa.eu/legal-content/EN/TXT/?uri=LEGISSUM%3Al33239.

13 See, for example, TEU Declarations 13 and 14, which declare the changes 'do not affect the responsibilities of Member States as they currently exist', and do not 'prejudice the specific character of the security and defence policy of member states'. For more on the Treaty of Lisbon, see http://www.europarl.europa.eu/factsheets/en/sheet/5/the-treaty-of-lisbon.

14 The mutual defence clause is Article 42.7 of the TEU. The mutual solidarity clause is in Part V, Title VII, Article 222 of the TFEU.

15 High Representative and European Commission, 'The EU's Comprehensive Approach to External Conflict and Crises', Joint Communication to the EU Parliament and Council, JOIN(2013) 30 final, 12 December 2013.

16 See, for example, the EC statement on enlargement as 'the Union's most successful foreign policy instrument'. Commission of the European Communities, 'Communication from the Commission: Wider Europe – Neighbourhood: A New Framework for Relations with our Eastern and Southern Neighbours', COM(2003) 104 final, Brussels, 11 March 2003, p. 5.

17 Romano Prodi, 'A Wider Europe – a Proximity Policy as the Key to Stability', speech to the Sixth ECSA-World Conference, Brussels, 5–6 December 2002.

18 See, for example, Hilmar Linnenkamp and Christian Molling, 'A Doable Agenda for the European Defence Council 2013', SWP Comments, no. 28, August 2013.

19 George Soros, 'The Future of Europe', remarks delivered at the Global Economic Symposium, Kiel, Germany, 10 January 2013.

20 Peter Spiegel, 'How the Euro was Saved', Financial Times, 11 May 2014, https://www.ft.com/content/f6f4d6b4-ca2e-11e3-ac05-00144feabdc0.

21 Ibid.

22 Mario Draghi, speech at the Global Investment Conference in London, 26 July 2012.

23 Thomas Wright, 'Europe's Lost Decade', Survival, vol. 55, no. 6, December 2013–January 2014, p. 7.

24 The crisis is sometimes portrayed as a sovereign-debt crisis, but some argue that the crisis was more often the cause of these deficits rather than vice versa. Spain and Ireland, for example, had fiscal surpluses and low debt-to-GDP ratios before the crisis hit. Meanwhile, Belgium and Italy, which had extraordinarily high debts, made it through without requiring a bailout. For more on this, see, for example, Joseph Stiglitz, 'How to Save a Broken Euro', Euractiv, 1 July 2014, https://www.euractiv.com/section/euro-finance/opinion/stiglitz-how-to-save-a-broken-euro/, or R.A. London, 'The Euro Crisis was not a Government-debt Crisis', Economist Free Exchange, 23 November 2015, https://www.economist.com/free-exchange/2015/11/23/the-euro-crisis-was-not-a-government-debt-crisis.

25 Only a month earlier, Spanish foreign minister Jose Manuel Garcia-Margallon had already publicly expressed his personal scepticism about the logic of sanctions. Explaining Spain's interest in mending ties, he had argued that the EU needed to take Russia's interests in Ukraine into account in its own interactions with Ukraine. See Andrew Rettman, 'Spain: Russia Sanctions Beneficial for No One', EUObserver, 10 March 2015, https://euobserver.com/foreign/127940.

26 Timothy Garton Ash, quoted in Neil Buckley and Andrew Byrne, 'The Rise and Rise of Viktor Orban', Financial Times, 25 January 2018, https://www.ft.com/content/dda50a3e-0095-11e8-9650-9c0ad2d7c5b5.

27 See, for example, the late 2017 threat by the Hungarian foreign minister to block every issue important to Ukraine in international organisations. For more on its motivation and consequences, see Peter Kreko and Patrik Szicherle, 'Why is Hungary blocking Ukraine's Western Integration?', Atlantic

Council UkraineAlert blog, 16 January 2018, https://www.atlanticcouncil.org/blogs/ukrainealert/why-is-hungary-blocking-ukraine-s-western-integration. Orbán's early political career was characterised by a fiercely anti-Russian stance. This shifted from around 2010 with his espousal of an 'Eastern Way'.

28 Emmanuel Macron, speech at Humboldt University, Berlin, 10 January 2017.

29 Angelos Chryssogelos, 'Euro Crisis Eroding EU Foreign Policy', Chatham House Expert Comment, 15 May 2015, https://www.chathamhouse.org/expert/comment/17679.

30 Statement by UNHCR Commissioner Navi Pillay on 12 February 2013, reported in Ashley Fantz, 'Syria Death Toll Probably at 70,000, U.N. Human Rights Official Says', CNN, 13 February 2013, https://edition.cnn.com/2013/02/12/world/meast/syria-death-toll/index.html.

31 Andrew Rettman, 'EU Sheds no Tears over Morsi's Departure', EUObserver, 4 July 2013, https://euobserver.com/foreign/120758.

32 'Joint Statement on Fighting near Gharyan, Libya', 4 April 2019, https://www.state.gov/r/pa/prs/ps/2019/04/290918.htm.

33 For a European Council briefing on how individual member states responded to this activation, see http://www.europarl.europa.eu/thinktank/en/document.html?reference=EPRS_BRI(2016)581408.

34 Julia Lisiecka, 'After the Arab Spring, What's Changed?', EU Institute for Security Studies, May 2017, https://www.iss.europa.eu/sites/default/files/EUISSFiles/SMS_3_Arab_Spring%20%281%29.pdf. In 2015, 84% of EU money came from just four donors – the EU (33%), Germany (22%), the UK (15%) and France (14%).

35 'European Neighbourhood Policy And Enlargement Negotiations: Southern Neighbourhood', https://ec.europa.eu/neighbourhood-enlargement/neighbourhood/southern-neighbourhood_en.

36 Foreign Fighters: An Updated Assessment of the Flow of Foreign Fighters into Syria and Iraq (New York: The Sofan Group, December 2015), available at http://soufangroup.com/wp-content/uploads/2015/12/TSG_ForeignFightersUpdate3.pdf.

37 Arab Human Development Report 2016: Youth and the Prospects for Human Development in a Changing Reality (New York: UN Development Programme, Regional Bureau for Arab States, 2016), pp. 175–6.

38 For a full timeline of these sanctions and their contents, see https://eeas.europa.eu/headquarters/headquarters-homepage/30963/eu-restrictive-measures-response-crisis-ukraine_en.

39 UN Office of the High Commissioner for Human Rights, Report on the Human Rights Situation in Ukraine 16 February to 15 May 2017, 15 May 2017, p. 2, available at https://www.refworld.org/docid/5940f16f4.html.

40 See the Global Internal Displacement Database at http://www.internal-displacement.org/database/. For more on this, see Beth Mitchneck, Jane Zavisca and Theodore P. Gerber, 'Europe's Forgotten Refugees', Foreign Affairs: Snapshot, 24 August 2016, https://www.foreignaffairs.com/articles/ukraine/2016-08-24/europes-forgotten-refugees-0.

41 Mike Elleman, 'The Secret to North Korea's ICBM Success', IISS Voices

blog, 14 August 2017, https://www.iiss.org/blogs/analysis/2017/08/north-korea-icbm-success.

[42] The increase in interceptions can also be attributed to NATO's enhancement of its air policing. See Damian Sharokov, 'NATO: Russian Aircraft Intercepted 110 Times above Baltic, in 2016', *Newsweek*, 4 January 2017, https://www.newsweek.com/nato-intercepted-110-russian-aircraft-around-baltic-2016-538444.

[43] Dmitri Trenin, 'The Revival of the Russian Military', *Foreign Affairs*, vol. 95, no. 3, May–June 2016, p. 28.

[44] For more on *Zapad*, see 'The wider implications of Zapad 2017', IISS Strategic Comments, vol. 24, no. 2, 17 January 2018.

[45] Jochen Rehrl, 'Migration and CSDP', in Jochen Rehrl (ed.), *Handbook on CSDP*, vol. 1, 3rd ed. (Vienna: Directorate for Security Policy, Austrian Ministry of Defence and Sports, 2017), p. 112.

[46] 'Irregular Migration via the Central Mediterranean: From Emergency Responses to Systemic Solutions', ESPC Strategic Notes, no. 22, 2 February 2017, https://ec.europa.eu/epsc/publications/strategic-notes/irregular-migration-central-mediterranean_en.

[47] For a current list of Schengen states who have reintroduced internal border controls, see https://ec.europa.eu/home-affairs/what-we-do/policies/borders-and-visas/schengen/reintroduction-border-control_en.

[48] International Organisation for Migration, 'Flow Monitoring: Europe', http://migration.iom.int/europe/. Data as of 27 August 2018.

[49] European Commission, 'Relocation: Commission refers the Czech Republic, Hungary and Poland to the Court of Justice', press release, 7 December 2017, http://europa.eu/rapid/press-release_IP-17-5002_en.htm.

[50] In 2017, in Italy alone, there were five hotspots operating across its main islands, offering a collective capacity of 7,450 'reception facilities'. For one brief on hotspots and the concerns surrounding them, see 'Hotspots at EU External Borders: State of Play', European Parliament briefing by the European Parliamentary Research Service, June 2018.

[51] Médecins Sans Frontières, 'Families Trapped on Islands on the Brink of a Humanitarian Emergency', press release, 5 December 2017, http://www.msf.org/en/article/greece-families-trapped-islands-brink-humanitarian-emergency.

[52] Office of the High Commissioner for Human Rights, press release, 14 November 2017, http://www.ohchr.org/EN/NewsEvents/Pages/DisplayNews.aspx?NewsID=22393&LangID=E.

[53] International Organisation for Migration, 'Flow Monitoring: Europe'.

[54] Ivan Krastev, 'Germany's Problem is Europe's Problem', *New York Times*, 4 October 2017, https://www.nytimes.com/2017/10/04/opinion/germany-europe-east-west.html.

[55] Amnesty International, 'EU: New Migration Plans "Dangerous and Self Serving"', press release, 29 June 2018, https://www.amnesty.org/en/latest/news/2018/06/eu-new-migration-plansdangerous-and-selfserving/.

[56] Boris Johnson, 'The Only Continent with Weaker Economic Growth than Europe is Antarctica', *Telegraph*, 29 May 2016, https://www.telegraph.co.uk/news/2016/05/29/the-only-continent-with-weaker-economic-growth-than-europe-is-an/.

[57] The Electoral Commission, 'EU Referendum Results', https://www.

electoralcommission.org.uk/find-information-by-subject/elections-and-referendums/past-elections-and-referendums/eu-referendum/electorate-and-count-information.

58 Discussion with British official, December 2015.

59 European External Action Service, 'Shared Vision, Common Action: A Stronger Europe – A Global Strategy for the European Union's Common Foreign and Security Policy', June 2016, available at http://europa.eu/globalstrategy/en.

60 G. John Ikenberry, 'The Plot against American Foreign Policy', *Foreign Affairs*, vol. 96, no. 3, May–June 2017, pp. 2–9.

61 'Remarks by Secretary Gates at the Security and Defense Agenda, Brussels, Belgium', 10 June 2011, http://archive.defense.gov/Transcripts/Transcript.aspx?TranscriptID=4839. For one take on this, see Hans Kundani and Jana Puglierin, 'Atlanticist and "Post Atlanticist" Wishful Thinking', GMF Policy Essay, 3 January 2018, http://www.gmfus.org/publications/atlanticist-and-post-atlanticist-wishful-thinking.

62 Heiko Maas, 'For a Balanced Trans-atlantic Partnership', *Handelsblatt*, 22 August 2018, available at https://www.auswaertiges-amt.de/en/newsroom/news/maas-handelsblatt/2129154.

63 Peter Wise, 'Portugal Grows at Fastest Rate Since 2000', *Financial Times*, 14 February 2018., https://www.ft.com/content/cd5642e2-1175-11e8-8cb6-b9ccc4c4dbbb

64 Charles Forelle, Pat Minczeski and Elliot Bentley, 'Greece's Debt Due', *Wall Street Journal*, 19 February 2015, http://graphics.wsj.com/greece-debt-timeline/.

65 Matt O'Brien, 'Greece's Economic Crisis is Over Only if You Don't Live There', *Washington Post*, 26 April 2018, https://www.washingtonpost.com/news/wonk/wp/2018/04/26/greeces-economic-crisis-is-over-only-if-you-dont-live-there/?utm_term=.1a99e4ed84cf.

66 Draghi, speech at the Global Investment Conference in London, 26 July 2012.

67 'Russian Security Chief Warns Ukraine Could Lose Statehood', Tass, 15 January 2019, http://tass.com/world/1040080.

68 Laura Smith-Spark, 'Illegal Migration to EU Falls to Lowest Level in 5 Years – but Spikes in Spain', CNN, https://edition.cnn.com/2019/01/05/europe/migrant-figures-drop-europe-intl/index.html.

69 International Organisation for Migration, 'Mediterranean Migrant Arrivals Reach 113,145 in 2018; Deaths Reach 2,242', press release, 21 December 2018, https://www.iom.int/news/mediterranean-migrant-arrivals-reach-113145-2018-deaths-reach-2242.

70 Drew Hinshaw and Anita Komuves, 'Hungary Bucks US Push to Curb Russian and Chinese Influence', *Wall Street Journal*, 27 January 2019, https://www.wsj.com/articles/hungary-bucks-u-s-push-to-curb-russian-and-chinese-influence-11548626080.

Chapter Two

1 Juncker repeatedly used the term 'poly-crisis' to describe the situation the EU faced.

2 Quoted in 'Konrad Adenauer and the European Integration', an Exhibition of the Archive for Christian Democratic Policy of the Konrad Adenauer Foundation, p.5, http://www.kas.de/upload/ACDP/GB_Katalog_KA.pdf. Adenauer was addressing a meeting of his CDU party in 1946.

3 Charles de Gaulle, speech in Strasbourg, France, 23 November 1959.

4 For one perspective, see Harold James, Jean-Pierre Landau and Markus Brunnermeier, *The Euro and the Battle of Ideas* (Princeton, NJ: Princeton University Press, 2016).

5 Lluis Orriols, 'El divorcio ideologico de Europa', eldario.es, 12 June 2013, http://www.eldiario.es/piedrasdepapel/gran-divorcio-ideologico-Europa_6_142145798.html.

6 'Renzi – Reminding Europe of What it Doesn't Have', *EUObserver*, 2 July 2014, https://euobserver.com/eu-election/124846.

7 Joint EU–US Statement on the Asia–Pacific Region, Phnom Penh, 12 July 2012, A328/12, available at https://www.consilium.europa.eu/uedocs/cms_Data/docs/pressdata/EN/foraff/131709.pdf.

8 Personal communications, Berlin, July 2012.

9 Jean-Claude Juncker, 'State of the Union 2015: Time for Honesty, Unity and Solidarity', Strasbourg, 9 September 2015, http://europa.eu/rapid/press-release_SPEECH-15-5614_en.htm.

10 'We Don't Want No Transfer Union', *The Economist*, 2 December 2010, https://www.economist.com/europe/2010/12/02/we-dont-want-no-transfer-union.

11 'Merkel Says Euro Bonds are "Absolutely Wrong"', Reuters, 15 September 2011, https://www.reuters.com/article/us-eurozone-germany-merkel/merkel-says-euro-bonds-are-absolutely-wrong-idUSTRE78E1KZ20110915.

12 For an interesting theory on a north–south governance divide, see Francis Fukuyama, *Political Order and Political Decay: From the Industrial Revolution to the Globalisation of Democracy* (New York: Farrar, Strauss and Giroux, 2014).

13 Anders Åslund, 'The IMF Still Misunderstands the Euro Crisis', ProjectSyndicate, 4 August 2016, https://www.project-syndicate.org/commentary/imf-euro-crisis-response-by-anders-aslund-2016-08?barrier=accesspaylog.

14 See, for example, comments by Guy Verhofstadt seeking greater involvement for the European Parliament in the negotiations over the next round of the EU's budget: 'This is the only parliament worldwide that has no say on income. That has to stop now.' 'Debate with the Prime Minister of Croatia, Andrej Plenković, on the Future of Europe', European Parliament, 6 February 2018.

15 Gideon Rachman, 'Block Juncker to Save Real Democracy in Europe', *Financial Times*, 2 June 2014, https://www.ft.com/content/cofae448-ea38-11e3-8dde-00144feabdco.

16 'Results of the 2014 European Elections', European Parliament, http://www.europarl.europa.eu/

elections2014-results/en/country-results-sk-2014.html.

17 See, for example, tensions through 2018 over the proposed integration of the European Stability Mechanism (established through intergovernmental treaty) into EU law in the form of a European Monetary Fund. 'Integration of the ESM into EU law by way of creating a European Monetary Fund (EMF)', http://www.europarl.europa.eu/legislative-train/theme-deeper-and-fairer-economic-and-monetary-union/file-integration-of-the-esm-into-eu-law-by-creating-an-emf.

18 For more on the historical evolution of the Eurogroup, see, for example, Uwe Putter, *The Eurogroup: How a Secretive Circle of Finance Ministers Shape European Economic Governance* (Manchester: Manchester University Press, 2006).

19 Björn Fägersten and Catharina Klingspor, 'The Implications of the Euro crisis for European Foreign Policy', UI Occasional Paper no. 22, November 2013, p. 8.

20 See, for example, the EEAS's own review of its activities, published in July 2013, available at http://europeanmemoranda.cabinetoffice.gov.uk/files/2014/04/External_action_servive(_EEAS_Review_July_2013).pdf, or the EU Auditors review of the EEAS in 2014, available at https://www.eca.europa.euLists/ECADocuments/SR14_11/SR14_11_EN.pdf, that specifically highlighted the problem of poor financial resources and planning at the outset of the EEAS.

21 See, for example, the Committee for Civilian Aspects of Crisis Management (CIVCOM), where member-state divisions have been on particular display.

22 See data from the International Institute for Strategic Studies, *The Military Balance*, various years; also statement by NATO Secretary-General Jens Stoltenberg, quoted by David Bond and Gemma Tetlow, 'UK Missed 2% Defence-spending Target, Report Claims', *Financial Times*, 14 February 2018, https://www.ft.com/content/c4005130-10dd-11e8-8cb6-b9ccc4c4dbbb.

23 Lucie Beraud-Sudreau, 'European Defence Spending: The New Consensus', IISS Military Balance blog, 15 February 2018, https://www.iiss.org/blogs/military-balance/2018/02/european-defence-spending. In 2017, European defence spending increased by 3.6% over 2016.

24 'To the Brink – and Back?', *Munich Security Report 2018*, February 2018.

25 Sven Biscop, 'The EU Global Strategy: Realpolitik with European Characteristics', Egmont Security Policy Brief, no. 75, June 2016.

26 See, for example, Eurobarometer survey 464b on the attitudes of EU citizens towards security, published by the EC on 12 December 2017, http://ec.europa.eu/commfrontoffice/publicopinion/index.cfm/Survey/getSurveyDetail/instruments/SPECIAL/surveyKy/1569.

27 Rachman, 'Block Juncker to Save Real Democracy in Europe'.

28 For more on the inherent tensions and problematic relationship between the two tracks of European integration, see Kathleen McNamara, 'A Less Perfect Union: Europe after the Greek Debt Crisis', *Foreign Affairs* Snapshot, 19 July 2015, https://www.foreignaffairs.com/articles/western-europe/2015-07-19/less-perfect-union.

29 Bruno Waterfield, 'Francois Hollande tells European Commission it can't

"Dictate" to France', *Telegraph*, 29 May 2013, http://www.telegraph.co.uk/finance/financialcrisis/10088005/Francois-Hollande-tells-European-Commission-it-cant-dictate-to-France.html.

30 European Commission, 'Towards a Sustainable and Fair Common European Asylum System' press release, 4 May 2016, http://europa.eu/rapid/press-release_IP-16-1620_en.htm.

31 For details of the proposed reform, see *ibid*.

32 The road map noted the EU's role as the first world's 'first responder'. In 2016, the EU granted asylum to and resettled three times as many refugees as the US, Canada and Australia combined. See European Commission, 'Migration: A Roadmap', https://ec.europa.eu/home-affairs/sites/homeaffairs/files/what-we-do/policies/european-agenda-migration/20171207_migration_a_roadmap_en.pdf.

33 Conversation with EC official, 12 February 2018.

34 For one example of the many articles praising this, see 'Rediscovering the Fundamental Value of EU Solidarity', *Irish Times*, 14 May 2018, https://www.irishtimes.com/opinion/editorial/rediscovering-the-fundamental-eu-value-of-solidarity-1.3493615.

35 For more details, see Stefan Lehne, 'Are Prime Ministers Taking Over EU Foreign Policy?', Carnegie Europe, 16 February 2015, https://carnegieeurope.eu/2015/02/16/are-prime-ministers-taking-over-eu-foreign-policy-pub-59070.

36 Alex Barker and Peter Spiegel, 'EU Sets Out Framework for Banking Union', *Financial Times*, 11 December 2013, https://www.ft.com/content/f65fa1ee-61e6-11e3-aa02-00144feabdc0.

37 Mark Bromley, *Export Controls, Human Security and Cyber-surveillance Technology: Examining the Proposed Changes to the EU Dual-use Regulation* (Stockholm: SIPRI, 2017).

38 See, for example, the European Commission's 2009 Defence Procurement Directive, transferred into national law in all EU member states by 2013, and its Transfers of Defence-Related Products Directive of the same year.

39 Poland remains legally committed to adopting the euro, but one reason it weathered the global financial crisis so well was because it had not yet done so. In 2012, one Polish commentator argued 'the main long-term threat [to the Polish economy] stems from the country's future participation in the euro'. Witold M. Orlowski, 'Poland has Survived the Economic Crisis Remarkably Well, but the Country Faces a Future Dilemma over Adopting the Euro', LSE EUROPP blog, 25 September 2012, https://blogs.lse.ac.uk/europpblog/2012/09/25/poland-economic-success-orlowski/.

40 'White Paper on the Future of Europe: Five Scenarios', 1 March 2017, https://ec.europa.eu/commission/white-paper-future-europe/white-paper-future-europe-five-scenarios_en.

41 David Herszenhorn, 'EU's Iran Fight is Not about Iran (or Trump)', Politico, 30 January 2019, https://www.politico.eu/article/eu-iran-fight-diplomacy-nuclear-deal/.

42 Discussions with German Foreign Office officials. See, for example, the warning of Polish President Andrzej Duda in September 2017 that, should countries be excluded from the inner core, it would mark the 'beginning of the end of the Union'.

43 For further discussion, see Emmanuel Morlon-Druol, 'Rethinking Franco-German Relations: A Historical Perspective', Bruegel, November 2017, http://bruegel.org/2017/11/rethinking-franco-german-relations-a-historical-perspective/.

44 François Heisbourg, 'The Union at Europe's Heart is Frayed', *Financial Times*, 20 January 2013, https://www.ft.com/content/871534b8-6005-11e2-8d8d-00144feab49a.

45 Quentin Peel and Hugh Carnegy, 'Europe: An Uneven Entente', *Financial Times*, 20 January 2013, https://www.ft.com/content/37c2ae62-6182-11e2-9545-00144feab49a.

46 Conversation with German Chancellery official, December 2015.

47 Conversation with former senior French MoD official, Brussels, January 2017.

48 For one take on shifting French interests in EU defence cooperation, see Claudia Major and Christian Mölling, 'France Moves from EU Defence to European Defence', Carnegie Strategic Europe blog, 7 December 2017, https://carnegieeurope.eu/strategic europe/74944.

49 'Flexing its Muscles', *The Economist*, 17 August 2013, https://www.economist.com/europe/2013/08/17/flexing-its-muscles.

50 Jana Kobzova, 'The Visgrad Group in Eastern Europe: An Actor Not a Leader (Yet)', V4 Review, 4 April 2012, http://visegradrevue.eu/?p=561.

51 For details on Germany's positioning towards the V4, see Andrea Gawrich and Maxim Stepanov, 'German Foreign Policy towards the Visegrad Countries', DGAP Analysis, 29 September 2014.

52 See Orbán's speech at the XXV Bálványos Free Summer University and Youth Camp, 26 July 2014, available at https://budapestbeacon.com/full-text-of-viktor-orbans-speech-at-baile-tusnad-tusnadfurdo-of-26-july-2014/.

53 See http://www.norden.org/en. For more on the difficulties of institutional cooperation in recent years, see Christian Opitz and Tobias Etzold, 'Seeking Renewed Relevance: Institutions of Nordic Cooperation in the Reform Process', SWP Comment 2018/C 03, January 2018.

54 For example, Catherine Gregout has argued that the Quint can serve a useful leadership purpose within the EU. Catherine Gregout, *European Foreign and Security Policy: States, Power, Institutions and American Hegemony* (Toronto: University of Toronto Press, 2010).

55 Conversation with UK diplomat, late February 2012. Campbell travelled to Brussels and London on 22–23 February. Confirmed in conversation with a former US State Department official at the IISS Shangri-la Dialogue, June 2012.

56 Conversations with several member-state diplomats at the time of both the Campbell visit and shortly after the Russell visit.

57 Jean-Claude Juncker, 'A New Start for Europe: My Agenda for Jobs, Growth, Fairness and Democratic Change', Strasbourg, 15 July 2014, https://ec.europa.eu/commission/sites/beta-political/files/juncker-political-guidelines-speech_en.pdf.

58 The European Commission recommended opening negotiations on EU accession with Serbia, and on a Partnership and Stabilisation Agreement with Kosovo. See European Commission, 'Serbia and Kosovo: Historic Agree-

ment Paves the Way for Decisive Progress in their EU Perspectives', press release, 22 April 2013, http://europa.eu/rapid/press-release_IP-13-347_en.htm.

59 Jean-Claude Juncker, 'The European Union: A Source of Stability in a Time of Crisis', 14th Norbert Schmelzer Lecture, The Hague, 3 March 2016.

60 'EU sees Us as Leader, We'll Work Even Harder – PM', B92.net, 7 February 2018, https://www.b92.net/eng/news/politics.php?yyyy=2018&mm=02&dd=07&nav_id=103434,

61 Federica Mogherini, press conference, 6 February 2018, https://eeas.europa.eu/headquarters/headquarters-homepage/39436/remarks-high-representativevice-president-federica-mogherini-college-read-out-present-western_en.

62 Robert-Jan Bartunek and Robin Emmott, 'EU Opens Door to Balkans with 2025 Target for Membership', Reuters, 6 February 2018, https://www.reuters.com/article/us-eu-balkans/eu-opens-door-to-balkans-with-2025-target-for-membership-idUSKBN1FQ1XE.

63 The result was a compromise text setting out 'a path towards opening accession negotiations in June 2019'. Jacopo Barigazzi, 'EU Ministers Postpone Albania and Macedonia Accession Decision', Politico, 26 June 2018, https://www.politico.eu/article/eu-european-union-ministers-general-affairs-council-postpone-albania-and-macedonia-accession-decision/.

64 Tanja Miscevic, 'The EU as Seen from Serbia', ECFR Commentary, 14 March 2018, https://www.ecfr.eu/article/commentary_the_eu_as_seen_from_serbia.

65 Florian Eder and Andrew Gray, 'Brussels' New Balkan Strategy:

Tough Love', Politico, 6 February 2018, https://www.politico.eu/article/europe-balkan-membership-new-strategy-tough-love/.

66 Ruben V. Atoyan et al., 'Public Infrastructure in the Western Balkans: Opportunities and Challenges', IMF Europe Department paper no. 18/02, 17 April 2018, p. 1.

67 These pre-accession mechanisms can be used without necessitating enlargement. Indeed, the term 'pre-accession assistance' is liberally used in the European Commission's 31-page proposal for the next multiannual budget, yet 'enlargement' does not appear once. Georgi Gotev, 'Commission Budget Proposal Hardly Makes EU Enlargement Possible', Euractiv, 2 May 2018, https://www.euractiv.com/section/enlargement/news/commission-budget-proposal-hardly-makes-eu-enlargement-possible/.

68 See, for example, Kemal Kirisci and Onur Bülbül, 'The EU and Turkey Need Each Other. Could Upgrading the Customs Union be the Key?', Brookings Order from Chaos blog, 29 August 2017, https://www.brookings.edu/blog/order-from-chaos/2017/08/29/the-eu-and-turkey-need-each-other-could-upgrading-the-customs-union-be-the-key/.

69 See, for example, Mehmet Ugur, 'Why the EU Should Not Upgrade the Customs Union with Turkey', Social Europe, 8 February 2018, https://www.socialeurope.eu/eu-not-upgrade-customs-union-turkey.

70 See the excellent book by Kemal Kirisci, Turkey and the West: Faultlines in a Troubled Alliance (Washington DC: Brookings Institution Press, 2017).

Chapter Three

1   The definition and objectives of the CFSP can be found in Articles 24 and 21.2 of the TEU respectively.

2   See, for example, an interview with Angela Merkel, 'Schwerwiegend und absolut nicht hinnehmbar', *Frankfurter Allgemeine Zeitung*, 10 September 2017, https://www.faz.net/aktuell/politik/inland/angela-merkel-scharfe-krtik-an-erdogan-im-f-a-s-interview-15191472.html.

3   Discussions with officials, various dates.

4   Italy also contributed to multilateral deployments, sending troops to the UN in Western Sahara, to the EU in CAR and to NATO in Tunisia. For more on this, see Amanda Lapo, 'Italy: Renewed Focus on Overseas Deployments', IISS Military Balance blog, 9 April 2018, https://www.iiss.org/blogs/military-balance/2018/04/italy-renewed-focus-overseas-deployments.

5   Florence Parly, Munich Security Conference, 16 February 2018, quoted in Judy Dempsey, 'Waiting in Munich for European Defence', Carnegie Strategic Europe blog, 16 February 2018, https://carnegieeurope.eu/strategiceurope/75568.

6   Mogherini, announcing the EU–UN second Brussels Conference on 'Supporting the Future of Syria and the Region', 24–25 April 2018, https://eeas.europa.eu/headquarters/headquarters-homepage/39966/syria-eu-un-co-chair-second-brussels-conference-24-25-april_en.

7   David M. Herszenhorn, 'Venezuela's Chaos Exposes EU Disarray on Foreign Policy', Politico, 4 February 2019, https://www.politico.eu/article/venezuela-president-inf-treaty-chaos-exposes-eu-disarray-on-foreign-policy-federica-mogherini/.

8   Emmanuel Macron, addressing a meeting of French ambassadors, 27 August 2018, quoted in 'France Calls On EU To Not Rely On U.S. Defense, Reach Out To Russia', Radio Free Europe/Radio Liberty, https://www.rferl.org/a/france-says-eu-should-not-rely-us-military-defense-reach-out-russia/29456958.html.

9   EUGS, p. 46.

10 Unanimous support is currently required for action on 'sensitive' issues including the CFSP. Article 31.2 of the TEU lists four areas where QMV is permitted. Article 31.3 contains a bridging clause, as yet unused, that allows the European Council unanimously to decide to act on the basis of QMV in other areas, with the support of an absolute majority of MEPs. National parliaments would also have to be notified. An option for 'constructive abstention' under Article 31.1 has only been used once, by Cyprus in 2008 to permit the establishment of EULEX Kosovo. Modest provisions for QMV are provided for with regard to the financing of a start-up fund for military operations (Article 41.3), to decisions of the EDA (Article 45.2) or to PESCO (Article 46).

11 Francis Fukuyama, *The End of History and the Last Man* (New York: The Free Press, 1992), p. xi.

12 John Chipman, speaking at an IISS workshop in Berlin, 27 June 2018.

13 Crispian Balmer, 'Italy Upset Over French Diplomatic Intervention in Libya', Reuters, 24 July 2017, https://www.reuters.com/article/us-italy-france-libya/italy-upset-over-french-

diplomatic-intervention-in-libya-idUSKBN1A926W. For more on the dynamics with Italy and Haftar, see Mattia Toaldo, 'Italy's Dilemmas in Libya', Aspenia Online, 19 September 2016, https://www.aspeniaonline.it/italys-dilemmas-in-libya/.

14 See, for example, 'As Clashes Rage in Libya's Tripoli, Italy Takes a Swipe at France', France24, 4 September 2018, https://www.france24.com/en/20180904-libya-elections-italy-france-salvini-macron-sarkozy-diplomacy.

15 Gideon Rachman, 'Middle-sized Powers must Unite to Preserve the World Order', *Financial Times*, 28 May 2018, https://www.ft.com/content/546ca388-625d-11e8-90c2-9563a0613e56.

16 See, for example, the list of countries aligning themselves with EU sanctions on Belarus at https://www.consilium.europa.eu/uedocs/cms_Data/docs/pressdata/en/cfsp/133277.pdf.

17 See the map on the website of the Estonian European Council Presidency at https://sanctionsmap.eu/#/main.

18 Clara Portela, 'The EU's Sanctions Against Syria: Conflict Management by other Means', Egmont Security Policy Brief, no. 38, September 2012, http://www.egmontinstitute. be/wp-content/uploads/2013/09/SPB38.pdf.

19 See, for example, Liu Jianxi, 'Time to Lift EU's Outdated Arms Embargo on China', *Global Times*, 31 May 2017, http://www.globaltimes.cn/content/1049431.shtml.

20 Clara Portela, 'Member States Resistance to EU Foreign Policy Sanctions', *European Foreign Affairs Review*, vol. 20, no. 2/1, p. 47, August 2015.

21 Robin Emmott, 'Siemens' Crimean Predicament Tests Limits of EU Sanctions', Reuters, 12 July 2017, https://www.reuters.com/article/us-ukraine-crisis-siemens-eu-idUSKBN19X1QE.

22 Ross Denton, 'Significant Changes to UK Sanctions Enforcement Come into Force', *Global Compliance News*, 9 April 2017, https://globalcompliancenews.com/uk-sanctions-enforcement-20170409/.

23 Adam Smith et al., '2017 Year End Sanctions Update', Gibson Dunn & Crutcher, 5 February 2018, https://www.gibsondunn.com/2017-year-end-sanctions-update/.

24 Nate Raymond, 'BNP Paribas Sentenced in $8.9 Billion Accord over Sanctions Violations', Reuters, 1 May 2015, https://www.reuters.com/article/us-bnp-paribas-settlement-sentencing/bnp-paribas-sentenced-in-8-9-billion-accord-over-sanctions-violations-idUSKBN0NM41K20150501.

25 Smith et al., '2017 Year End Sanctions Update'.

26 Population Reference Bureau, '2017 World Population Data Sheet', https://www.prb.org/2017-world-population-data-sheet/.

27 Peter Korzun, 'Marshall Plan with Africa: New EU Foreign Policy Priority', *Strategic Culture Foundation Online Journal*, 1 December 2017, https://www.strategic-culture.org/news/2017/12/01/marshall-plan-with-africa-new-eu-foreign-policy-priority.html.

28 Alex Duval Smith, 'France's Macron Outlines New Approach to African Policy', BBC News, 28 November 2017, https://www.bbc.co.uk/news/world-africa-42151353.

29 Figures as of 9 June 2018. For more details on the EU Trust Fund for Africa, see https://ec.europa.

eu/trustfundforafrica/content/
homepage_en.

30 Jacques Poos, quoted in Alan Riding,
'Conflict in Yugoslavia: Europeans
Send High-level Team', *New York
Times*, 29 June 1991, https://www.
nytimes.com/1991/06/29/world/
conflict-in-yugoslavia-europeans-
send-high-level-team.html.

31 Ben Scott, Stefan Heumann and
Phillipe Lorenz, *Artificial Intelligence
and Foreign Policy* (Berlin: Stiftung Fur
Neue Verantwortung, January 2018).

32 'Foreign Investment Screening and
the China Factor', Rasmussen Global
memo, 16 November 2017, p. 1,
available at https://rasmussenglobal.
com/media/foreign-investment-
screening-china-factor-memo.

33 'China Talks of Building a "Digital
Silk Road"', *The Economist*, 31 May
2018, https://www.economist.com/
china/2018/05/31/china-talks-of-
building-a-digital-silk-road.

34 For further discussion, and on the
strategy in general, see 'Made in China
2025', MERICS Papers on China, no. 2,
December 2016.

35 *Ibid.*, p. 6.

36 Adam Segal, 'Why Does Everyone
Hate Made in China 2025?', CFR blog,
28 March 2018, https://www.cfr.org/
blog/why-does-everyone-hate-made-
china-2025.

37 China's ambitions are outlined in
China's 2017 New Generation AI
Development Plan and Three Year
Action Plan on this issue. See, for
example, Elsa Kania, 'China's AI
Agenda Advances', *Diplomat*, 14
February 2018, https://thediplomat.
com/2018/02/chinas-ai-agenda-
advances/. For more on the European
Commission AI strategy and its failure
to match up to China, see Caroline

Meinhardt et al., 'Europe's AI Strategy
is No Match for China's Global
Dominance', MERICS blog, 29 June
2018, https://www.merics.org/en/blog/
europes-ai-strategy-no-match-chinas-
drive-global-dominance.

38 Guy Chazan, 'Germany Withdraws
Approval for Chinese Takeover of
Tech Group', *Financial Times*, 24
October 2016, https://www.ft.com/
content/f1b3e52e-99b0-11e6-8f9b-70e3
cabccfae.

39 Shawn Donnan, 'Obama Blocks
Chinese Takeover of Tech Group',
Financial Times, 3 December 2016,
https://www.ft.com/content/0c940900-
b8e2-11e6-ba85-95d1533d9a62.

40 'Foreign Investment Screening and the
China Factor'.

41 Gisela Grieger, ''EU Framework for
FDI Screening', European Parliament
Research Service, January 2018, p.2,
http://www.europarl.europa.eu/EPRS/
EPRS-Briefing-614667-EU-framework-
FDI-screening-FINAL.pdf.

42 See, for example, Theodore H.
Moran, 'CFIUS and National
Security: Challenges for the US
and Opportunities for the EU',
draft paper, Peterson Institute for
International Economics, 21 February
2017, https://piie.com/commentary/
speeches-papers/cfius-and-national-
security-challenges-united-states-
opportunities.

43 'Demistifying Chinese Investment in
Australia', KPMG/University of Sydney
report, May 2017, https://home.kpmg.
com/au/en/home/insights/2017/05/
demystifying-chinese-investment-in-
australia-may-2017.html.

44 See, for example, 'France, Germany,
Italy Urge Rethink of Foreign
Investment in EU', Reuters, 14 February
2017, https://www.reuters.com/article/

uk-eu-trade-france/france-germany-italy-urge-rethink-of-foreign-investment-in-eu-idUKKBN15T1ND.

45 For further discussion, see Mathew P. Goodman and Ely Ratner, 'A Better Way to Challenge China on Trade', *Foreign Affairs* Snapshot, 22 March 2018, https://www.foreignaffairs.com/articles/china/2018-03-22/better-way-challenge-china-trade.

Chapter Four

1 Joint Declaration on European Defence issued at the British–French Summit, Saint-Malo, 3–4 December 1998, https://www.cvce.eu/en/obj/franco_british_st_malo_declaration_4_december_1998-en-f3cd16fb-fc37-4d52-936f-c8e9bc80f24f.html.

2 'Juncker: EU Military Forces? All Squawk, No Bite', AFP, 7 May 2015, https://www.defensenews.com/home/2015/05/07/juncker-eu-military-forces-all-squawk-no-bite/.

3 For more details on these constraints and developments, see Chapter Five. See also, for example, Daniel Keohane, 'Constrained Leadership: Germany's New Defence Policy', *CSS Analyses in Security Policy*, no. 201, December 2016.

4 Tobias Buck, 'Hardware: Submarines that Cannot Sail Expose the Impact of Budget Cuts', *Financial Times*, 15 February 2018, https://www.ft.com/content/36e2cd40-0fdf-11e8-940e-08320fc2a277.

5 *Ibid.*

6 Mark Francois, *'Filling the Ranks': A Report for the Prime Minister on the State of Recruiting for the United Kingdom Armed Forces*, September 2017, available at https://www.markfrancois.com/filling-ranks.

7 Richard Barrons, Evidence to UK Commons Defence Committee, National Security Capability Review HC556, 14 November 2017.

8 Problems with night-vision equipment, winter clothing and body armour were reported in the German Ministry of Defence's annual *Report on the Operational Readiness of the Bundeswehr's Primary Weapons Systems: 2017*.

9 EEAS, 'Shared Vision, Common Action', p. 4.

10 2018 and 2019 figures are budget requests. The European Deterrence Initiative was launched by Obama as the European Reassurance Initiative. In 2016, its budget was US$789m. For further details, see Lucie Béraud-Sudreau, 'The US and its NATO Allies: Cost and Value', IISS Military Balance blog, 9 July 2018, https://www.iiss.org/blogs/military-balance/2018/07/us-and-nato-allies-costs-and-value.

11 See EEAS, 'Fact Sheet: Strengthening the Civilian Side of the EU's CSDP', 19 November 2018, https://eeas.europa.eu/headquarters/headquarters-homepage/54030/factsheet-strengthening-civilian-side-eus-common-security-and-defence-policy_en.

12 European Commission, *European Defence Action Plan*, Communication from the European Commission to the European Parliament et al., COM(2016) 950 final, 30 November 2016.

13 Available at http://club.bruxelles2.eu/wp-content/uploads/2016/09/let-fra-all-defensefeuiileroute@fr160911en.pdf.

14 Jacopo Barigazzi, 'Mogherini Hails "Historic" EU Defense Pact', Politico, 13 November 2017, https://www.politico.eu/article/federica-mogherini-defense-hails-historic-eu-defense-pact-as-23-countries-sign-up/.

15 See, for example, 'Third Progress Report on the Implementation of the Common Set of Proposals Endorsed by EU and NATO Councils on 6 December 2016 and 5 December 2017', 6 June 2018, https://www.nato.int/nato_static_fl2014/assets/pdf/pdf_2018_06/20180608_180608-3rd-Joint-progress-report-EU-NATO-eng.pdf.

16 Nick Whitney, 'How to Stop the Demilitarization of Europe', ECFR Policy Brief, 8 November 2011, p. 2. For CARD, see European Council, 'Council Conclusions on Implementing the EU Global Strategy in the area of Security and Defence', 14149/16, 14 November 2016.

17 For further discussion, see Julia Himmlich, 'Can CARD Change European Thinking about Defence Capabilities?', European Leadership Network, September 2017, available at https://www.europeanleadershipnetwork.org/policy-brief/can-card-change-european-thinking-about-capabilities/.

18 See https://www.bruxelles2.eu/wp-content/uploads/2018/11/carte-pesco-2ndvague-b2.jpeg.

19 Claudia Major and Christian Mölling, 'France Moves from EU Defence to European Defence', Carnegie Europe, 7 December 2017, https://carnegieeurope.eu/strategiceurope/74944.

20 Steven Erlanger, 'US Revives Concerns about European Defence Plans, Rattling NATO Allies', New York Times, 18 February 2018, https://www.nytimes.com/2018/02/18/world/europe/nato-europe-us-.html.

21 Madeleine Albright at a NATO ministerial meeting, Brussels, 8 December 1998, quoted in Robert E. Hunter, The European Security and Defence Policy – NATO's Companion or Competitor? (Santa Monica, CA: RAND, 2002), ch. 6.

22 Jonathan Caverley, 'America's Arms Sales Policy: Security Abroad, not Jobs at Home', War on the Rocks, 6 April 2018, https://warontherocks.com/2018/04/americas-arms-sales-policy-security-abroad-not-jobs-at-home/.

23 Non-executive missions do not have a mandate to conduct governmental or executive tasks in support of, or indeed in the absence of, a government. They focus on tasks such as capacity-building and training and constitute around half of EU military operations, but just 13% of EU personnel deployed under CSDP (2017 figures).

24 International Institute for Strategic Studies, The Military Balance 2018 (Abingdon: Routledge for the IISS, 2018), p. 73.

25 For more on developments in this sector, see ibid.

26 Article 346(1)(b) of the TFEU reads 'any Member State may take such measures as it considers necessary for the protection of the essential interests of its security which are connected with the production of or trade in arms, munitions and war material; such measures shall not adversely affect the conditions of competition in the internal market regarding products which are not intended for specifically military purposes'.

27 Article 24.3 of the TEU commits member states to support the EU's external and security policy 'actively

and unreservedly in a spirit of loyalty and mutual solidarity'. It also requires them to refrain from any activity likely to undermine the effectiveness of the EU 'as a cohesive force in international relations'. See Steven Blockmans, *Differentiation in CFSP: Potential and Limits* (Rome: Istituto Affari Internazionali, 8 March 2017), p. 10.

28 IISS, *Military Balance 2018*, p. 67.

29 Figures cited by NATO Secretary General Jens Stoltenberg in February 2018. He referred to 15 states, but the US and the UK are not (or will not be) EU member states. See David Bond and Gemma Tetlow, 'UK missed 2% Defence-spending Target, Report Claims', *Financial Times*, 14 February 2018, https://www.ft.com/content/c4005130-10dd-11e8-8cb6-b9ccc4c4dbbb.

30 Anne-Slyvaine Chassany, 'France to Increase Military Spending', *Financial Times*, 8 February 2018, https://www.ft.com/content/fede4e5a-0cb0-11e8-8eb7-42f857ea9f09.

31 UK House of Commons Public Accounts Committee, 'MoD Lacks Funds to Buy All the Equipment It Says It Needs', 11 May 2018, https://www.parliament.uk/business/committees/committees-a-z/commons-select/public-accounts-committee/news-parliament-2017/defence-equipment-plan-2018-report-published-27-17-19/.

32 Austin Davis and Maximiliane Koschyk, 'Germany Plans Military Spending Hike but is it Enough to Please NATO?', *Deutsche Welle*, 6 February 2019, https://www.dw.com/en/germany-plans-military-spending-hike-but-is-it-enough-to-appease-nato/a-47394560.

33 For the 2024 spending estimate, see Kevin Koerner, 'German Defence Policy: Towards a More Integrated Framework', *Deutsche Bank Research Germany Monitor*, 8 August 2017.

34 For more details, see IISS, *Military Balance 2018*. Although capital expenses account for almost half of Romania's 2017 defence spending, this is intended to change in the coming years, with an increased focus on procurement.

35 Amanda Lapo, 'Italy: Renewed Focus on Overseas Deployments', IISS Military Balance blog, 9 April 2018, https://www.iiss.org/blogs/military-balance/2018/04/italy-renewed-focus-overseas-deployments.

36 Elisabeth Braw, 'The Future of Italy's Military Footprint', RUSI Commentary, 12 June 2018, https://rusi.org/commentary/future-italys-international-military-footprint.

37 Details on current military operations are taken from the website of Italy's Ministry of Defence, 7 March 2019, https://www.difesa.it/EN/Operations/Pagine/MilitaryOperations.aspx.

38 Donald Trump, 'Remarks by President Trump at NATO Unveiling of the Article 5 and Berlin Wall Memorials – Brussels, Belgium', 25 May 2017, https://www.whitehouse.gov/briefings-statements/remarks-president-trump-nato-unveiling-article-5-berlin-wall-memorials-brussels-belgium/.

39 EEAS, 'Fact Sheet: Strengthening the Civilian Side of the EU's CSDP', https://eeas.europa.eu/headquarters/headquarters-homepage/54030/factsheet-strengthening-civilian-side-eus-common-security-and-defence-policy_en.

40 Sebastian Moffet, 'EU Considers Sending 200 Troops to Train in Mali', Reuters, 30 October 2012, https://www.reuters.com/article/us-mali-crisis-eu/eu-considers-sending-

200-troops-to-train-mali-army-idUSBRE89T1DB20121030.

41 Michael Shurkin, *France's War in Mali: Lessons for an Expeditionary Army* (Santa Monica, CA: RAND, 2014).

42 UK Ministry of Defence, 'RAF Helicopters Ready to Support French in Mali', 16 August 2018, https://www.gov.uk/government/news/raf-helicopters-ready-to-support-french-in-mali.

43 'EU Doubles Sahel Force Funding amid Urgent Appeal from African Leaders', France24.com, 3 March 2018, https://www.france24.com/en/20180223-eu-boost-funding-g5-joint-military-force-fighting-jihadists-west-africa-sahel.

44 Richard Reeve, *Mali on the Brink* (London: Peace Direct, 2018).

45 For latest deployment details, see http://eunavfor.eu/deployed-units/surface-vessels/.

46 'Somalia Wants More Help from NATO', *Maritime Executive*, 19 March 2017, https://www.maritime-executive.com/article/somalia-wants-more-help-from-nato.

47 Testimony of Major-General Charlie Stickland to the UK House of Lords Select Committee on the European Union, External Affairs Publication, cited in House of Lords European Union Committee, *Brexit: Common Security and Defence Policy Operations*, HL Paper 132, 14 May 2018, paras 80, 83.

48 The EU provides some 60% of all emergency aid to Somalia. For more on reasons behind the success of *Atalanta*, see House of Lords European Union Committee, *Brexit: Common Security and Defence Policy Operations*, ch. 2.

49 EUCAP Niger is the only CSDP mission specifically to include counter-terrorism in its mandate as of 2018, but other missions have clearly been informed by terrorism concerns.

50 Discussions with EU officials, Brussels, 2018.

51 See https://euvsdisinfo.eu/disinfo-review/.

Chapter Five

1 Jean-Claude Juncker, 'Catching the Wind in Our Sails', State of the Union Address 2017, http://europa.eu/rapid/attachment/SPEECH-17-3165/en/EN-FR-DE-Speech.pdf.

2 Arthur Benz, 'An Asymmetric Two-Level Game. Parliaments in the Euro Crisis', in Ben Crum and John Erik Fossum (eds), *Practices of Inter-Parliamentary Coordination in International Politics: The European Union and Beyond* (Colchester: ECPR Press, 2013), pp. 125–40.

3 Herman Van Rompuy, 'Towards a Genuine Economic and Monetary Union', Report to the European Council, 29 June 2012, https://www.consilium.europa.eu/media/21570/131201.pdf.

4 Jean-Claude Juncker et al., *Completing Europe's Economic and Monetary Union* (Brussels: European Commission, 2015), p. 17, https://ec.europa.eu/commission/sites/beta-political/files/5-presidents-report_en.pdf.

5 Alastair Macdonald, 'Don't be Shy: EU Ombudsman Urges States to End Secrecy of Debates', Reuters, 13 February 2018, https://uk.reuters.com/article/uk-eu-transparency/dont-be-shy-eu-ombudsman-urges-states-to-end-

secrecy-of-debates-idUKKBN1FX0VT?f eedType=RSS&feedName=worldNews.

6   For an argument on the illogicality of such abstentions, see 'Weedkiller Row Sums up the EU's Image Problem', *Financial Times*, 28 November 2017, https://www.ft.com/content/03340022-d434-11e7-a303-9060cb1e5f44.

7   European Commission, 'Subsidiarity Control Mechanism', https://ec.europa.eu/info/law-making-process/how-eu-laws-are-adopted/relations-national-parliaments/subsidiarity-control_en#howitworks.

8   Freedom House's 2019 report recorded a net drop in global freedom for the 13th consecutive year. See *Freedom in the World 2019: Democracy in Retreat* (Washington DC: Freedom House, 2019).

9   Simon Shuster, 'The Populists', *Time*, 7 December 2016, http://time.com/time-person-of-the-year-populism/.

10 Orbán quoted in Patrick Kingsley, 'As West Fears the Rise of Autocrats, Hungary Shows What is Possible', *New York Times*, 10 February 2018, https://www.nytimes.com/2018/02/10/world/europe/hungary-orban-democracy-far-right.html.

11 Kingsley, 'As West Fears the Rise of Autocrats, Hungary Shows What's Possible'. Ignatieff moved the main campus out of the country after becoming a particular target for Orbán's attention.

12 'European Governments in Melt-down over an Inoffensive Migration Compact', *The Economist*, 6 December 2018, https://www.economist.com/europe/2018/12/06/european-governments-in-melt-down-over-an-inoffensive-migration-compact.

13 William Galston, 'The Rise of Populism and the Collapse of the Centre-left', Brookings Order from Chaos blog, 8 March 2018, https://www.brookings.edu/blog/order-from-chaos/2018/03/08/the-rise-of-european-populism-and-the-collapse-of-the-center-left/.

14 Tom Batchelor, 'Hungary's Prime Minister Viktor Orban Praises Donald Trump's "America First" Nationalism', *Independent*, 23 January 2017, https://www.independent.co.uk/news/world/europe/donald-trump-nationalist-hungary-pm-viktor-orban-praise-america-first-a7542361.html.

15 Kay-Alexander Scholz, 'Germany's Right-wing AfD and Donald Trump', *Deutsche Welle*, 1 February 2017, https://www.dw.com/en/germanys-right-wing-afd-and-donald-trump/a-37373538.

16 Henry Olsen, 'Lessons from Italy's Election, Part 1: Death of the "Ins"', The Feed blog, 19 March 2018, https://unherd.com/the-feed-blog/lessons-italys-election-part-1-death-ins/.

17 Donald Trump interview on 'Face the Nation', CBS News, 15 July 2018, https://www.cbsnews.com/news/full-transcript-face-the-nation-july-15-2018/; 'Remarks by President Trump and President Putin of the Russian Federation in Joint Press Conference', Helsinki, 16 July 2018, https://www.whitehouse.gov/briefings-statements/remarks-president-trump-president-putin-russian-federation-joint-press-conference.

18 Some two weeks later Trump did go on record confirming his commitment to Article 5. Robbie Gramer, 'Trump Discovers Article 5 after Disastrous NATO Visit', *Foreign Policy*, 9 June 2017, https://foreignpolicy.com/2017/06/09/trump-discovers-article-5-after-

disastrous-nato-visit-brussels-visit-transatlantic-relationship-europe/.

19 On 14 January 2019, the *New York Times* reported that Trump had repeatedly discussed pulling the US out of NATO. Sarah Sanders argued in the press briefing that followed that this story was meaningless.

20 Mattias Maatthijs, 'The Three Faces of German Leadership', *Survival*, vol. 58, no. 2, April–May 2016, pp. 135–54.

21 'Merkel Ally Demands that Britain "Contribute" to EU Success', *Spiegel Online*, 15 November 2011, https://www.spiegel.de/international/europe/now-europe-is-speaking-german-merkel-ally-demands-that-britain-contribute-to-eu-success-a-798009.html.

22 Nancy Gibbs, 'Person of the Year: Angela Merkel', *Time*, 9 December 2015, http://time.com/time-person-of-the-year-2015-angela-merkel-choice/?iid=toc.

23 See, for example, Jens Boysen-Hogrefe, 'Low Bond Yields have Saved the German Government €80 Billion in Interest since 2009', *Kiel Focus*, June 2013, https://www.ifw-kiel.de/media/kiel-institute-focus/2013/kiel-institute-focus-22.

24 Timothy Garton Ash, 'Everywhere the European Project is Stalling. It Needs a New German Engine', *Guardian*, 15 June 2011, https://www.theguardian.com/commentisfree/2011/jun/15/european-project-new-german-engine. On the same theme of leadership, in November 2015, the *Economist* labelled Angela Merkel 'the indispensable European'.

25 'Libya Crisis Leaves Berlin Isolated', *Spiegel Online*, 28 March 2011, https://www.spiegel.de/international/germany/a-serious-mistake-of-historic-dimensions-libya-crisis-leaves-berlin-isolated-a-753498.html.

26 Radoslaw Sikorski, 'Poland and the Future of the European Union', speech at the Allianz Forum, Berlin, 28 November 2011, available at http://www.mfa.gov.pl/resource/33ce6061-ec12-4da1-a145-01e2995c6302:JCR.

27 Markus Kaim and Constanze Stelzenmüller (eds), *New Power, New Responsibility: Elements of a German Foreign and Security Policy for a Changing World* (Berlin and Washington DC: SWP and GMF, 2013).

28 Joachim Gauck, 'Germany's Role in the World: Reflections on Responsibility, Norms and Alliances', speech at the Munich Security Conference, 31 January 2014, available at http://www.bundespraesident.de/SharedDocs/Reden/EN/JoachimGauck/Reden/2014/140131-Munich-Security-Conference.html.

29 Angela Merkel, 'Introduction', in *White Paper on German Security Policy and the Future of the Bundeswehr* (Berlin: German Federal Ministry of Defence, 2016), p. 6.

30 *White Paper on German Security Policy and the Future of the Bundeswehr*, p. 49.

31 *Ibid.*, p. 6.

32 See https://peacekeeping.un.org/en/mission/minusma.

33 'Todesfälle in der Bundeswehr', 31 January 2019, https://www.bundeswehr.de/portal/a/bwde/start/gedenken/todesfaelle_in_der_bundeswehr.

34 For more on German fighting in Kunduz, see Berthold Kohler, 'Der Krieg ganz nahe', *Frankfurter Allgemeine Zeitung*, 16 November 2009, https://www.faz.net/aktuell/politik/ausland/afghanistan-dem-krieg-ganz-nahe-1885883.html.

35 Hans Kundani, 'Afghanistan Deployment Forces More Assertive Bundeswehr', *Spiegel Online*, 1 November 2011, https://www.spiegel. de/international/germany/no-longer-the-aggressive-camping-organization-afghanistan-deployment-forges-more-assertive-bundeswehr-a-794189.html.

36 See, for example, the public-outreach elements of the 2014 Review run by the Policy Planning staff in the German Federal Foreign Office.

37 Janosch Delcker, 'Martin Schulz Warns of New Arms Race', Politico, 13 March 2017, https://www.politico.eu/article/martin-schulz-warns-of-new-arms-race-donald-trump-angela-merkel-election-germany-2017/.

38 Speech by Foreign Minister Sigmar Gabriel at the Munich Security Conference, German Federal Foreign Office, 17 February 2018, https://www.auswaertiges-amt.de/en/newsroom/news/rede-muenchner-sicherheitskonferenz/1602662.

39 For an excellent argument along these lines, see Jana Puglierin, 'Stuck in a Holding Pattern', *Berlin Policy Journal*, September–October 2018.

40 Ursula von der Leyen, 'The World Still Needs NATO', *New York Times*, 18 January 2019, https://www.nytimes.com/2019/01/18/opinion/nato-european-union-america.html.

41 Bastian Giegerich, 'The Long Road to Readiness', *Berlin Policy Journal*, September–October 2018. Figures reflect combined spending on procurement, research, development and testing.

42 According to the 2017 'Bühler Paper' of the German MoD, current investments in capability developments should see the Bundeswehr fully equipped by 2032. See 'Bis zu den Sternen', *Frankfurter Allgemeine Zeitung*, 18 April 2017, https://edition.faz.net/faz-edition/politik/2017-04-19/3jsfcxcjdtmu86eamcqcnzoe/.

43 In January 2017, Germany's armed forces formally numbered 185,000, but payroll showed closer to 178,000. Justyna Gotkowska, 'Germany's Security Policy and the Trump Administration: Modified Rhetoric and Moderate Commitments', *OSW Commentary*, no. 232, 22 February 2017.

44 Wolfgang Wagner et al.,'Politicization, Party Politics and Military Missions', WZB discussion paper, no. SP IV 2017-101, Berlin Social Science Centre, January 2017, p. 13.

45 For more on the history of this collaboration, see Douglas Barrie, 'Franco-German Defence Aerospace Cooperation: To the Future and Back', IISS Military Balance blog, 14 May 2018, https://www.iiss.org/blogs/military-balance/2018/05/franco-german-defence-aerospace-cooperation.

46 Ursula von der Leyen, speech at the Munich Security Conference, 16 February 2018. For an example of the 3% target, see Wolfgang Ischinger, 'Mehr Eigenverantwortung in und für Europa', *Deutschlands Neue Verantwortung*, 17 February 2018, http://www.deutschlands-verantwortung.de/beitraege/mehr-eigenverantwortung-in-und-f%C3%BCr-europa.

47 For more on Germany's ODA record, see https://donortracker.org/country/germany. For more on the history of the 0.7% threshold, see http://www.oecd.org/dac/stats/the07odagnitarget-ahistory.htm.

48 See, for example, the tweet by former SPD candidate for chancellor and previous president of the European

Parliament, Martin Schulz, 13 July 2018, https://twitter.com/MartinSchulz/status/1017816041907539968.

49 House of Lords European Union Committee, *Brexit: Common Security and Defence Policy Operations*, HL Paper 132, 14 May 2018, pp. 3, 18.

50 Theresa May, speech at the Munich Security Conference, 17 February 2018, https://www.gov.uk/government/speeches/pm-speech-at-munich-security-conference-17-february-2018.

51 For more on this, see Torben Schutz and Christian Mölling, 'Fostering a Defence-industrial Base for Europe: The Impact of Brexit', IISS and DGAP, June 2018, https://www.iiss.org/-/media/images/comment/military-balance-blog/2018/june/fostering-a-defence-industrial-base-for-europe-iiss-dgap.ashx.

52 This balance of attention is reflected in the UK government's September 2017 strategy paper on a future partnership on foreign policy, defence and development, available at https://www.gov.uk/government/publications/foreign-policy-defence-and-development-a-future-partnership-paper. The most substantive entry outlining the areas for cooperation falls not on foreign policy (two pages), or on development cooperation (two pages), but on defence and security cooperation (five pages).

53 House of Lords European Union Committee, *Brexit: Sanctions Policy*, HL Paper 50, 17 December 2017, p. 2.

54 See, for example, 'Benjamin Kienzle: Written Evidence', House of Lords European Union Committee, External Affairs Subcommittee, BSP0010, 1 September 2017, http://data.parliament.uk/writtenevidence/committeeevidence.svc/evidencedocument/eu-external-affairs-subcommittee/brexit-sanctions-policy/written/70459.html.

55 See Bastian Giegerich and Kristian Mölling, 'The United Kingdom's Contribution to European Security and Defence', IISS and DGAP, February 2018, https://dgap.org/en/article/getFullPDF/30724.

56 For more on this, see James Black et al., *Defence and Security after Brexit*: *Compendium Report* (Santa Monica, CA: RAND, 2017), pp. 127–8.

57 Giegerich and Mölling, 'The United Kingdom's Contribution to European Security and Defence'.

58 UK Defence Department official, Berlin, 30 November 2017.

59 Peter Round, Bastian Giegerich and Christian Mölling, 'European Strategic Autonomy after Brexit', IISS and DGAP, June 2018, https://www.iiss.org/-/media/images/comment/military-balance-blog/2018/june/european-strategic-autonomy-and-brexit-iiss-dgap.ashx.

60 Yvonni-Stefania Efstathiou, 'European Defence Spending gets a Boost from the EU', IISS Military Balance blog, 17 June 2018, https://www.iiss.org/blogs/military-balance/2018/06/eu-boosts-european-defence-spending.

61 'The Defence Capability Review: Equipment', Briefing Paper 08112, House of Commons Library, 17 October 2017.

62 See, for example, the menu of tasks outlined in 'Common Set of New Proposals on the Implementation of the Joint Declaration Signed by the President of the European Council, the President of the European Commission and the Secretary General of the North Atlantic Treaty Organisation', 5 December 2017, https://www.nato.int/

cps/en/natohq/official_texts_149522. htm.

63 It is difficult to calculate the proportion since a lot of US defence spending is in pursuit of US defence interests beyond NATO, while the same is true on a smaller scale for countries such as Canada, France, Turkey and the UK.

Conclusion

1   European Commission, 'The EU Pledges €2 Million to Assist Victims of Violence in the Philippines', 16 August 2018, https://ec.europa.eu/echo/news/eu-pledges-2-million-assist-victims-violence-philippines_en.

2   For one analysis of these centres, see Ralf Trapp, 'The EU's CBRN Centres of Excellence Initiative after Six Years', EU Non-Proliferation Consortium paper no. 55, February 2017.

3   See, for example, European Commission, 'Resilience, Deterrence and Defence: Building Strong Cyber Security for the EU', Joint Communication to the European Council and Parliament, 13 September 2017.

4   For more on the history of the Comprehensive Approach, see, for example, Fernanda Faria, 'What EU Comprehensive Approach?', European Centre for Development Policy Management, briefing note 71, 2014.

5   See, for example, European Council, 'Enhanced EU Security Cooperation in and with Asia – Council Conclusions', 9265/1/8 REV 1, 28 May 2018.

6   Douglas Barrie et al, 'Protecting Europe: Meeting the EU's Military Level of Ambition in the Context of Brexit', IISS and DGAP, November 2018, https://www.iiss.org/-/media/images/comment/analysis/2018/november/protecting-europe-meeting-the-eu-military-level-of-ambition-in-the-context-of-brexit-iiss-dgap.ashx.

7   For Tusk's 14 April 2018 tweet, see https://twitter.com/eucopresident/status/985044176923394048; for Mogherini's tweet, see https://twitter.com/federicamog/status/985101957525331969.

8   For a strong argument along these lines, see Volker Perthes, 'Sustaining Europe's Security Trio', *Project Syndicate*, 28 August 2018, https://www.project-syndicate.org/commentary/france-germany-britain-security-cooperation-by-volker-perthes-2018-08.

9   Ursula von der Leyen, speech to the Bundestag, 21 March 2018, https://www.bundesregierung.de/breg-de/service/bulletin/rede-der-bundesministerin-der-verteidigung-dr-ursula-von-der-leyen--862360.

10 Steven Hill, 'Post-Brexit: EU Still a Superpower', *Globalist*, 27 June 2016, https://www.theglobalist.com/post-brexit-eu-still-a-superpower/.

11 Anders Aslund, 'One Thing G7 Leaders Won't be Discussing Today? Europe's Giant Innovation Fail', *Washington Post*, 26 May 2017, https://www.washingtonpost.com/news/democracy-post/wp/2017/05/26/one-thing-g7-leaders-wont-be-discussing-today-europes-giant-innovation-fail/?utm_term=.4c3deff9d373.

INDEX

Adelphi books are published six times a year by Routledge Journals, an imprint of Taylor & Francis, 4 Park Square, Milton Park, Abingdon, Oxfordshire OX14 4RN, UK.

A subscription to the institution print edition, ISSN 1944-5571, includes free access for any number of concurrent users across a local area network to the online edition, ISSN 1944-558X. Taylor & Francis has a flexible approach to subscriptions enabling us to match individual libraries' requirements. This journal is available via a traditional institutional subscription (either print with free online access, or online-only at a discount) or as part of our libraries, subject collections or archives. For more information on our sales packages please visit www.tandfonline.com/page/librarians.

2019 Annual Adelphi Subscription Rates			
Institution	£785	US$1,376	€1,451
Individual	£269	US$460	€368
Online only	£667	US$1,170	€986

Dollar rates apply to subscribers outside Europe. Euro rates apply to all subscribers in Europe except the UK and the Republic of Ireland where the pound sterling price applies. All subscriptions are payable in advance and all rates include postage. Journals are sent by air to the USA, Canada, Mexico, India, Japan and Australasia. Subscriptions are entered on an annual basis, i.e. January to December. Payment may be made by sterling cheque, dollar cheque, international money order, National Giro, or credit card (Amex, Visa, Mastercard).

For a complete and up-to-date guide to Taylor & Francis journals and books publishing programmes, and details of advertising in our journals, visit our website: http://www.tandfonline.com.

Ordering information:
USA/Canada: Taylor & Francis Inc., Journals Department, 530 Walnut Street, Suite 850, Philadelphia, PA 19106, USA. **UK/Europe/Rest of World:** Routledge Journals, T&F Customer Services, T&F Informa UK Ltd., Sheepen Place, Colchester, Essex, CO3 3LP, UK.

Advertising enquiries to:
USA/Canada: The Advertising Manager, Taylor & Francis Inc., 530 Walnut Street, Suite 850, Philadelphia, PA 19106, USA. Tel: +1 (800) 354 1420. Fax: +1 (215) 207 0050. **UK/Europe/Rest of World**: The Advertising Manager, Routledge Journals, Taylor & Francis, 4 Park Square, Milton Park, Abingdon, Oxfordshire OX14 4RN, UK. Tel: +44 (0) 20 7017 6000. Fax: +44 (0) 20 7017 6336.